GOD AND JETFIRE

GOD
AND
JETFIRE

CONFESSIONS OF A BIRTH MOTHER

AMY SEEK

FARRAR, STRAUS AND GIROUX
NEW YORK

Farrar, Straus and Giroux
18 West 18th Street, New York 10011

Printed in the United States of America
First edition, 2015

Library of Congress Cataloging-in-Publication Data
Seek, Amy, 1977–
  God and Jetfire : confessions of a birth mother / Amy Seek. — 1st Edition.
     pages   cm
  ISBN 978-0-374-16445-4 (hardback) — ISBN 978-0-374-71382-9 (e-book)
  1. Open adoption.   2. Motherhood.   3. Families.   I. Title.

HV875 .S375 2015
306.874—dc23
[B]

                                                    2014044643

Designed by Abby Kagan

Farrar, Straus and Giroux books may be purchased for educational, business,
or promotional use. For information on bulk purchases, please contact the
Macmillan Corporate and Premium Sales Department at 1-800-221-7945,
extension 5442, or write to specialmarkets@macmillan.com.

www.fsgbooks.com
www.twitter.com/fsgbooks • www.facebook.com/fsgbooks

1   3   5   7   9   10   8   6   4   2

For my family—all of it

GOD AND JETFIRE

ZERO

My son and I were lying on my bed, looking up at the ceiling and speculating about eternity. It was just like when I was his age, ten or eleven; I'd stare up and think: Eternity means for*ever*. And ever. And ever and ever and ever and ever. Eternity means I'd still be saying "and ever" from the last time I lost myself in the scaleless white, trying to make sense of eternity.

At some point I turned toward him. He looked at me without lifting his head from the pillow. I reached over and brushed his hair behind his ear.

"I wanted you. You know that? I really wanted you." I paused, pressing his face with my palm. He held my gaze for a moment.

"Yeah . . . ," he said, knowing that. Then he turned back, squinted, and addressed the ceiling. "But *why?*"

I might have thought it was the question I was always waiting for. The one that would free me to share the whole story: how he came to be and why I gave him up, and how everything had been shaped by his absence. There was so much I wanted to tell him, so much I wanted to know, but every month and then year that passed, I kept having to remind myself that he was just a child. He would need time. Time to build muscle and learn to walk and eat lots of breakfasts and get the training wheels taken off his bike, and earn an allowance and spend it a million times, and practice cursive and pass notes in class, and ponder lots of different careers—maybe even go to college and get married—before we could talk about those things.

And the way he studied the ceiling, I could tell he meant something else. He was asking everyone's question. It was the question, Why *everything*? Why consciousness? Why time? Why desire; why love? He wasn't hurt, and he wasn't looking for an answer. The question wasn't for me. I turned back to the ceiling and asked it with him.

It was just like him to contemplate such things. And it was very much him: lying there, skeptical slits of eyes piercing the ceiling, weight so real he sank into my duvet. It was exciting to have him there with me, and it was fun to be cohorts confronting the universe together. But the most fantastic thing was touching him. No one was watching, and I wasn't thinking about whether it was okay or whether it made him or anyone else uncomfortable, or whether I was allowed to express my love like that, without restraint. I didn't think about anything at all! I just reached over and combed through the blond mop, bent the warm, rubbery flap of his ear, as it felt natural to do—as I had, in fact, never once done. He had never been to my apartment, and we had never lain like that. I'd never said those true words, making sure he understood. I'd never let my affection flow straight from my heart, through my outstretched arm, and land so solidly and without hesitation. I'd never enjoyed that relief—profound, even as he turned and let it roll to the side, his mother's love, imponderable as eternity, shedding it as a son will do.

If I could have, I'd have turned to my other side and put his question to my father. But when I woke, there was just the west, buildings gleaming pink, illuminated by sunrise. And another eternity to contemplate: I would never, ever, *ever* be my son's mother.

ONE

A sympathetic Jesus hovered just above the head of the woman who was telling me my baby would be born in July. I had to tilt my head to see him fully, down to his toes. His eyes were sad and his soft mouth was mute. In his outstretched palms, he held a tiny red baby curled up in the fetal position. The woman leaned toward us with an elbow on the desk. "Don't you know what happens when you have premarital sex without a condom?" After three tests at home and one in the pink-painted bathroom to her right, I still had an urge to look behind me at the pregnant girl she was leveling with. I couldn't believe she was speaking to me. *Me!*—who was, myself, an accident, as my sister often reminded me. The woman held her fingers two inches apart. On the basis of the dates I gave her she informed us that I was eight weeks pregnant.

I sat silently and waited. The walls and bookshelves shimmered, deflated, like surfaces loosely attached to brittle frames. I wanted the woman to talk forever, pointing at diagrams and unfolding brochures. Then I would never have to leave this place, and time wouldn't proceed past this moment. If I was pregnant, it was just barely, and I simply wouldn't take a single step further.

I'd left the third test on the side of the sink in my apartment. My hands were shaking as I stumbled out of the bathroom, at once blinded and liberated by the impossibility. I couldn't be pregnant. I *couldn't* be. My mind raced, lurching for certainties to anchor me—I was too young, I was only in my second year of college, I didn't have any money, I had my whole life ahead of me—as if reason could cure my body of its delusions.

I opened the phone book to the unthinkable first few pages, those that stick close to the cover, concealed, as you thumb for wonderfully innocuous middle things like Plumbers and Laundromats. Between Abortion and Advertising, I discovered a dark world of resources I'd never had reason to know about, and, overwhelmed, I returned to the bathroom to reexamine the device—compelled, then hesitant, to look. Jevn arrived as trembling and incredulous as I was, but he reminded me we already knew the options. There wasn't some brand-new way of dealing with pregnancy, and there was no one to call until we knew what we were going to do.

I called anyway, frantically, picking a number at random. I needed to say it: *I'm pregnant.* To hear it, to see it land somewhere and stick. I wanted to speak with a professional in the field and be presented with the full range of options. But the woman on the line wasn't moved by my urgency and wouldn't indulge my disbelief. She wanted me to call back when I was prepared to schedule an abortion. I scanned the thin pages and dialed another number. The receptionist invited me to come to the center that afternoon; I could take another test, just to be sure, and someone would be there to help me process it all. It was a Christian ministry, but we could correct for their bias, I told Jevn. I just needed to talk to someone. And that's how we ended up here.

I looked at the woman unblinking, waiting for her to flip through her paperwork, admit the mistake, and agree with me: it couldn't be true. I wanted things to be returned solidly to their proper places, all the softened surfaces filled full again. She put her pamphlets resolutely aside. She said we were a beautiful couple; we should get married and have the baby. I felt Jevn shift as if to get up, but I couldn't leave yet. This could not be the end of our conversation! I hadn't even accepted the premise that I was pregnant; I couldn't admit this conclusion. We'd never even spoken about marriage! Until just days ago, I'd been planning our breakup. Steeling myself for it, speaking it through in my mind, assuring myself it was best. But Jevn was putting on his coat. Reluctantly, I put on mine. We smiled as we shut the door.

Jevn walked ahead of me across the parking lot to the car. He could fit his entire apartment in that tiny car, his long row of books that lined its perimeter, his perfectly weighted silverware, his Aalto vases, even his bed, which he'd built to come apart for that purpose. I didn't know there were cars with heated seats until I met Jevn. I grew up with empty dashboard panels for luxuries I could only imagine.

I asked him to walk slower, but he was propelled by the forward swinging of his broad shoulders, and I moved my feet just to catch myself from falling. With each step, I divided the future into halves and halves, approaching a moment I hoped to never reach.

The Yellow Pages were folded behind the windshield. I'd ripped out the whole first chapter and written directions in the margins. We were somewhere in the suburbs, north of the university, near a drive-through bank kitty-corner from a Kohl's. Jevn drove like he did everything, with a determination that intimidated me. It was December; my seat was on high.

I had certain ideas about what life should look like at my age, thanks to my mother, and they didn't include a baby. There were just forests of bamboo, clear water and high cliffsides, a dangerous motorbike and wind so strong you couldn't keep a hairdo—and, most intriguing of all: men who would drink champagne out of your shoe. Glimpses she gave me of her time working overseas before she met my dad. What many years lay ahead of me! What mysteries of the world must unfold before I might find myself in circumstances like those, propping my bike on its stand, slipping off my shoes so the men could drink! Marriage and family might have been somewhere in the hazy distance, but I wasn't dreaming about them. And that's why I kept breaking up with Jevn. Committing to a boy meant deciding too many other things about the future. I'd only made it as far north as Cincinnati for college; there wasn't a place I could think of I didn't still want to see.

Dad would pass the phone to Mom whenever the subject turned to romance, but she wasn't anything like my roommate's mom my first year of school, who sent her leopard-print underwear in the mail to help her snatch up a man. And so I was nothing like my other roommate, who would cry, curled up on the carpet of her bedroom with her best friend, because, at age twenty-one, no one had yet made them brides. My mother put all boys in one category: they were a phase. Like letting my sister shave one half of my head, like huffing Scotchgard and falling in love with the Karate Kid, boys were a thing I'd look back on, laugh and cover my mouth and not be able to believe I did that. Phases were important, because they're part of growing up, but my mother didn't pay much attention to interests of mine she knew would pass. She was already old by the time I was born, she already had white hair and people thought she was my grandmother. Her ambivalence about boys made me embarrassed to care about them at all. It was why I always called them "boys." She didn't have to tell me not to waste time with them; she *really* didn't have to tell me not to get pregnant.

The top of Jevn's head almost touched the ceiling of the car. Bending down to see out his side window, he filled its frame like someone who'd been stuffed into a television set. The highway ran along the Mill Creek Valley, which emptied into the Ohio River as it curved around the southern edge of the city. Just on the other side was Kentucky, and, beyond that, the South I was always trying to get away from.

I'd always feared somehow getting stuck there, becoming one of those girls I used to see in the Kmart parking lot. Girls with stringy long hair who couldn't carry their own toddlers for their girth and didn't teach them not to cuss. They emerged wearing flip-flops from long maroon cars with hot vinyl seats, shorts inching asymmetrically up the insides of their thighs while they shopped for microwaves, boxes of Coke, and dirty birthday cards. They were the girls who had the sons who sat on the front porches of half-fallen homes on rural roads that didn't have curbs, who called at me as I jogged past: "Yewanna run? . . . *We* kin make ye' run."

Pure products of the mountains, I grew up among them, I carpooled with them to school in smoke-filled hatchbacks, but I begged for braces to fix the gap between my front teeth so no one in my future would know where I'd come from and send me back. I was an accident, so I knew I didn't belong in the world at all, but I especially didn't belong in Tennessee.

But soon after I got to Cincinnati, I realized it was just an extension of Kentucky, whose southeastern hills wove right back into the mountains of Tennessee. It was like I just couldn't escape the South, hard as I tried.

We got off the highway and onto the gridded streets of the university neighborhood. As we neared my apartment, I tried to make sense of it. Eight weeks pregnant. Due in July. I tried to work out what it should mean to me by imagining what it might mean to other people. My mother was Catholic, so I knew she'd be disappointed, and could guess at least one option she wouldn't approve of. And my dad wasn't anything, but I was pretty sure I knew what he'd say.

Biiiiiig bucks!

He'd lean back and smile with both thumbs up when he said it, as if to say: it must be so much fun to spend money you didn't work your fingers to the bone to earn! Besides all the lost dreams, the dropping out of school, the flying Confederate flags—having a baby was expensive. And he'd always tried to curb my expensive tastes. He used to tell me that if he let me spend money the way I wanted to, our whole family would end up on the street eating dog food. My siblings were content to be potato-sack bears and old-laundry-basket worms-in-apples, but I wanted a store-bought, trademarked, two-piece vinyl Halloween costume with a plastic mask. I wanted a real Barbie and real Breyer horses. My desire for things knew no bounds. And so my father worked carefully every day to thread a fear of poverty into my most basic wiring.

What I begged for most was a grand piano. One with keys you could plunge your fingers in like the muddy bottom of a pond; one with worlds to plumb before you sank to somewhere solid. Our piano was an Everett upright that was fine for Christmas carols, but for real music it was just like diving into the shallow end.

Biiiiiig bucks meant no, and that that was the end of the conversation. Dad made me get a job at Pizza Plus so I could earn my own grand piano and, he hoped, see what a future in music would really look like—no doubt similar to single motherhood. Poverty always appeared the same way in my imagination: sitting on the curb eating a big bag of dog food, kibble by kibble.

Jevn dropped me off at my apartment. I don't remember if we said a single word, or if we were both just speechless. It was almost the end of the school term, so we had plenty of things to get back to.

TWO

The first time I ever saw him I was shocked by his beauty. Very tall and tan, white-blond hair and shadowy blue eyes. I lost my breath—that first time, and every time I'd see him. I was content to admire him from a distance, but sometimes when he'd come around the corner I'd actually jump in surprise, which only drew his attention. He began to leave things on my desk in studio. Long strips of industrial felt, aluminum tubes with torn ends, crumpled sheets of lead, tiny dunes of broken glass. I don't know how I knew it was him. He had a name for me, before he knew my name, and he'd say it softly, like an owl, after we'd pass each other in the hallway.

Wooomb.

This began after the pumpkin-carving competition in my first architecture studio in college. Jack-o'-lanterns in the manner of famous architects. I picked Louis Kahn, whom I'd never heard of, and read his famous conversation with a brick. The architect asks what the brick wants to be, and the brick responds, "An arch!" It's one of the most well-known fairy tales in architecture school literature, the point of which is that we should let materials be what they want to be. Bricks do well stacked heavily on top of one another in compression; they do not make good curtain walls, as another famous architect later demonstrated on our very own campus.

I couldn't understand why an architect would want to do otherwise, but I resolved to stay true to my material. I opened the pumpkin up like a belly from the side, revealing within it a tall, narrow gourd, which I cut open and splayed to reveal a small, pale white pumpkin. Each fleshy layer revealed the pumpkin-y nature of my pumpkin; each was backlit with candles, and water pooled in the bottom like a bodily fluid.

The judges favored the jack-o'-lanterns that had square windows and an architectural sense of structure. More like buildings and less like the midpoint of an open heart surgery. Technically, I was still a piano major.

Jevn was one of the judges. After that, I'd see him. I'd jump. He'd say, *Wooomb*.

Then he was there again, recruited to teach my architecture history review sessions, which met only before tests to revisit material our professor had covered in class. But what Jevn liked to talk about instead was architects' deaths. Borromini fell on his sword, but not as you'd expect. On the long axis of the oval of his chest. Kind of significant, when you think about San Carlo alle Quattro Fontane. Right? He would glance around the room. We'd all be mad because it was never the material we were going to be tested on.

Late one night before a review session, he came into my studio and asked if I was indeed in his class (he supposedly couldn't remember). He wanted my assistance with a task having to do with slides and projectors. I followed him to his office, the only office belonging to an undergraduate, and after a long pause, he told me I seemed like someone who had a brother. I said I did. Two years older. Mikey. Jevn was reclining in his swivel chair and I was standing in front of his desk. And he just went silent and watched me.

I remember two other things about that conversation. His using the words *reindeer* and *clouds*, and although I'd learned those words many, many years ago, my not knowing what he was talking about. I also remember that I asked him what his favorite book was. It was a dense philosophical text I later read, but at the time I only understood the part about felt. It pointed out that felt, unlike woven textiles, gets its strength not through organized structures but through disorder; tangling. The sociopolitical implications were lost on me, but I took it as a small sign of our connection. My family were sheep farmers, and I'd made felt, rubbing handfuls of raw wool between my palms in soapy water until big clouds of it, piled on the floor and across the kitchen table, became thick fabric. I didn't understand Jevn, but I knew firsthand about that special resilience born of complex and messy knots. And that seemed like some kind of auspicious starting point.

I didn't understand much about architecture either that first year. I thought architects were kind of like civil servants, like postmen or plumbers. An architect's job, it seemed to me, was to put buildings where buildings were needed: hospitals for refugees in war-torn countries, homes for families after tornadoes and hurricanes. Architects used mundane materials to create humble things, which were not even about themselves but the empty space inside them. And people who really needed buildings often couldn't afford them, so ideally architecture should be free.

Architecture was definitely not something to be passionate about. But students would stay up all night working with the kind of dedication I thought existed only in music school. I couldn't tell what they were working so hard on. After the pumpkins, we were supposed to design a building for a site that overlooked downtown. I'd been there lots of times to watch storms come in from the west over the river valley, and I didn't think that place would be at all improved by architecture. I proposed instead that they demolish the bathrooms already on site and do a little landscaping. I put in time like a good civil servant and then slipped away to play piano. I thought it couldn't be the least of the tools in an architect's toolbelt: to know when architecture was not called for. There were so many vacant buildings just down the hill.

At the end of that first term, my class presented our designs on the grand staircase of the school for everyone to see. I wasn't nervous about speaking in front of my classmates or my professors; I only hoped Jevn wouldn't pass by. But he did, just as I was explaining my empty set of drawings, my inadvertent argument against architecture. The next day, by my drafting board I found a tiny pile of one-sixteenth-inch basswood sticks cut into equal one-inch lengths.

It was soon after that that I saw him standing on the sidewalk near my apartment one afternoon, his arms full of books.

"I thought you'd like these," he said as he handed them to me, and I realized he'd been waiting for me to get home. How did he know where I lived? And how did he know what I'd like?

That spring was magical. I didn't know from experience how special it was to fall in love, but I felt it, a fullness in my chest as I walked past the park feeling stupidly aligned with the chirping birds and the early morning frogs and the fog. Feeling like college was just a fascinating backdrop for something even bigger.

At school Jevn was serious and reserved; no one would believe the way he danced on his bed and mouthed the words to "Rocky Mountain High." Mouthed, not sang. He carefully selected the things in the world he would love, and I considered my position extremely privileged, dancing on the bed with him, knocking him down but still failing to stop the mouthing. He said it was the way I smiled all the time that made him want to know me.

But I kept him at a distance to protect myself. First it was because I wanted independence. Then it was because I was in love and scared he'd figure out I wasn't as smart or talented as he was. I practiced losing him so I'd be ready for it; I went to Europe for the summer without him even though he wanted us to go together. I cheated on him, and though he didn't believe I'd done it because I liked him so much it terrified me, he still forgave me. I chipped away at us with small complaints—I said we were getting boring, always taking the same walk through the same woods to the same restaurant. He said, "I think repetition has everything to do with a heartbeat."

His name was pronounced "Yehn," and it meant *steady*. He was born in the United States, but he was Norwegian by blood, and his rituals seemed Scandinavian. Getting up religiously before sunrise to take a long, pensive bath, folded into the tub but gazing out the windows like he was floating in a forest lake in Finland. Reading for hours, sun still dawning—not books for school, but his own readings on philosophy and art. He worked so hard he would fall asleep sitting up any time his attention wasn't needed; screen saver, he called it. His dad was an alcoholic, and he'd taken refuge in an architecture internship in high school, devoting himself to beautiful lines and to men who stood steady themselves. When he decided he liked something, he didn't waver.

I trusted him so early on and so absolutely that I often forgot myself. When he'd drop me off, I'd be surprised to be alone, as if I'd been gone for a long time and hadn't anticipated my own return. I was happy when, the first time I visited his apartment, he had three vases on his mantel, and I thought: *Those are* ugly! I realized it was one of the few times I'd heard my own voice in his presence. But it took only a few more months of architecture school for me to learn they were very famous vases, by Alvar Aalto, and I grew to appreciate them so much that when I went to Europe without him, I made a pilgrimage to the factory in Finland where they were made, and because I couldn't afford one, I scooped up by-products of their fabrication off the factory floor to take home as a memento.

It scared me, how naturally I disappeared. How easily, how fully, architecture school, and Jevn, supplanted my natural instincts. He couldn't understand why being myself meant I couldn't be with him, and I couldn't explain it. I didn't understand it, either. It was simpler for us to break up.

By the time we found out I was pregnant, we had been dating for two years. I was twenty-two. Twice eleven, Jevn's favorite number. He said we were like the number eleven. Eleven is special because of all kinds of ancient ideas about numbers I still don't understand, but also because of its shape. Two solid rectangles with an invisible rectangle in between. That invisible rectangle exists only when the two solid ones stand close by. Jevn called it "the third," and he said that was what was special about us, the thing that wasn't him and wasn't me, but emerged only out of our proximity. Even if I wasn't as talented as he was, I thought, I at least helped make that third thing he liked so much.

THREE

I *am pregnant.*
Typing the words, it felt as if I was forging an impossible reality. *Don't tell Mom. I'm not sure what I'm going to do yet.*
It made my heart beat fast. But it also felt like something I could easily change. Backspace backspace backspace backspace.

The words slipped away when I pressed send, and I forgot them. My sister was twelve hours ahead in China, where she taught at a university. She coughed black soot and had to boil her drinking water, and she'd learned to speak Chinese tones so musically I couldn't recognize her voice within them. Four years older, Julie was my closest friend, though she was also the one, throughout my childhood, who was always reminding me I wasn't meant to be here.

My dad did it, too. When they'd tell me how I fell into a swimming pool as an infant but didn't cough or cry when they rescued me, Mom would say I must have been a water baby, born to swim, but Dad would say, *I don't know why your mother got so upset that day: you were an accident anyway!* And many times, I heard the story about my brother toddling into the living room, where he discovered me for the first time, the only point of which was to illustrate how neither here nor there was my arrival. *There's a little baby in there!* he said, which everyone thought was adorable. And so, incidentally, I began.

No one had meant to bring me here, I'd just slipped in somehow. It got confirmed all the time: pedestrians cut me off diagonally on busy sidewalks. Subway doors snapped on my nose. People stepped in front of me in line to buy tickets or board the plane. My speech teacher said I had to speak twice as loud because I was narrow and easy to ignore. I was occupying space meant for other things, too precarious myself to supply someone else's foundation.

Jevn and I were going to meet in the morning. I was supposed to decide what I wanted to do. I put the cast-iron skillet on the stove and, invigorated by its familiar weight, the ancient sound of crackling oil, I silently perfected my argument: why I could not be pregnant. Maybe, if I explained everything, that woman could recalibrate the test.

I couldn't even picture a child. Pregnancy was just an end, the vertigo of all my fears made absolute certainties. Shouldn't it take some kind of definite pull, a sustained desire, to draw another soul into the world? Or excesses of love and life and wisdom so overflowing it takes another whole person to contain it all? It should at least require collaborative skill, but I could barely design a building; how could we have inadvertently concocted a *child*?

But if I really was pregnant, then maybe it meant something. I'd taken smaller things as signs. Once when Jevn drove me to the doctor for a sore throat, the prescription was mistakenly written out to me with his last name. It had seemed like an artifact from the future, evidence from beyond that we were meant to be. I put that orange pill bottle in a drawer where I stored things I meant to keep forever, like my cat's tooth, and my own tooth, and a turquoise cross given to me by my grandmother. And the pieces of those ugly vases.

But, no. I was an accident. And being born and giving birth stitch a person into a history, puncture the fabric of the universe, anchor heels and hands firmly in the earth. They make a person part of a lineage, and lines, as I learned in trigonometry, have direction and intent. They don't float like points, without mass or orientation; they split the sky, they distinguish here from there, they begin to tell a story. I couldn't be pregnant because that would mean I had to be here, a stitch in the seam, connecting everyone.

In the morning my sister wrote she would come back from China and help me raise the baby; we could live on our family's sheep farm. She said, of the options, abortion may be simple, but there was the day after that, and the day after that. *Maybe if Jevn pays child support and you don't work for a year? You know you were an accident, right?*

And then Jevn was knocking at my door, before I was ready to hear what he'd decided or tell him what I'd decided, or talk about any of this like it was real. I opened the door, and he stood there surprisingly fresh and energetic. He slipped in nervously, as if he had something to say. He was smiling and avoiding my eyes. His shallow breath made me hope he'd thought of something new. He said he'd gotten up early and taken a shower. He said he'd found himself—smiling. And then he began to float foreign images in front of my mind: keep the child, read it books, take it hiking, wait at the bus stop. He said he thought we should do it: be a family. Me, him, and the third.

I don't know what happened then.

I said no. Listened to myself say it. He said he watched himself hear it. I said it definitively and without qualification. I said *never*. And though I'd broken up with him countless other times, it was only then that I could see I finally lost him. His bright eyes became gray hollows. He paced my apartment, too large for it, and made me cower.

◎ ◎ ◎

Then a darkness like no nightmare overtook us. The enemy was unknown and invisible, and so we lashed out blindly at each other. Old wounds reopened. I pushed him away. I wanted him out. I wanted to rid myself of the trust and affection that had imprisoned me for so long. I struggled to regain my footing. I couldn't think clearly with him in front of me, demanding certainty, but I was terrified to be left alone. I pounded my fear into the flesh of his chest, the meat of his shoulders, but as hard as my fists fell, the darkness only deepened.

Whenever things were difficult before, usually with school, he would remind me to breathe. Or he would say, *Remember the river.* Not any river in particular. He had his rivers, the ones that barreled through mountains in Colorado, and I had mine, that wound through the valleys of East Tennessee. We were both aliens in the flatlands of Ohio. He would tell me to lift my feet and let the water carry me. Don't waste energy struggling, just go where it takes me.

It was an easy image for him, because his natural instincts were like a deep-coursed stream. When he let go, he went far and made beautiful things. He encouraged me, always wanting to know what I was drawing, or thinking about, or building. He said that I had the most important thing to start with: sensitivity. But I didn't have a river. A palm reader showed me the fine, intricate, and undifferentiated webbing of my hands, the absence of a single strong line. Mine was a spring that ran across an unarticulated landscape, spreading and dividing when it encountered the smallest obstruction. She said it meant there wasn't a single direction for me; I could do anything, but I would never be sure about it.

Not knowing where I was going was a frightening but familiar feeling, full of potential. But it was a violent event for Jevn's river to change course. And yet, he'd done it; in one night, he'd devoted himself to a new direction. We would have a child. But now I was sending him coursing into the unknown, and I could no longer see into him. I saw only fear—the blank blindness of a panicked animal.

Pacing around my apartment, he charged forth powerfully in a new direction. If we weren't going to keep the baby together, he wanted to get rid of it. He didn't want me to raise the child as a single mother, because then he'd become a father as absent as his own. I insisted there had to be another way, and I wasn't ready to decide anything. Reduced to our reflexes, Jevn closed and concealed himself; I opened.

We fought wildly, for days. Not getting anywhere. All we knew was something big was going to happen. We were bound together and flying off a cliff, fighting only over how to land. He slammed his hand on the phone every time I reached for it to call my mother, though I still didn't think I could tell her. He thought we should figure things out for ourselves. He held the knob of the bathroom door so I couldn't come out until I made a decision. In between and in shock, we went to class, and I would spend the time forgetting that there was a decision to be made.

It was hard to believe I'd returned from my first trip to Europe just three months earlier. I was supposed to be asserting my independence, but I was so often calculating time zones, searching for pay phones and moments when Jevn and I could talk. I'd spent the summer in school in Copenhagen and then traveled all over by train. I'd brought very few things home with me, but one was a children's book I found in Venice. The title was *Oh!* and there were no words within it. As the pages unfolded, a coffee cup printed across the leaves stretched into a cruise ship; a pipe became the tail of a cat brushing its teeth. None of the objects were what you thought at first. And I guessed you were supposed to say "oh!" every time you realized that. When I found it, I was sunburned and hungry and lonely, but I was also happy, and I thought: this is the story of wrong trains and kind strangers and surprise vistas where you weren't supposed to be. There isn't some big right way for things to happen; things just unfold weightlessly, and we're left standing before the surprising story of our lives, little of it as we planned, every inch of it precious, with nothing much to say but "oh!" I was going to save that book for someday after all my travels were through, when I was too old to jog Mediterranean cliffsides and sleep in train stations, when I would get married and have children, at which point I would give it to them, and I would tell them all about life's charming twists and turns.

Memories like that would return to me sometimes when we were fighting, like a flash of light on the waves giving sudden orientation, and I'd feel sure that things were somehow going to be okay.

"Why does everything have to be *sugarcoated* for you?" Jevn demanded. This was not a wrong turn in Paris. He insisted that I make a decision, and so I did. I made a decision and then a phone call—but I waited for him to leave to do it.

He picked me up the next morning, and we drove less than a mile to the other side of the university. We pulled into a gravel parking lot behind a Mexican restaurant I had been to once and a stately segment of row houses. A small brick building sat in the far corner of the lot, and signs pointed to the surgery entrance at the basement level in back. We parked beside the Dumpsters and entered a tiny vestibule. An armed security guard scanned us with a handheld metal detector, and we edged around the door into reception, where two girls sat low behind a counter. *The Price Is Right* on the television in the waiting room; a man seated, inexplicably laughing. One of the girls filed my credit card in a long drawer that looked like it was drawn from a library's card catalog. In its place she handed me a device that, she explained, would vibrate when the doctor was ready for me.

I asked whether there wasn't something between now and surgery, some kind of counseling or preparation? She said that the clinic offered counseling over the phone and that I had already had it. They were young and in the middle of a conversation.

The windows in the waiting room looked out to the bumpers of cars parked at the level above us. Cars pulled in and out, flashing light fast around the perimeter of the room, and we could see feet clicking toward the upper entrance of the women's center. We took seats against the wall; the weight of the earth pressed against it on the other side. Bob Barker stood, microphone in hand, as a contestant pulled down hard on the big wheel, and the little device in my lap started to shake. I told Jevn that I didn't know what we should do, but I thought I'd probably never smile again. The sun was low and the seats of the Saab were warm on our very fast car ride home, during which I understood what he meant when he said he couldn't be responsible for that.

For the next few days, we clung to what we knew with certainty: we had to finish the school term. But I was exhausted and anxious, and so I asked Jevn to build my model. We were broken up but bound. I gave him my drawings, and he sat at the little table beside my drafting board in my apartment and began to lay out measurements on a piece of chipboard.

I picked up the pencil I had left there days ago. I traced the lines, trying to find the feeling that had originally shaped them, a threshold to that time when their contours were my biggest concern. Now it appeared they'd been drawn by someone else.

"Is this roofline supposed to meet this one?" he asked, but I didn't know. I hadn't decided. I designed with my eyes closed, like a mole digging where the ground was softest, asking myself if the space should open out left, open right. Should there be light, should there be shelter. Jevn thought about the quickest, simplest way to build things. The best material, the most efficient construction sequence. He cut similar pieces at the same time, using a jig for speed and precision. He would lay out all the parts before he assembled them. What resulted was always beautiful.

He worked furiously at the table. I hated how he glanced at me as I handed him my long metal ruler. Sitting there, he required me to make my many unmade decisions, and in very little time the questions that had consumed me during the school term were given certain, unremarkable dimension, and the thing I'd allowed to remain a rich mystery for ten weeks began to look like a building. I ran into the bathroom to throw up. He continued to measure and cut, measure, cut, and he finished my model in half the time it would have taken me.

I stepped into my shower and let the water pummel me. The north light of the frosted windows glowed; their rusted, wet cranks made muddy dust on the yellow tiles of the sill. I pressed my stomach with the palm of my hand. Nothing was visible there, but a small certainty began to develop inside me. A pebble dropped into my infinite lightness. A tiny weight that pulls a flying curtain flat. Two unstoppable inches and a hardening of my abdomen. When I moved, my muscles gently tightened around it, the weight of certainty, the early seed of a lifelong grief.

Don't have an abortion, come to Tennessee; the only time I could remember my mother telling me exactly what to do. *There are no accidents, hooray for that!* my sister wrote from China. Jevn shuffled large sheets of cardboard outside the bathroom door, and I imagined the larger forces of the universe pausing for a moment to focus attention on me—not to destroy me, but to utilize me for an event as old as time, as vital as the nitrogen cycle.

FOUR

My favorite way to leave the architecture school was through the doors on the sixth floor. The ground on that side swelled to meet them, and in the summer, you could sit on the slope and bake in the warmth. The cold air of the new building, the fluorescent lights, and the doubts and fears harbored there would dissipate like trapped spirits set free in the body-temperature bath of sunset. I was so often struck by the sunset there that my friends would imitate me, falling over on the hillside, arms flung wide in a backward embrace. Desire so great it's its own inversion. *It's so beautiful!* they would say, mocking me.

But now it was winter, and passing through those doors for the last time that term gave no relief at all.

A narrow stand of bamboo grew along the side of my apartment building, screening it from the fraternity house next door and creating a breezy tunnel to my stoop. Bamboo filled my wide south window, and when the sun set it cast a shimmering shadow on the wall above my mattress, a few inches above the floor. At night I gazed up through the veil of torn leaves to the sky, and I could lean out and touch the tall stalks from my doorstep. Inside, a turquoise wingback chair given to me by a neighbor stood tall in the corner, and a bulbous blue Eames chair left by the last tenant was its round counterpart. On my desk, the Yellow Pages were folded where I'd left them.

Jevn and I had each told our mothers. In a moment when my fears about our situation outweighed my terror about what she'd say, I'd exhaled the words *Mom—I'm pregnant* before I'd even uttered hello. I don't know how Jevn told his mother. I only knew that the year before, she'd given me and her daughter-in-law the same red cardigan for Christmas, but in the past few days she'd started calling me to talk about Jevn's talent and potential and how I was putting them both at risk. She kept telling me how simple abortion was.

Within the pages I'd torn from the phone book, I found a listing for Catholic Social Services and called to make an appointment. There were private lawyers and agencies, but I didn't want to talk to anyone who might have commercial interests in my pregnancy. And I was comfortable with Catholics. I'd spent a thousand Sundays gazing up at the timber ribs that swelled to support the ceiling of my mother's church. I'd appreciate a perspective that was bigger minded in a situation like this.

But Jevn didn't join me when I drove downtown. He didn't think I could do adoption. He said I was too sensitive. He reminded me: I couldn't eat animals; I picked earthworms off the sidewalk after it rained. How could I possibly abandon a baby? But adoption seemed like our only choice. The only option that didn't kill anything, wouldn't deprive anyone of a father, and wouldn't require *biiiiiig* bucks.

◎ ◎ ◎

The receptionist directed me to take a seat in the lobby. Her cushiony arms resting unmoved against the desk assured me that mine was a problem solved every day in this place. Molly appeared and introduced herself. She led me down the corridor and into a counseling room. I sat down in an armchair. She perched herself on the sofa and smiled. She was in her late twenties and pretty. She leaned toward me, brown hair brushing her shoulders as she spoke.

"Tell me why you're here today."

She asked questions that were easy to answer. I told her the stock stories of my life: I was born in Tennessee, I had come to Ohio to study piano at the conservatory but had recently switched majors to architecture. Those stories were like old friends, and it eased my mind to remember them.

She listened closely, nodding with warmth, and then, as if it was simply another background question for her file, she asked, "Do you have any experience with adoption?" She might have asked what I thought about modern art or the conflict in Yugoslavia.

"My uncle was adopted, and I think a friend of my brother's," I told her. It seemed unremarkable that certain characters would be cast into families by means other than birth. Being adopted seemed like a benign abnormality, similar to being foreign or an only child, or to having divorced parents or freckles, or to moving a lot because of your dad's job; all vast mysteries of other people's lives I didn't have the imagination to ponder.

"Do you know anyone who has *placed* a child for adoption?"

I shook my head no, but it almost seemed like a trick question. The whole *point* of adoption was that the baby doesn't have a mother—that's why it needs a home. The whole point was that the mother is gone.

"That's understandable. Women who place their children often don't talk about it."

I'd never even thought about it. All of those children had mothers.

Not once had I considered Uncle Johnny's real mother or the woman who must have given up my brother's friend. The story I'd heard about my uncle was that he'd just shown up in the shed and stayed, so Grandma adopted him. That's what adoption meant. You were *added* to a family. Adoption was a means of *getting* children, it was not a way to lose them.

Molly handed me some work sheets to take home that would help me think about the decision. They were printed on blue and green and pink paper, FAQs about adoption. *How soon after the birth can the baby be placed in its adoptive home? Will my medical bills be covered by the agency, the adoptive parents, or both? Will I be able to see my baby in the hospital?*

But I was thinking about Uncle Johnny. I'd observed the way his short nose and wide face didn't match any of ours, but I'd never wondered who it was he looked like. His smoky voice and hearty laugh, his *heyyy, hon!* belonged to some other family, but I hadn't had the flicker of a thought: *Whose?* His mother was standing right in front of me every time I hugged him, and yet I hadn't seen her once; how had she accomplished such utter invisibility?

"We refer to them as birth mothers, for lack of a better term."

A *birth* mother—it seemed like some kind of fantastic, magical character. The shadow of the coatrack you couldn't see, the wrinkles in a son's face that assemble and disappear, a ghostly presence that slips across the side of the wall. If I was going to take on this role, the invisible member of adoption, I would have to understand the special sleights, the extraordinary hiding places.

Molly asked if I'd ever heard of open adoption. It sounded like some kind of *improved* adoption. Adoption had of course evolved along with dentistry and flight and calculators and war. Allowances had been studied and generous contingencies put in place. By now, they'd have devised ways to make what used to be hard about adoption easier.

"Open adoption basically means that the mother can know the family who adopts her child." Molly explained that Catholic Social Services was at the forefront of a whole open adoption movement I hadn't heard about. "That contact gives the adopted child access to information about its history. The parents gain the confidence of knowing they were specifically chosen by the birth mother to raise her child. And the birth mother gets to see that her child is happy and safe."

This all seemed sensible and exactly as it should be.

It was brand-new information, but it registered easily, as if I'd always known it. Open adoption seemed perfectly suited to the modern world and the kind of hybrid solution I was looking for. It wasn't once and for all like abortion, and it wasn't being a single parent or getting married too young, but it wasn't just giving up a baby, either. It was some mix of other things. These ideas I stored to think about later, with other thoughts I hadn't fully processed: that I was pregnant, that I was going to have a baby, that it was already two inches big inside me.

"You don't need to make a decision today. We want you to feel comfortable with whatever you decide, and there's still plenty of time."

Molly reassured me, in that imitation living room, with giant inoperable windows overlooking the Ohio River Valley, with her shoulder-length brown hair and her handouts xeroxed on blue and green and pink colored paper, on the fifth floor of a professional building in downtown Cincinnati, that everything would be okay, that people made adoption plans every day, that I was not too late for anything, that what she'd presented to me was a sound option. Adoption had a beautiful economy. It was like any biological process refined over millennia in which the by-product of one system becomes a building block of another. A special symbiosis. It drew on everything virtuous in human nature: love and selflessness and generosity. Things we should always want to cultivate. Molly would prepare me, and when the time came I would know what to do. It was a straight-forward process, one that had steps; all I needed to do was take them.

Molly stopped short of what I wanted her to tell me. I wanted her to tell me I had the look of a girl who could give up her baby. I wanted her to assure me, in her professional opinion, given my ambitions and history and constitution, that this was what I should do. Even though, as we agreed to meet again after Christmas, I knew Jevn was right.

FIVE

We left for the holidays without making a decision. I couldn't remember how I'd ever decided anything. I'd changed majors three times, but those hadn't felt like decisions. I'd started out in political science at a college in Virginia, but when I met with the dean she was wearing false eyelashes, and it wasn't a decision; I just knew when she blinked that I had to go to music school. I switched majors to architecture a couple of years later because I happened to overhear a conversation between two architects, and it sounded so honest. Something about the "dimensions of the foundation." People do not need modern reproductions of early polyphony, I realized at that moment; they need *buildings*.

I didn't really think I was making decisions then. To decide means to cut something off—you have to lose something. But I was never weighing one thing over another. There was never some haunting regret. I was just blown like a seed.

But every step, even the littlest ones, forever changed the picture of my entire universe. During my summer overseas, I'd abandoned entire countries for the sake of a chapel in Todi, entire landscapes for a garden in Tivoli. I went to the Mediterranean coast instead of exploring Mantua. Because of a dream along the way, I bought a ticket to China. Who knows why I let those things be my guide? Who knows what I hadn't seen as a result?

I was deciding all the time. We're always at a fork in the road, abandoning a universe of possibilities for the sake of just one, on the basis of inadequate information. And still we continue, as though a thousand futures were not crumbling with every step.

The heat of the interstate rippled the horizon as the soft ridges of East Tennessee came into view. I was accustomed to a high horizon, purple mountains in every direction; it felt as if they secured gravity in our little valley, like stones holding down the picnic-blanket edges of our town. Jevn wasn't coming home with me for Christmas as we'd planned in the fall. We hadn't even had to talk about it to know those plans had changed. I opened the creaky front door and dropped my bags in the hallway. My dad was in the kitchen, standing at the counter shelling peanuts out of the red canister Mom kept them in. He looked at me for a moment before he opened his arms.

"Does someone need a hug from her daddy?"

I'd never called him *Daddy*. I just wanted things to be normal. He made a high-pitched *mmmmm!!* sound when I squeezed him around his fat middle and patted me on my shoulder blades. He asked me if I wanted any peanuts, but he didn't mention my pregnancy, and he said nothing about Jevn. I'm not sure what I expected. I was glad he wasn't angry, but I wanted something more from him. I'd always wanted him to take my boyfriends aside and whisper manly threats in their ears, like the beautifully hot-tempered fathers and brothers in movies did. Like the Dukes did for Daisy. Like my brother had done only once, when I kicked Jeff Howl's bike while he was on it, and Mikey threatened to beat him up when Jeff tried to chase me down and kill me. I'd felt so deeply validated, cowering behind my brother while he defended me—all the more because I didn't know why I'd done it in the first place.

But when my dad met Jevn the first time, he just asked, *How do you suppose trees manage to grow taller than thirty-two feet? Atmospheric pressure keeps water from rising above that height, don't you know.* He wasn't even trying to intimidate him, there was just no Internet then.

Even when our neighbor pulled a knife on him, calling him a Yank, after we moved in—it only provoked him to clarify that Maryland, where he grew up, was actually south of the Mason-Dixon. Not that that mattered much to them, because Maryland still fought with the Union in the Civil War. We were still Yankees among Confederates, heathens in the Bible Belt.

It just wasn't in his nature to beat people up, or talk about my love life, or give advice. The only rule he ever instituted was, don't kill spiders. And he didn't have to say it twice. When the biggest, wolfiest spider showed up on my pillow once, he helped me find a wide-mouthed jar but sent me back upstairs solo. I flinched every time it leapt dry and furrily at the glass, but he knew I'd find a home for it in the brush across the street, because he said so few things, but he said that. Spiders are good; don't kill them. He didn't tell me not to kill ants, but one time in the garden he said that the earth would collapse if they went extinct. And structures were his expertise. Who knows what minuscule, squishable things hold up this whole entire universe? So I didn't kill ants, either.

When Mom came down the stairs in her robe, Dad put a handful of peanuts in his pocket and went outside. She hugged me and listed the leftovers that were in the refrigerator. I was dreading our conversation, too, and so I took control of it right away.

"I had a meeting at Catholic Social Services," I said as she put a loaf of bread on the countertop. I explained the logistics of the adoption process to avoid the unspeakable other things my pregnancy brought up. Boys. Money. Religion. Mom was Catholic, but she wasn't dogmatic about it, and I thought her own daughter's crisis pregnancy might test her conviction. But I was glad she'd been so certain about abortion. I already knew I couldn't do it, and now we didn't even have to talk about it. "They do open adoption, where you actually get to know the family who adopts the child. You pick them out from a bunch of letters couples have written, and you try to find people you think would make good parents."

She sat down at the table next to me. I repeated everything I had learned from Molly. How it was free, how the child would go to a couple who needed it, and how there was a whole process that had been perfected. "I have a meeting with Molly when I get back to Cincinnati," I said, to let her know I'd already begun the process. By the time I'd told her everything, I'd convinced us both that I was going to do adoption.

"It's going to be hard," my mother said. "I think you'll just have to think about the couple it's going to help." Then she got up and quietly returned to the countertop. *Enjoy the last of the chocolate milk*, I remembered her saying once as she put the square metal container away. Nestlé was somehow depriving the children in Africa of breast milk, so we weren't going to buy anything from that company anymore. If we were hungry for chocolate milk, we should just think about how hungry those babies must be. Feelings were a luxury of the modern age, and you could minimize them by remembering what real suffering looks like.

"Maybe we can stop by the Natural Foods Store and get you some prenatal vitamins," she said, back to the comforting terrain of the practical. It didn't occur to me then that my old roommate's mother, who sent her the leopard-print underwear, would have probably offered to help raise the baby. And her father would have definitely beaten Jevn up.

She leaned over and kissed me on the top of my head and went back upstairs to put on her makeup. She left two sandwiches on the countertop, one for me and one for my dad.

Outside, Dad was partway through the process of replacing the driveway by hand, breaking up the concrete and carting the debris a quarter of a mile away by wheelbarrow to a busy road, along which he piled the chunks to stabilize the slope. All our cars were parked on the street, including the station wagon neighborhood teenagers were always offering to buy. It had a special suspension system, good for crash-up derbies. But Dad was saving it for a crash-up derby himself. The back door had fallen off, so he'd tied the canoe to the roof like an external spine and dangled the door from the cantilevered canoe behind. Driving cars into the ground was one of his money-saving strategies; we had cars abandoned all over town. When one broke down, we could walk to another, cross our fingers it might start.

He offered the sledgehammer to my brother, who had just pulled up, home from college himself. I'd told him my news over the phone, but he hadn't said much in response. I don't think he knew what to say. He hugged me hello in a way that told me he hadn't forgotten, and I stood back as he took a swing. It fell dull and heavy on the concrete. Dad took the sledgehammer back to demonstrate his technique. It struck with a solid metallic thud. Between swings, he leaned back proudly and smiled. "And some people pay *big bucks* for a gym membership!"

And then everything was normal. There was nothing more to talk about. My sister was still in China, but otherwise it felt like any other Christmas. We piled into the car and drove out to our land in the country as usual. Thirteen acres of pasture where we'd planted four thousand white pines and Douglas firs when we were little—Dad's backup plan in case his engineering practice failed. All those saplings grew into a solid block of forest by the time we were teenagers, but we'd drag a tree out of it at Christmastime to make good on the investment.

That night, Mom put the old shoeboxes full of ornaments on the coffee table, and we rummaged through them, decorating the tree. Most of the ornaments were from Germany and France, where my parents were living when they met. Both were working for the army, Mom as a teacher, Dad as an engineer. Our whole house was decorated with trinkets from other places: street artists' renderings of Vienna and Strasbourg, a camel saddle from Egypt, a glass clown from Murano. As much as I loved the mountains of Tennessee, I always knew it was just one place in the world, and I always knew I would be leaving.

"Isn't that a beautiful fire?" Dad leaned back from the fireplace, his hands behind his head, and invited us to admire it with him. I untangled a beaded angel I'd made in Indian Princesses, a father-daughter bonding organization we used to attend. He recognized it and smiled. We'd gone on a camping trip, during which the fathers told the daughters there were escaped convicts on the loose in the woods, and then a couple of fathers put on scary masks and came banging on the windows of our cabin late at night, and we stacked our mattresses ten high and scrambled to the top but only narrowly escaped their grasp as they reached for our ankles from the bottom. There was a lot of beer and poker, some canoeing and swinging on vines, and then there was the last-minute craft, Dad's fat fingers beading an angel to persuade Mom we'd had a weekend of quality time. Which, of course, we had.

That night before Midnight Mass, I called Jevn. We wished each other Merry Christmas. I told him my family supported the idea of adoption and I was feeling really hopeful about it. But Jevn said that his mother had been telling him more about abortion. It wasn't too late. She was a nurse, and she'd assisted with abortions. She was really worried, like he was, about whether I'd be able to go through with adoption. And what were my plans if I couldn't?

I didn't have an answer; the only answer was I had to do it.

I stood between my mother and brother at church, the only Catholic church for miles. Dad stood on my brother's other side, wearing the wool jacket he kept just for that annual occasion when he'd dutifully accompany us to Midnight Mass. At the Our Father, we all took hands to pray. I was comforted by the familiar motions, though I never knew much about what they meant. I remembered some of our born-again neighbors telling me you don't take anything with you when you die, not your parents, or your siblings, or your pets. Definitely not your possessions. Definitely not the hills of Tennessee, or anywhere else you might love. When they said God's ways were not our ways, I thought that was the least my way of all God's ways. Because I wanted to keep all those things.

When we got to the middle of the Our Father, we always lifted our hands, hand in hand, together, for the words "For thine is the kingdom." It was an expression of submission to God's ways. But then it was an incongruous gesture, and for that reason it was always my favorite moment in the Mass. We were lifting our hands in surrender, but we were grasping them, hand in hand, like a human chain. With our mouths we admitted we don't make the rules, we may all die alone, but with a hundred clasped hands held high, we objected: we are going to hold on tight. It was a losing battle, our will against his, but we raised our clenched fists to God, as if we could hold on to anything.

◉ ◉ ◉

Only secretly did I enjoy a new pleasure over the holidays. Having someone together with me while I rolled out cookie dough with my brother. Within me to share a taste of my mother's roasted vegetables and squash soup. Swaddled in my ski pants and thick wool sweater when we went skiing in West Virginia before I headed back to school. Someone who fell with me, careful as I was not to fall, when a skier came out of nowhere saying *sorry, sorry, sorry* beneath me as we all three slid down the hill. Someone who demanded pickles, just like on TV.

And someone who joined us for a last hike in the mountains, where Dad did what he always did out in the woods. He'd wander off the trail, studying one tree after another, from top to bottom. He'd press at a trunk inquisitively. When he found a good one, he'd press more until the tree began to move almost imperceptibly back and forth, and at that same tiny rhythm he'd push back. Soon the top of the tree would be whipping in large arcs, knocking through the canopy, and it would start to crack a few feet above where it met the ground. We were so used to him doing it, we didn't even turn around when we heard it fall, but sometimes we'd chop it up and roll it down the mountain for firewood.

"Just a lovely day, isn't it?" he asked me. It was sunny and not cold at all, though colder on the mountaintop than back at home. I told him about my internship that was coming up in January. My program consisted of alternating internship quarters and quarters in school, year-round for six years. Kids went all over the world for their internships, but I'd found a job in Cincinnati so I could be with Jevn, who would be in school. We'd made that plan before I got pregnant.

Dad liked to hear about architecture school. Architects' ignorance about construction made his engineering work more challenging, but he was amused by stories about this ignorance in its earliest stages of development. And he was always willing to help with my structures assignments. Design a column to be crushed, a bridge to be broken. You know a material best by knowing how it breaks.

"I was thinking," he said, "it was nice with your mother and me, that when we had you kiddies she could take off from teaching, and I could work on making the money. And that we'd done all the traveling we wanted to do beforehand. I'd think it would be awfully hard to be a single mother—"

"I *know*, Dad." I stopped him from nearing the subject, in his indirect way. "That's what we already decided. I'm doing adoption."

And we had already established that hard and easy didn't matter. It wasn't about how it felt. It was about the facts, that a child needs certain things I couldn't give it. It was up to me to manage the emotional part.

He went silent and cracked some peanuts out of his pocket, offering one to me. He stepped off to the side and pressed at another trunk. Looked up the column to its leafless top. All that weight seemed weightless when it was woven within the other branches, reaching to the sky.

"What is it that makes it fall?" I asked.

"Oh, oh. Well. It's called resonance. Just the particular frequency of a material where it has a bigger amplitude." He waved his hand back and forth, imitating the tree. "When you apply pressure at a certain rhythm, a small amount of force can generate a whole lot of oscillation." His hand waved in bigger arcs. "Enough oscillation, and the material fails. It's in everything's nature to break. You just have to find the right force." He pressed a few more times until there was a splintering, shifting deep inside the trunk. He looked at me and smiled, raising and wiggling his eyebrows. He scrambled backward as the tree came crashing down.

SIX

olly brought a small stack of colorful packets into the room
and sat down. Some were almost books, their cardstock cov-
ers bound with lace ribbons, and some were just a few pages
stapled at the corner. There were beaming faces on the front pages, ecstatic fonts and cute margin art. "Hi! We're Rob and Robin!!" they cried
out from some strange and wonderful place, out of cozy windows where
fuzzy felt shutters were stuck to fuzzy felt walls. A primary instrument
of open adoption, these were letters written by waiting couples to an unknown pregnant girl, kept on file by the agency for moments like this,
when one stops in, contemplating the impossible.

Jevn hadn't gotten back from Colorado, but I'd begun to take the steps:
I set up prenatal appointments at the university hospital and arranged
my second meeting with Molly. I bought groceries and a pregnancy
cookbook; I took the vitamins Mom had bought for me in Tennessee.
On the phone, I told Jevn I could do adoption. All the while, I was still
trying to convince myself that I was pregnant.

Molly handed me several letters, along with a work sheet she pulled
from a folder, and left me to look at them. I had in my hands a bumpy
pile of what could be my child's parents. The exercise would be as simple
as this: for each potential family, a check box for yes and one for no, and

three empty lines to accommodate an explanation. This was open adoption: you go into a little room with your ballpoint pen and a work sheet and come out with a completed form and a family for your child.

Dear Birth Mother, Our names are Kevin and Kate, and we are in our late twenties.

There was a heart-shaped photo of a brunette couple, china cabinet in the background, flowered border along the top of the wall behind them. Her wrist fell over his shoulder and her hand lay perfectly flat at his chest, as if to display her diamond ring.

We were high school sweethearts and have a very tender loving stable and supportive marriage.

I turned the page.

There was a photograph of Kevin sitting in the branches of a tree; it was affixed with football helmet and baseball glove stickers. His round, gold-rimmed glasses and wide face reminded me of my high school boyfriend. *Kevin is an attorney and works in a local law firm not far from home*, the caption said.

On the next page, there was a photo of Kate, limp-wristed and pulled up so close to the piano her belly was touching the keys. The photo was attached with music note and flower stickers.

I put the profile on the sofa beside me and looked at the next. Carl and Denise's letter had a light blue ribbon border and a soft pink rose in the corner. Its tone was direct and earnest. *While having a hysterectomy was certainly not something we wished for, we don't see it as the end of the world.* They described their home as *a four-bedroom house in a subdivision outside of a large metropolitan area*, and they had a three-year-old adopted daughter. Denise said Carl could always make her laugh; Carl said that Denise had an *irresistible childish joy.* They loved to travel; their daughter had already seen the Shedd Aquarium, FAO Schwarz, the Ghirardelli Chocolate factory, and Lake Tahoe!

I put them on top of Kevin and Kate.

Rob and Lori had wide smiles and giant plaid shirts. *We both love children and have been through four years of infertility treatment trying to start our family.* There was a photo of five indistinguishable heads bobbing in a lake. Handwritten below it, *swimming with friends.* Along the margins were colorful flowers overlaid with romantic fragments of script, as if their own seventeen-page message was printed on the palimpsest of a love letter from the days of inkwells and wax seals. There was a picture of Lori's brother kissing a llama. A picture of a mobile home with vast lengths of plastic siding where windows should have been. A cat and the handwritten text *precious*—the name of the cat, or maybe just the nature of its blissful curled-up-ness. A blurry picture of a deer, maybe in their yard, and a yellowed photo of a barge loaded with people, with the caption *boat parade*.

Molly returned and quietly closed the door.

"You'll have more time to look at these; I just wanted you to get an idea of the kinds of letters couples write. You're very early on in this process."

This Process had Early Stages and Late Stages. I was sitting comfortably within known boundaries.

She said my options wouldn't be limited to the twenty or so couples she had on file, who were all Catholic couples living in southwest Ohio. There were many more couples, in other places across the United States. She advised me to go "online," where I could search for open adoption agencies. They would send their own files of Dear Birth Mother letters, and if I found a couple I liked, Molly would work with their agency to represent me.

"How many profiles do people usually look at before they find a family?"

"It really just depends; everyone's different. Did you have any questions about those?"

"No," I said, shaking my head. The couples piled in my lap seemed perfectly nice. From what I could tell, they were ready for parenthood in exactly the ways I wasn't. They were married and had houses and jobs and incomes. But they weren't simply "waiting adoptive families," the way I'd imagined them. I'd pictured them like the starving children in Africa my mother would tell me about: a homogeneous mass of people who were deserving inasmuch as they were in need. I thought I would cast my baby into the void of human heartbreak and know that, whatever it cost me, it was at least doing something good for someone who deserved it. But these were not homogeneous people at all! They had their own hair colors and names and neighborhoods and brothers who kissed llamas. They would have smells and jukeboxes and three-car garages. They might blast the air-conditioning, or heat the swimming pool, or watch enormous televisions in finished basements with parquet floors and windows that looked out to the undersides of holly bushes. There were so many things to watch out for.

Molly said that open adoption means you get to *know* the couple who adopts your child. That *knowing* had seemed simple and good. I'd know their names and addresses and what they looked like. Knowing seemed like a form of protection I'd retain as a parent. I'd have a window, like a guardian angel, into my child's life. But now knowing seemed dangerous and complicated. That window opened wide. I'd know the pattern of the wallpaper in the kitchen and the color of the carpet—and I would feel responsible for it, and for everything it signified. Everything I saw, I was choosing for my child. They'd be adopting my baby, but I'd be adopting the burden of every last detail of their lives, and I wouldn't be able to ignore it any more than I wanted to shut that window to my child. But once I signed the papers, the entire future would be set in motion, and I wouldn't be able to do anything about it.

When Jevn returned from Colorado, I told him that the meeting with Molly had been promising. I could feel a new distance between us, and I tried to think about how to love him in the right way—the new, broken-up but having a baby way. How to not hate him and his potential. But on my twenty-third birthday, it felt more like the old days. He took me to see *Island of the Sharks* at the Omnimax in the old art deco train station. The entrance was punctuated by fountains and pools and terraces and sculpture, and as we walked along them, I asked him to slow down; my tailbone was still hurting from my fall on the ski slopes. But I was always asking him to slow down. Sometimes I'd refer to the saying *Don't walk behind me; I may not lead. Don't walk in front of me; I may not follow.* "Just walk beside me and be my friend."

"Maybe you should just be my friend and speed up!"

The old train hall was sheltered by a monumental dome. We went to opposite corners of the arch, spoke softly to each other, and waited. His secret message would go bouncing up into the ceiling only to arrive at my ear, perfectly preserved as a whisper. After the film, we drove downtown for dinner at my favorite restaurant. It felt like we'd forgotten about all the complications and returned momentarily to our relationship in a prior form.

"I like you," he would say simply, his smile gaping open. He meant something precise; simple and full of wonder. "I smile when I think about you."

He often looked at me like he was a dog inspecting a curious object he thought might play with him at any moment. Like he was ready to burst into a run to chase it, and he could hardly wait for it to move, and his excitement wasn't diminished when it didn't.

For the two years we were together, we spent a lot of time apart, Jevn on internship, me overseas or in Tennessee. *I dreamed of you last night*, he wrote in one of his letters. *We were buying a board game for you.* In one of my letters I drew the James River, where I'd gone exploring abandoned canal locks and pump rooms with my brother, as a long line running along the edge of the page. In the next letter, he suggested we make a pact. We would traverse the world by river.

"Did you forget our pact?" he would ask in his letters that followed. Not because he thought I had. I think just because vulnerability was one of those exciting new territories he wanted to explore with me. When we were back in the same city, he named our pact "We have questions for God." He was acknowledging my inability to pin down my ambiguous and uncertain faith, and he was enjoying, himself, having someone to ask such questions with. He folded the paper that detailed our itinerary.

"How many times should I fold it? One for you . . . one for me . . . and one for the third." When he unfolded it there were eight panels made by the creases, for the number of deserts we were going to see by river.

That weekend after my birthday, I went to his apartment to get some of the things I'd stored there when I was overseas. The narrow door of the closet where I kept them opened to a space ten feet deep. He often offered it to me as a sublet; we joked that I could put a bed in there and a little lamp. Like a pocket he could keep me in.

I noticed he had taken down our pictures from the windowsill.

Pictures he'd framed between two sheets of glass with small metal clips. The two of us at a cabin in the mountains by the Arkansas River, me wearing one of his gigantic wool sweaters, smiling for the timer on his camera before we took a long walk. When I closed the door, I told myself there wouldn't be time, for a very, very long time, to think about this relationship again.

Jevn joined me for my next appointment with Molly, but I sat mostly silent so she could ask him all the background questions she had already asked me. I looked to the floor to give them privacy.

I was afraid he wouldn't trust Molly or speak openly with her, and that later he would tell me I couldn't possibly give up a baby. And, knowing he had given it a chance, I might believe him and then we wouldn't have any options left. I looked up occasionally at Molly, willing her to be broad-minded, to capture Jevn's attention, to gain his trust.

She sensed his reserve. She matched his rhythms and tenor. And soon she began talking about things that concerned both of us, so I straightened in my seat.

"Given what you both know about open adoption, can you tell me a little bit about what you think could be the advantages? Do you think you would like to have a relationship of some kind with your child?"

I waited to hear Jevn's response.

"I think this child will be a very sensitive and special person," he said. "Yes, I very much want to be around it, and get to know it, and have it know my family."

I was surprised to hear him talk about it like that, like he was already thinking of it as a real person, someone to get to know. If it was real to anyone, it should have been me. I was the one with regular appointments in the maternity ward, where patients were all called *Mama*, where every woman was defined by the promise of a child within her. I was the one nodding in disbelief as they recorded its heart rate, estimated a due date, and told me I already wasn't consuming enough calories. I was the one who agreed to start eating an egg every day to build brain cells in a thing I still couldn't think of as an independent "it" I'd like my family to know.

"Do you have any feelings about parenting the child? Obviously, you'd get to know it best if you remained its father."

"I would love to be its father—I think we'd both be good parents. And I'm not sure Amy can give up a child. This child." Jevn spoke very slowly. "But we've talked about it. Neither of us is ready for parenting. A child needs two parents, and we've agreed we can't be together and be those two parents. Adoption seems the most loving option in our situation."

Jevn often held his thumb and index finger a tiny distance apart when he spoke so that you would understand how deliberate he was being about his words. The half an inch he held horizontally in space seemed to register the degree of precision that distinguished his idea from other ideas, even those just a tiny distance away. He was admitting a margin of error, a dubious relationship between word and idea, but by admitting it, he was also telling you he was more careful than most people, and that the slowness of his speech was not for him, it was for you.

"And Amy might still be my friend," he added.

Molly smiled at me, at this. But I didn't take any comfort in the thought of some distant time when we'd be able to be friends.

"Ideally, you will be able to know the child in some way as it grows up," Molly said. "That's what we hope for. But there are no guarantees, and I want you to be very clear about this." She uncrossed her legs and leaned forward, her hands in prayer between her knees. "There is nothing legally binding about ongoing openness in an open adoption. There's not a state in the country that can enforce openness. You will get to choose a family—in that way your adoption will certainly be 'open'—but once you sign a Permanent Surrender, you will have no legal protections to ensure you can see your child. If the parents decide they don't want you to have contact with the child, for any reason, that will be perfectly within their rights."

She softened as she continued. "In light of that, are you at all worried about how you'll feel after placing your child? Particularly given how strong your feelings seem to be for each other and for this child?"

"Yes, of course," Jevn said, "it will be difficult knowing that it's in the world somewhere without me. I think, no matter what, I'll always be wondering about it. Especially if it ends up not being an open adoption. But I just want the best for it. I really want to find a good family."

"Well, these are important things to consider. If you feel you wouldn't be able to give the baby up without openness, we have to really think about whether adoption is the right plan for you, or whether it might be best to think about parenting." Molly turned to me. "What about you, Amy? We've talked about a lot of this before, but what are your feelings at this point?"

My feelings were located almost entirely behind my belly button, a satisfying knot that reached along the back side of my heart and all the way up to the hollow between my collarbones. This would transform unpredictably into a dramatic hunger and then a violent, nauseating heartburn. An excruciating compulsion to eat and a fierce impulse to vomit, with only a tiny window in between during which I could cast food at the thing everyone said was inside me. I did not have any well-reasoned things to say.

"I definitely feel concern. And excitement." And disbelief, feral hunger, and heartburn.

"Last time we met I asked you to think about the advantages of parenting; do you want to talk about that?"

"Yeah, I've been thinking about it," I said. "I just know that if I kept it, even if I didn't have money, and I didn't finish school, and I struggled forever, I'd find a way to make sure things worked out. I wouldn't have to worry about whether I'd chosen the right parents—and there would never be a day when it realized it was abandoned."

Molly turned her head slightly, so that one side of her face was advancing toward me faster than the other.

"I want to make sure you understand that adoption is not abandonment, Amy. It's a very important distinction. You're considering a plan for adoption so your child can have the *best possible situation* to grow up in." Her head nodded with each important word. "You're making a *parenting* decision when you place your child for adoption. That's completely different from abandonment."

I nodded, I know, I know, I know. I understood there was language I was supposed to use—*plan for adoption, placing my child*—but I wanted to use harder, more honest-sounding language. Language that wouldn't let me trick myself into thinking I was doing something more noble than I was. Abandoning my baby to llama kissers.

"The two of you are intelligent and resourceful, and you work well together, am I right in seeing that? Do you agree?"

I waited, but Jevn was silent. We had started a project together, collecting aluminum cans from the design studios. We'd bought special containers and drilled can-sized holes in the lids and spray-painted recycling symbols on them. We would borrow a truck every few weeks and take the cans to be recycled. We made a pretty good team doing that, I thought. But maybe Jevn felt differently.

"You seem to communicate well, which is one of the most important measures of a relationship. And you've been working together functionally up to this point. I know this could be a very sensitive question, but is there any way you can imagine parenting the child together?"

"Our relationship is complex enough not to have to add another layer of complexity," Jevn said definitively. Just a couple of weeks ago he could imagine it, I thought. But then I didn't want her to return us to that moment we were now pretending never happened.

"And there are so many families waiting to adopt," I added. It was easier to think of some other fresh, new couple, not us. Infinitely complicated us. I had to hope there was, in fact, a generic mass of good and worthy waiting families somewhere. I just hadn't found them yet.

Molly sent us home with our workbooks and asked us to spend time thinking about keeping our child. The workbook asked questions to test our preparedness for having a family. *Are you really ready to have a child? Do you know the basic needs of a child? Can your apartment accommodate a child? Do you have transportation? Do you have a babysitter? How often would you need one? Will your family help? Do you have the money to support a child (including rent, taxes, insurance, utilities, water, garbage collection, telephone, furniture, house repairs, cleaning supplies, groceries, eating out, gas, oil, automobile repairs, doctor, dentist, drugs, clothes, laundry, dry cleaning, tuition, books, special instructional fees, union dues, subscriptions, haircuts, entertainment, alimony, child's allowance, miscellaneous debts, cigarettes, hobbies, babysitters, Christmas, special occasions, church, and charity)? What dreams do you have for your life and could a child fit into them? Are there any compromises that might allow you to have all the things you want?*

Having a child, according to the workbook, was a matter of figuring out a certain set of logistics, and you would need to be very organized and begin the process a long time in advance of getting pregnant. But even if you had everything in place, down to the money set aside for cigarettes, it still seemed to me you did not necessarily have a reason to have a child. What was a good reason to have a child? What justification could there be for keeping one? Surely every couple would fail on some test of preparedness—but should we all give up our babies, if we couldn't tick every box? And if some couple really was ready, should that alone entitle them to take my child? Nature certainly wasn't paying attention to anyone's readiness.

And it seemed to me that giving up a child would likely bring about issues I wasn't any more prepared to deal with than I was the logistics of parenthood. Why didn't my workbook ask: *Was I really ready to lose a child?*

I didn't fill out the answers. The answers were obvious. No, I wasn't ready. Yes, every single one of my dreams precluded having a child at twenty-three. The questions did their job. They forced me to look closely at a future I was in important ways not equipped for and scared me back. I went online at the computer lab and began requesting "Dear Birth Mother" letters from every agency I could find. As the profiles streamed in, in thick packages that arrived on my stoop, Jevn and I spent hours reviewing them, and I began to send envelopes full of letters to my sister in China to scan for potential candidates.

SEVEN

The architecture building was buried in a hillside that sloped steeply from my favorite exit down to the street, and a signature landscape architect had put some signature ripples in the lawn on its way down. Only two floors peeped out from the top of the hill, but four stories were buried underground and opened like a geode into the interior of campus. The building had reputedly been constructed without a single 90-degree angle between any two planes; walls met floors and each other at various angles, some so closely approximating 90 degrees they didn't seem avant-garde at all, and some so acute they became dusty no-man's-lands into which no furniture could be squeezed. Room numbers were out of sequence and nested, such that 6206 was hidden inside a hallway accessed by 6104. The building was clad in a synthetic material painted pink and baby blue; the window mullions were Frank Lloyd Wright red.

I drove past it many times when I was in the conservatory. I thought it was a derelict elementary school, swallowed over time by an insatiable university campus and slated for demolition. I would soon learn about deconstructivism and that the building had just had its forty-million-dollar ribbon cutting.

"Hey," I said, greeting Jevn in the computer lab.

"Hey," he exhaled, leaning back in his chair, not looking up from the screen. I sat down at the computer beside him.

I didn't ask him about school, and he didn't ask about my internship, which had just started that week. It was the kind of architecture I'd hoped to do when I signed up for architecture school. Free design work for people who needed it. But most of the projects were on hold awaiting funding, and I spent a lot of time gazing out the storefront windows. The only thing that really broke up the day was eating my afternoon egg, which I shut myself in the tiny bathroom at the back of the office to do. I became a vegan when I was twelve, so I hadn't eaten an egg in ten years. I'd crack the shell on the sink and wrap the pieces in toilet paper. Then I'd swallow it like a pill. I'd face myself in the mirror, amid drawings stored along the side of the sink and behind the toilet, waiting for the fan to suck up the smell. I didn't mind the slow days; I could conserve energy for what felt like my real job, which began late in the afternoon when I pedaled back up Vine Street toward home.

We sat side by side in the back rows of the lab so other students couldn't see what we were working on. The Web was new—a haphazard database of incomplete information you stumbled upon using search terms: *open adoption*; *adoption agencies in Ohio*. We printed agency web pages and profiles we liked to read more closely later.

"I was thinking it would be nice if they came from the mountains," Jevn said quietly, and because we always disagreed about whose mountains were better, I knew he meant, specifically, the sharp young Rockies, not the refined old Appalachians. We agreed our child shouldn't grow up in Ohio.

"Yeah, and be outside a lot," I responded. Both of us loved to hike and ride bikes. I ran as often as I could, and Jevn liked to ski and cycle so much, he had come to school in Ohio to keep from being distracted by those things. "It could also be really good for them to have a child already, so we could be sure it would have a sibling," I said. That was one very important thing I wouldn't be able to provide, were I to become a single parent.

"Yeah," he agreed, "and if the sibling is adopted, we'd get to see what kind of relationship they have with the other birth parents."

It felt like progress to visualize them.

We both read quietly through profiles to ourselves. Most couples said that they were Christian. I used to think I was a Christian, too, but our neighbors back in Tennessee were always correcting me. They said my whole family was going to hell. My mother because on top of being Catholic, she let a whole range of social justice issues in this world distract her from her future in the next. My dad because he wasn't religious at all. Like the devil, he enjoyed nothing so much as fire, and he would chop our neighbors' dead trees down for them, just so he could have the kindling. And the rest of us, because we were somewhere in between.

But those neighbors never stopped trying to save me. I'd play Barbies with the girl down the street, and one night her mother knocked on her bedroom door and asked: Do I want to be saved and go to heaven, or not, and suffer eternal punishment in hell? They had illustrated hell for me on many occasions: fire and extreme heat, no family, no friends, no Barbies, no pets. Everything you don't like—for ever and ever and ever and ever and ever and ever. I remember the dim lights and the quiet as they waited for my answer. They'd described heaven, too. Praising God forever. Crowns and gold and gates and glory and seraphim and cherubim. I didn't want heaven or hell; I wanted to be propped in front of my friend's four big-screen televisions in her living room, each one encased in faux wood and standing on its own four faux-wood feet, cable blaring from the one that worked, with boxes of Coke and Sprite stacked as tall as her father against the wall. Anywhere but cornered on the bed listening to my friend's mother talk about the devil, whom I knew to live at the bottom of the hill, before the woods, where the ground was soft and moss instead of grass grew by a tiny creek—more a fissure in the ground that appeared and disappeared—and where it was dark no matter what the time of day. Where we would eventually drink whiskey and try cigarettes. I may not have known much about God, but I knew well to avoid the devil. I lost my hustle whenever the ball rolled down the hill in that direction. I made things as easy as possible and prayed the prayer. But getting saved didn't mean much more than I was trusted to play with my friend, and then only until I turned twelve and became a vegan, at which point I was abandoned to the devil for good.

I'd spent a lot of time in college trying to untangle it all. I'd even broken up with Jevn over it, saying I needed to figure out God and to do that I needed to be free of Jevn's influence. I thought it could be a touchy subject now, but it was important to me; I wanted my child to have space on reserve for such important questions.

"I want them to be Christian," I told him.

"Not Bible thumpers," he qualified, by way of agreement.

Most of the things we wanted we didn't really have to talk about. They were complicated and nuanced things, but it was basically just us, a little more prepared and about ten years older. We weren't talking anymore about whether I could do adoption; we were just working hard to find a family we could do it with. Until we found them, the only decision we were making was that the baby was going to be born. There was still time to think about the rest.

"They should recycle," I said.

"Of course."

By early February, I had *no* piles and *maybe* piles, *Jevn-needs-to-look-at* and *Jevn-likes* piles. But they mixed together in my memory and got shuffled around as I stepped over them in my apartment. The letters had much the same structure; in the About Him and About Her sections, couples described themselves in long lists of benign adjectives: romantic, wacky, tender, fun, forgiving, encouraging, likes to laugh, a friend to everyone, a heart of pure gold. They wrote of gratifying careers and told stories of how they met and became best friends. They shared dreams of apple-picking, cooking s'mores over the fire, and driving to the farm for balled and burlapped Christmas trees to be planted in the yard come January. The About Our Home section read like a real estate listing: three bedrooms, two and a half baths, on three acres and a cul-de-sac with a fully fenced-in backyard just waiting for a swing set!

Photographs were strewn throughout—in Florida swimming with a dolphin, him backlit by the Planet Hollywood sign, her backlit by the Planet Hollywood sign, snowmobiling in Aspen, professional photos with his hand expressively positioned on her stomach, occasionally an idyllic picture of the Eiffel Tower or a beach in the Bahamas, with neither of them in the frame to suggest they were there to see it. Several couples shared their photos of the Magic Kingdom, all taken from approximately the same location. There were photographs shot in a single day by the kind of photographer who directs you to rotate your head on your neck in exceptional ways, who'd arranged the couple in various still lifes: beaming between the forked branches of a tree, sitting on rocks beside a small waterfall, donning different-colored raincoats and, inexplicably, sunglasses.

There were zany photos of her, standing on her head in the living room (*Mindy has flipped!*); him leaning proudly against the hood of his stock car (*Vrrrrroom!*). Photographs had been cut out with pinking shears and surrounded with glittery stickers hand-stuck to the page. Captions were often handwritten with arbitrary capitalization, framed by thought bubbles, and more often than not terminated with exclamation points: *Birthday time is Fun time!* Margins featured baby rattles, stacked blocks, and teddy bears. In one case, an actual rattle was attached to the letter's cover, securing its position at the top of the pile. Sometimes there were appendices, with letters of recommendation from mothers and fathers and good friends and siblings of the hopeful couple, vouching for their "constant, effortless, and plentiful smiles. What sweeter emotions could a child be given?"

I was escorted in a jolly promenade through happy homes and histories, through a world rendered elementary, where quotation marks designated common phrases and important words were written in all caps. *Todd likes to "kid around," loves "TOOLS" and is quite handy around the house!* Where sincerity was tempered with lightness: *Interior decorating is her passion—she moves the furniture around occasionally to keep me on my toes* (and, in case I did not get the joke: *HA HA!*). Couples made random declarations, as if cornered awkwardly at a cocktail party—*Dressing alike is Fun!*—and fumbled for words, often seeming to forget I was literate and a native speaker of English. Sometimes the uncomfortably self-promotional nature of the form was playfully averted, as with a letter written as a screenplay in which the couple was endorsed, between antics, by their cats, Tillie, Simon, and Bingo.

None of the couples had chosen adoption out of concern for the unwanted children of the world, the way we fertile girls with noble principles sometimes imagined we'd do. Every single one was driven to it by misfortunes they mentioned only briefly. Complex stories inflected toward the positive. *After five years of infertility treatments, two surgeries, fertility drugs, numerous tests and doctor visits, we believe adoption is the answer to our prayers!*

I had so many questions. I wondered how it felt to know their child wouldn't look like the partner they said they loved so much. I wanted to know how their relationship had survived the blow of infertility—it couldn't be their common interest in old movies (*Rick makes the popcorn!*). Maybe it wasn't the place for stripped-bare authenticity, but I found myself wanting to scratch through the polish and explore territory not sanctioned by the agency template. In a situation like ours, with so little time to make such a big commitment, honesty was expedient. I wanted a candid glimpse of the couple. Special signals and particular stories to give me some flicker of an instinct that I'd found someone with whom I could share a future.

Instead they lured me with loose praise, congratulating me for my strength and thanking me for my generosity. They assured me that giving them my baby would be *the most unselfish and mature choice* I would ever make. They tugged at my heartstrings with e-mail addresses like childofourdreams@aol.com and overwhelmed themselves with premature and cumbersome gratitude: *Words are simply inadequate to describe the joy we will experience when we are told that you have made our dreams come true.* They said they admired my courage. They knew I had a hard decision to make. But little did they know I was praying for a miscarriage! That the trinkets of the world they dreamed about by day—rattles and blue bears and birthday cakes—happened to moonlight in my nightmares.

It was only on the topic of openness that the tone of the letters changed. They read like legal contracts written just to be revoked: "We are willing to pursue a level of openness that would be mutually beneficial and comfortable for all involved." Some said that they would be willing to keep in touch through letters and photos, which seemed to suggest I wouldn't get to see my child in person again. One couple offered a *commitment to openness to sharing every progress* of the child's life, but didn't specify what might constitute sharing (would they send letters through the adoption agency? Could we share an actual experience together?) or progress (the child's first step? Or high school graduation—maybe with no progresses in between?). The whole phrase *commitment to openness to sharing* was so strangely layered, it was surely not to be mistaken for *commitment to openness*.

But shouldn't they be cultivating visions of openness that had the same neon joy and optimism as their idealized dreams of parenthood? If they could imagine rocking my baby to sleep every night, was it so difficult to think about having me over for lunch now and then? I thought that some of the warmth and affection they somehow already felt for my child might spill over to me by association. Or out of gratitude for my courage and generosity.

My sister was the first to call it: *vultures*. She wrote from China, in response to the letters I'd sent her. She said all those long nights waiting for a baby, they weren't dreaming of a birth mother. They were only feigning compassion as they hovered, gliding in graceful circles as they waited to dive in. They wouldn't dare admit that I was merely a means to an end. That as soon as I supplied the vital ingredient to create their family, they would perceive me as a threat to it. That we were natural enemies.

Her mistrust was disheartening, but I knew that there were deep dynamics in play, and I was prepared to be vigilant. I understood the advantage of my position. We were tall, well educated, and white; we didn't do drugs; we'd decided on adoption together and had the support of our families; and we planned to give up our child as a newborn—all of these things, Molly said, would be highly desirable to potential couples. The only sensible thing was to make the most of that, to scrutinize everyone fully, to indulge every doubt, and to demand all the information they were reluctant to give us. Because after we signed the papers, the asymmetry of our positions would be fully reversed.

The letters closed in the spirit of their openings, full of joy and excitement, with easy promises about how much affection the couples had to offer. Couples assured me my baby would be loved and cherished *with all their hearts*, and I wanted to believe them—but by then I'd grown so wary that even those guarantees, so grandiose, so sweeping, so certain, gave me pause. It had been among the very few things I hadn't doubted: I hadn't doubted that the couple who adopted my child would be well equipped to parent, and I never thought my child would be adopted and not loved. Tragedy of tragedies.

I went to visit Molly alone one afternoon when Jevn had class, but I didn't talk about my worries. I knew she'd tell me what I could easily tell myself, that writing a Dear Birth Mother letter is difficult, that couples have no idea how to represent themselves, that their letter is only the first step in getting to know them. She addressed my concerns all the same. We had arrived at the chapter in our workbook called Entitlement; Molly explained that it could be a long, hard process for love to develop between an adoptive parent and a child.

"I'm sure it seems strange, since you can see how much they want a family. But it's not automatic. Adoptive couples go through so much scrutiny and red tape—it can be hard for them to really accept the child as their own."

The midwinter gray pressed against the windows of the counseling room as she spoke, and from my seat the skyline wasn't visible to orient me. Openness was at that moment the least of my concerns. I needed to know my child would be loved. But how could a couple make such a promise?

"Adoptive parents need to feel entitled to parent in order to feel free to love. But because they don't have the baby growing inside them like you do, they have to accept their parenthood on the basis of legal procedure—and that's really difficult. It can feel abstract and shallow compared with your connection, and it can make bonding with the child challenging."

I got it, and I even felt sympathy for it. Adoptive parents wouldn't be biologically duped to love. After persuading me of their worthiness to parent my child, they would have to persuade themselves of the same. After bypassing nature to acquire a child, they would have to work against nature to love it. And yet every single couple gave me a guarantee of their love. This was a high-stakes experiment; how could we be sure they would succeed?

"Openness can really help," Molly said. "Adoptive parents benefit so much from knowing that, of all your options, you chose them. You are able, personally, to give them permission to parent the child. No one at an agency or in court can do that with the same authority."

She told me other ways Jevn and I could help. We could let them name the child, for example. We could let them stand by at the hospital to meet the baby right after delivery. We could have a formal "entrustment ceremony," like a wedding, during which our friends and families would gather to witness our bequeathal of parental rights to the couple.

Of course they could name it, I thought. And they'd be welcome to be at the hospital. And yes, we could have a ceremony—with poems from Kahlil Gibran and scripture and coffee and refreshments, whatever it takes. Why would I not do everything possible to help the family to whom I was giving my child succeed in loving it?

That night I returned, as usual, to the profiles, and I really thought I could see it, that struggle to find a way to love. Sheldon and Toni offered what they called a *forever home* and a *forever family*, and though I was insulted by the implication I had only transient and trivial things to offer, I realized that if a couple thought that, they'd feel *more* than entitled—they'd feel *obligated* to parent. Just as I consoled myself with the image of all the worthy families in need of babies, they were working toward entitlement by imagining all the poor babies in need of homes. What would it do to us, I wondered, to know the actual facts of one another?

And perhaps the couple who'd given detailed specifications for what they wanted in a child—*no African Americans, but a Caucasian-Asian mix is an acceptable alternative if Caucasian isn't available, and disabled is okay if disability is mild or medically correctible*—were just being realistic about the limits of their love. Maybe they felt they could only guarantee love if the child resembled them—or perhaps they thought the baby might need such deception, like a nestling who will only accept food from a convincing puppet bird. Better they be sure than take on a child they couldn't love.

But was it not enough that I'd let them name the baby, and be there at the birth, and tell them, wholeheartedly, that I'd chosen them? This was the advantage, Molly assured me, of openness. I could give them entitlement and free them to love in a single stroke.

"But with openness," Molly had said, "they also see your pain," and the way she said it, it was a warning. The window of open adoption would open both ways. They would feel responsible for my sadness, which I'd struggle to hide, while the very thing that would enable me to overcome it, and give them my child, and let them name it and be at the hospital—a selfless, strong, and unconditional love—would be an ever-present measure of their own love. My presence could strengthen the structure of their family, but it would have an unpredictable capacity to bring it down. Which explained why some couples negated me even in their letter addressed to me—Bill and Julia, for one, assured me: *this will be* our *child, not our* adopted *child.* Entitlement was just more assuredly achieved in the absence, real or imagined, of the birth mother.

And maybe that was why, the way Molly said it, it sounded like I had some kind of responsibility. As if, although I might not be able to make myself perfectly invisible, I would need to make certain things invisible. But whatever the complexities, what was certain was that the structure had to stand. I couldn't give my child away without confidence that it would be loved, and I wouldn't sacrifice that love for my privilege to peer in the window.

Exhausted, I put the profiles aside and stood up to make dinner. Even more difficult than weighing all our possible futures was imagining the child I was doing it for. The couples seemed to have a clearer image of my baby than I did, but I felt sure we were all just speaking in a kind of code. For them, a child stood for happiness and meaning, the fulfillment of their expectations, but for me the baby was *me.* My protective instincts weren't maternal; maternity had simply given me permission to guard myself as I never had before. I had no independent desire for my child, no separate compulsion to love or care for it, no faith that it would ever be anything but the hardness in my abdomen and a massive distraction from architecture school. I wondered how I could make good decisions for a thing I couldn't see or feel or understand.

My mother called, and I told her, just for fun, that I was thinking about names. Eventually I'd let the couple name it, so they could feel Entitled, but maybe if I could name it for now, I could begin to see it as a person, the way Jevn did. I'd exercise my own entitlement in preparation for passing it on. It was funny to think about naming my belly a human name, like the horse I knew named Stephen. Jevn joked "Alf" or "Thor," because the baby would be half Norwegian, but I couldn't imagine actually naming a thing with such indecipherable boundaries. It felt as rational as naming a mosquito bite.

I was sautéing onions to put in my stomach to feed an imaginary person who would supposedly gobble them up along with everything else I put in there. Everything was another exercise in imagining the unimaginable. But my mother didn't want any part of the fun. She was afraid I was second-guessing my decision. I should be concentrating on finding the family I was going to give my child to. She reminded me it was not my child to name.

EIGHT

Jevn had started saying that we should "heal apart" so that when this was all over, we wouldn't find ourselves clinging to each other for support. And I'd agreed, defensively. We would work as a team to find parents for our child, but there could be no good argument for entangling and confusing and complicating our relationship, becoming emotionally enmeshed. Still, as important as it might be, I'd have put healing apart at the very end of my list of important things to do. It would have followed finding a family, having a baby, giving it up for adoption, and not failing out of architecture school. Sometimes I even thought putting off "healing apart" for now and entangling each other in support could make some of those other tasks easier to do. Other times, finding myself alone would give me a surge of strength I didn't know I had.

We'd say goodbye in the computer lab or amid piles of profiles in my apartment at night. I had to remind myself that the answer was somewhere ahead of me in the terrifying darkness, not in the comfort of the past, still near enough to touch. One night after he left, anxious for progress, I reached out to one of the couples in my *maybe* pile.

Hello!
  I found your webpage on the internet, and I'd like to get to know more

about your family. I am a 23-year-old student studying architecture and
piano. I am 3 months pregnant. My boyfriend and I have broken up and
are considering adoption. The baby is healthy, and I am healthy—no
drugs or smoking, etc. I am vegetarian. No health problems in the families
either. I'll be getting a test soon to find out about Down syndrome and
some other diseases. Please let me know if you are still trying to adopt a
child. I hope to talk to you soon.

So long—Amy

I didn't really believe there could be someone out there on the other end. I
cc'd Jevn, and I pressed send, and those words, like my childhood prayers
for a horse, were instantly absorbed by the night.

I went to bed eager for oblivion, and soon I was floating on my back
in a pool of water. With my toes, I could feel the thickness of the black
lane stripes below me. Everything was all the same—the same temperature, the same wet softness—and it didn't seem to matter what I
decided about anything. I oriented myself and looked for a side of the
pool to get out, but the yellow walls of the dome above it had shrunk
to meet the edges. There was nothing to hold on to, nowhere to climb
out. I looked down to discover the slick bottom had disappeared, and
far below my feet there was an endless network of pipes generating
machine-shaped currents, sucking in, pushing out, churning into an
infinite turquoise darkness.

My nightmares were often about drowning. It was like I really was a
water baby, always looking for the world I was really meant for. Those
pipes and fans and pumps were planted in my memory from the many
times my father took me to job sites—dams and coal refineries and water
treatment tanks and chicken feed processing plants—to interest me in
engineering and to remind me that piano was not a viable career. Those
places below the ground and beyond chain-link fences made the world
we live in seem like a thin veil over a spinning, churning reality.

When I awoke, I was alone. And I'd gotten a response.

Erica and George were a little older, like my parents had been when they
had kids. They had a son through an open adoption. They were Christian. They were environmentalists by profession. They were working

on a project in Norway, Jevn's ancestral home. And their permanent residence was in Maryland, not far from my grandparents' sheep farm. But most of all, most incredibly, they were flesh and blood and alive somewhere, tapping back against the glass!

I wrote back right away. Jevn joined our conversation, too. With each exchange, my fears dissipated. And soon I realized that the key to open adoption, even more than I'd understood before, was to find the right couple. It wasn't simply that the right couple would make giving up the child *possible*. With the right couple, open adoption would be *easy*. Knowing them would mean liking them. My prior fears were supplanted by a wild generosity; I would not only give them my child—I'd get pregnant again to give more children away to couples like them! But when I mentioned making some kind of commitment, Erica said she'd read that most birth mothers don't settle on a couple until after the fifth month of pregnancy. I was only in my third, so they wanted to give us time to look around. They did what first loves do—they broke my heart, but they gave me hope for what might be out there, and they opened the door for others to come in.

I kept my tiny roundness concealed beneath my hoodie and oversized T-shirt, but with the adoption process fully under way, I began to tell my friends about it, starting with Sleepy Amy, who took me camping in the freezing rain to help me enjoy my last days of mobility and freedom. She had long black hair and she smiled easily. People called her Sleepy Amy to distinguish her from me. She would fall asleep in the middle of studio, right on her desk or beneath it, and I loved the way she was always undermining everything we were doing there all the time.

But I dreaded explaining it all to everyone else. They'd express concern, but I'd know what they were really thinking. My classmates would be happy to have me taken out of the competition in studio; Christian friends would think I'd gotten what I deserved. I thought about skipping town. Moving to the farm or to a state no one thinks about. But even if I could escape Ohio, I couldn't escape the thing growing inside me. Even strangers on the street would think they knew the whole story. They wouldn't realize that I was studying architecture and had a plan for everything.

And so I did the only thing I could. I began to talk about it. Eagerly.

Openly. I would tell everyone everything, fearlessly outlining the details, omitting nothing. I'd grant them their fears and hypotheses and concerns, and then I'd silence them with certainty. I'd educate them about a kind of adoption they'd never even heard of. The only way to resist being talked about would be to talk about myself and to fill in the juicy details generously. My only armor would be appearing free of doubt. And, over time, I began to build around myself a scaffolding of friends, and colleagues, and professors, and counselors, confident and fully informed about my plan. The only thing I'd admit was that it wouldn't be easy. But, then, neither was architecture school.

"I'm pregnant—but I'm doing adoption," I would say before they could give me advice. It would be as if I planned the whole thing, pregnancy and adoption, like a giant impressive two-part side project I'd taken on out of excess ambition. By the middle of February, I had said this so many times, to so many people, it was a mantra that no longer had any meaning to me.

I wouldn't say, "I'm giving up my child for adoption." Not because Molly told me not to, but because at that point I wasn't giving up a child. I was going to counseling, learning about the adoption process, eating an egg every day, reading books about adopted children, scanning profiles at night, and consulting with Jevn on everything. Adoption couldn't be done until after the birth, because my parental rights wouldn't exist until the baby did. In the meantime, I was doing adoption. Everything anyone could ask me to do.

One evening, Jevn and I met at my apartment for our first phone call with Beth and Ken, a couple from Idaho. We had started spending long evenings on the phone with couples, and late nights sending e-mails. Beth told us about their recent trip to Lake Tahoe and how happy they were to be back. I remembered that their profile had included a photo of a backyard deck, so I asked if they ate meals out there in the summer. Beth said that they didn't. "Unfortunately, we have a lot of bugs in the summer."

I looked across to Jevn, to see if he was thinking what I was thinking.

I was thinking about eating supper serenaded by crickets under the canopy of maples my dad had planted, on the deck he'd built to extend into them, often still wrapped in towels in our swimsuits after a long day at the pool he'd built in a cow pasture close to our house together with several of our neighbors who shared it with us. Summer was comprised of pilgrimages to the pool and suppers on the deck. And I'm sure there were also bugs. Most likely *lots* of them.

Jevn wasn't looking at me, but he bore the burden of the rest of that conversation. I couldn't think of anything else to say.

The conversations we had with couples were often about parenting, which I'd never thought so much about. One evening Mike and Terri described the way they disciplined their two-year-old daughter by holding her tight when she was upset, no matter how loud she screamed, because they wanted her to know they'd be there for her through all of her emotions. I told them my dad thought emotions came from not getting enough sleep. He'd put me in my room and pull the vinyl window shade, but the foggy light of day would seep through the rip and around the curled edges and turn everything deep red. I'd never really thought about it before, but what a difference it would have made to have someone sit with me and talk through it, whatever it was. That was something adoption would do effortlessly, correct faults that ran like deep ruts in a family, persisting through generations.

I hadn't felt at ease with Mike until that moment, but sensing the start of a connection, I asked about the love of travel they mentioned in their profile. Mike said that they'd traveled a lot. They didn't like to eat strange food or spend time in unfamiliar countries, but there was a certain beach in Florida they liked to go to every summer, a place where they liked the restaurants and where everyone knew them. It sounded nice, but it didn't sound like *travel* to me. Travel was exactly about not knowing or being known, and I couldn't help but doubt how well they'd manage in the foreign territory of open adoption.

I could never know what would sink my heart. I'd set out with so much hope, internalizing couples' stories, falling asleep imagining their hometowns, straining excitedly to see how far down the road I could picture us all together—but there was always a point when some detail, some way they would say something, would put out the spark. Our conversations led us fast into couples' most intimate spaces, their profoundest hopes and disappointments, and there were times I couldn't get out fast enough. Jevn would sigh and shake his head in frustration at me.

If this were a closed adoption, we'd have been finished a long time ago, and sometimes I wanted Molly to take the decision away from me. I couldn't know whether my criteria would be more effective than pulling a nice couple at random from the files. I felt guilty for scrutinizing people so mercilessly, couples that had been approved for adoption by every measurable standard. Who was I to say they weren't good enough? If I wasn't fit to parent, was I fit to select parents for my child? But no one was setting the rules, and the field was as wide as the Ohio horizon. The only things guiding us were measures we created, ideals even we couldn't pinpoint, instincts I couldn't begin to temper. Molly would assure us, frustrating as it was, guilty as I felt, they were enough, and they would lead us to someone.

We decided we'd give ourselves until the end of March. That was when I would return to school, and we'd both be too busy to be on the phone with couples all the time. It also gave us three months before my due date in July to get to know the couple well. If something happened to make us change our minds, it gave us time to figure out what we were going to do.

One night after a session with Molly, we walked down the hill to the pizza place to fill out the medical history forms she'd given us—vital information for our official record, to remain permanently accessible to our child. We were seated at a table next to the fireplace, and though our medical histories would be delicately, inextricably intertwined in our child, as we completed the forms, we might have been any two students thrown together on a school project. Our child a collaboration as unromantic as collecting aluminum cans from the architecture studios.

When our pizza arrived, we put away the papers, and I remembered the package I'd gotten in the mail earlier that day. I pulled it out of my backpack.

"We got photos from Dave and Laura," I said, showing him the envelope. Inside were ten glossy color photos, professionally done, along with a long handwritten letter. They wrote about trying with IVF for years and how they had contemplated divorce on account of it. Laura had almost died in surgery after a fertility procedure. They said IVF clinics deal hope, and they were addicted. It repulsed me. I couldn't imagine risking my life or spending thousands of dollars just for a chance to have a baby. "I still don't like them," I told Jevn. I couldn't help it.

"Maybe they'd appreciate a baby more because of what they've been through."

"They're *putting* themselves through it! I want them to have come to terms with adoption before they adopt my child!" He was so fair, so generous in his assessment of people, I was terrified it would be up to me alone to find their faults. "Aren't you worried about what kind of people they'd be?"

"Maybe that's a question we should be asking everyone: how they've dealt with infertility," Jevn said. "Maybe we should write down all the questions we want couples to answer."

That was a big problem with this process. We were managing vastly different information about so many different people. I was finding myself comparing one wife's strange laugh on the phone to someone else's job in sports management, to another person's large extended family.

"Okay." I tore out a sheet of notebook paper. *How have you dealt with infertility?* I wrote. "Maybe something like What's your biggest struggle as a couple?" I wanted to know what really sustained them. If I was giving up my child in part so that Jevn wouldn't become an absent father, I needed to feel confident that the adoptive parents were going to stay together.

"And, Are you still trying to have biological children?" Jevn suggested.

"I think we should ask some general things, too. Like, Are you happy? What are you passionate about?" I added, writing both questions down.

"Do you have a TV?" he suggested. Neither of us did.

"No, they probably all have TVs. Maybe, How much TV do you watch?"

"Where do you keep your TV?" he said. He was right. That would tell us more. I wrote it down. And that got me thinking.

"What songs do you sing to yourself while you're washing the dishes?" I said. "I know what my mother would sing: 'You Are My Sunshine.' Dad would probably sing 'Blueberry Hill,' or 'I Want to Hold Your Hand.' He'd sing that one on walks because he was too embarrassed to just hold hands without asking." Those songs took me fast to the deep interiors of my childhood. I wanted to know what my child would overhear, and be filled by, and remember.

"I know what you'd sing," Jevn said, smiling. He was probably about to make fun of me.

"You wouldn't sing at all! You'd just mouth constantly!" I went on the attack, remembering all the times he'd taken my hands and stepped lightly on his toes and bent his height over like a crescent moon as he looked into my eyes and mouthed the Jayhawks, *I'd run away! I'd run away with you, baby!*

"Do you build things?" he suggested, and I wrote it down. Of course that question. Jevn often spent vacations on a friend's property, building cabins and saunas by hand, using rock climbing gear to hoist himself along half-built structures. He always came back burned and full of fish he caught in the river. Between Jevn and my father, our child would probably be oriented toward making stuff.

"They should build fires!" I said. I had so many fire memories. Halfway through my childhood, our area got annexed by the city and instituted fire safety regulations, so the fire department was often called to our house, where dad had planted a forest for the exact purpose of producing firewood. We'd have elaborate systems of ropes to guide the fall and then epic bonfires. And, always eventually, the fire department.

"Yeah, definitely," Jevn said, thinking. I also remembered shivering in bed, and the smell of the wood, waiting for Jevn to get the fire going, that time I joined him at the cabin by the Arkansas. And the thick steam from the oatmeal rising up into the rafters when I finally got up to make breakfast.

"What do you do with holey socks?" I said as I wrote.

Jevn laughed. "What's the right answer to that one?"

"I don't know—it could be a lot of things!"

This was open adoption. We had more than a hundred families to choose from, all of them approved for parenting by every state and agency standard. But it came down to things no agency could measure. And everything we'd be able to give our child we were giving in these moments, thinking hard about what we wanted its life to look like, and harder about how to find it. We would standardize our data to manage the unmanageable. We composed questions that poked and prodded in places we thought we'd find life. Questions we weren't sure how we wanted answered. Others that were deal-breakers. We wrote down every question we could think of.

What kitchen appliances do you own? Will your children share a bedroom?

Describe a few of your T-shirts. What did you last give someone as a gift? What is the best time of day? How is your family imperfect? Do you ever build a fire? Do you get dessert? Do you drink Coke? What do you like most about your job? What do you do on a typical Sunday? Thursday? What is fun? How much time do you spend outside each day? What was the last show you saw at a museum or theater? Who was your favorite teacher? Describe your faith without using the word church. What would you say if your child told you he was an atheist? What are your quiet hours? Will you buy a car for your child when it turns sixteen? How old is your furniture? Who is your favorite relative? Do you speak any foreign languages? What do you use your basement for? Do you get any magazines or newspapers? Do you ever sleep late? How would you react if your twenty-two-year-old daughter told you she was pregnant? Who does the housework? Do you have a boat? Plane? Snowmobile? What were you like as a student? What volunteer work do you do? How do you celebrate your anniversary? Do you have a basketball hoop? Will your children have chores? Do you listen to the radio? What toys will you buy for your children? What would you do if your child got a D in school? How do you feel about divorce?

For whatever its faults, we'd embarked on a process that put all the mysteries of human attraction back on the scales. It affirmed us as parents, best-equipped, for reasons only nature knew, to make decisions for our child. And facing the piles of profiles that night, I had hope. If there were jukeboxes and llamas, there were bound to be tuning forks and telescopes. We just had to find them.

When the lines of the paper were full, we rotated the page and wrote sideways in the margins. I wrote some; Jevn pulled the page back to himself and wrote others. And after one very thick-crusted pizza, we'd compiled a total of 111 questions.

NINE

Of course I couldn't tell him what I thought about at night. That although I still couldn't imagine having a child, I liked to think about showing the world to someone who was new to it. I could imagine an allegiance as deep as family and hard work that means so much you can't feel its hardness. I could imagine how easy it would be for me to offer all the things I struggled to find in couples—things more important than readiness or financial security. I could imagine not worrying about couples from Minnesota and Michigan anymore. And I could imagine Jevn, in time, getting over it.

Then I would remember dog food.

It was expensive to have a child. The couples were always describing their big garages, their flexible work schedules, their fenced-in backyards and college funds. Like they knew money was the Achilles' heel for an accidental mother. None of the invaluable things I had to give mattered in the end, because what I didn't have was money. I made a hundred dollars a week working in the dean's office during the school term; a couple of thousand dollars at most from an internship. I was halfway through the money my dad had saved to help with my first four years of college. Their expensive desires got them babies; mine got me dog food—which I had tasted in the basement once, fishing a kibble out of the big green bag. It was oily and gritty, and I couldn't swallow.

One afternoon I left work early for a prenatal appointment at the university hospital. The baby was healthy, and my midwife congratulated me for gaining a lot of weight in the two weeks since I'd seen her. I told her I'd added milkshakes to my daily diet. *Mama's finally putting some meat on those bones!* she teased me, and I left feeling proud of myself, like I'd really accomplished something.

On the way home, I stopped in to see the woman I worked for in the dean's office. Cherry was in her sixties and had the disposition of her name. She was cheery and efficient, and small pops and clicks came from her dentures when she spoke. The plastic rims of her glasses and the chain that kept them around her neck were always bumping an earring or a string of pearls or her teeth between her pale pink lips as she pulled her glasses down to give me direction. She was a secretary from the old school; she used an electric typewriter and knew proper shorthand. She was sitting at her desk opening a stack of mail with a long, silver letter opener when I arrived. She took a moment to place me.

"Well, *hi*, Amy! Come in, come in! I didn't expect to see you!"

I stood in front of her desk, as I often did, chatting with her as she arranged things on her blotter and tended the phone, gazing at me blankly when it would ring and she'd put the receiver to her ear. I told her about my internship, and she said it sounded perfectly suited to me. Then I told her I was pregnant, and the smile drained from her eyes. She lowered her glasses to the very tip of her nose and raised her penciled-in eyebrows. She paused for a long time, reading me. "Well," she said, sighing, "you are about to learn the difference between men and women."

I could tell she meant something other than the most important difference, which I already knew about: that the baby would come out of me.

Not that that lesson was easy. Jevn and I had just signed up for the free childbirth classes Molly had told us about, and in our first session, the teacher showed us that difference in graphic detail. We sat in front of the television on the carpeted floor of a windowless basement at a crisis pregnancy center. Besides Jevn and me, there were ten unwed girls and about half as many boyfriends. They were not in college or college-bound. They were definitely not studying architecture. But they were mostly unlike us because they planned to keep their babies.

The scene in the video wasn't at all like what I'd seen in movies or on television, where women in labor were always screaming at and hitting their husbands, or squeezing their hands until they flinched. Childbirth on TV made you understand it was the worst pain you could ever imagine, and it was always the time when women got back at men for that difference. And for some reason that moment—when the wife reaches out across the divide to strangle her husband—was always accompanied by a laugh track.

But the birth we watched that evening in class wasn't a hilarious, bungled race to the hospital. The couple reclined comfortably in bed at home. There weren't any doctors or nurses. When a contraction came, the mother moaned a little and her husband cradled her head until she fell silent. But in the end, and what left me speechless, was the last sound she made; it was arresting and sincere: the outraged bellow of a large animal, betrayed by its body. A massive head, a horror you never see on television, a bulging perineum, some feces, blood, and other liquids.

A person came out of a person! It spontaneously erupted from someone's insides, starting with its black hair, which bobbled in and out for a couple of contractions, and then its face and slick shoulders. It abandoned its container violently, like a parasite discharged from its host, leaving the mother a quiet, crumpled mass, her head tilted back on the pillow.

I scanned the room; we could all refuse to do this together.

"Did you see that?" The teacher rewound the video. "Okay, right—there, you guys, that squeeze? That's called the fetal Heimlich."

She pulled her hair to the side with one hand as she picked up a posterboard diagram of a baby, emerging through the mother's pelvis. "This is when Mom's perineum presses the baby's rib cage and forces mucus and amniotic fluid out of its mouth and nose, so it's ready to breathe. No suctioning required!" she said emphatically. "This doesn't happen in medicated labors, guys. You have to have a mom whose uterine muscles are awake and alert!"

After class, I introduced myself to the teacher, who reminded me her name was Nina. I told her I didn't want it coming out of me, I didn't want blood, I didn't want to be naked. I didn't want candles. There had to be another way. A new and improved, in-between, hybrid way.

"Listen to you!" She put her hand solidly on my upper arm and held it there. "Believe me, you're gonna be fine."

It wasn't hard like architecture school, or hard like a piano audition. It wasn't even hard like carefully crafting an open adoption with your ex-boyfriend. It was impossible—like having a large and living creature burst out of you through your uterus.

Nina invited me to come to her house that Saturday, where she had me sit on her sofa and watch fifty births on video, *Clockwork Orange*–style, one immediately after the other. The films spanned the spectrum of geography and culture: African squatting births, births in the rice paddies of China during which farmer-mothers momentarily interrupt their rhythmic threshing to retrieve the newborn from between their legs, New Age water births in places like Vermont and California. Across the world, women were having babies; perineums on every continent deployed the fetal Heimlich; babies from Vancouver to Indonesia sought the breast; moms everywhere were casting off their clothes and letting babies spill out of them.

When the videos were finished, Nina put her laundry basket on the floor and sat down beside me. "Well . . . ?" she said, smiling and then laughing. I told her that I thought I might let the baby come out that way, but I still refused to be naked when I did. No maternal stupor could make me forget that civilized people wear clothes. She took me under her wing; she said she'd make sure of it.

Nina told me stories from her own single motherhood that gave me confidence about adoption. She'd gotten pregnant when she was sixteen. Her parents kicked her out of the house, so she lived in a car and then a domestic violence shelter, and then she moved in with a motorcycle gang. One day she called 911 after one of the gang's children fell down the stairs and cracked its skull. The authorities discovered illegal ID–making equipment, and after that, the gang started threatening her, so she changed her identity and hid for several years. Eventually, she began dating a pastor and thought she was finally safe, but she discovered he was molesting her daughter. Twenty years later, she was still running from the gang, still holding multiple jobs and struggling to support herself and three daughters. She had long blond hair and crisp bangs, like a second-grade school picture, but underneath them she was worn.

She started teaching free childbirth classes to single moms because she thought she could at least help them get a healthy start. She said pregnancy and birth were as much a part of a mother's relationship with her child as the lifetime to follow, and if I really was going to go through with an adoption, I had all the more reason to make the most of my short time with my child.

"Your baby's going to be beautiful," she said. She seemed to have limitless energy for other people. "And you're going to find the right family. You will. I'm praying for you." She rubbed my knee hard, like someone whose job it is to touch people's bodies. "Here, eat some grapes."

A few days later, my structures professor's wife invited me to dinner, and a studio professor offered me her old maternity clothes. I started being approached by mothers in the grocery store and on the street. They told me swimming would relieve the pressure on my back. That primrose oil would prevent stretch marks. Mothers everywhere were emerging to advise me. It was as if I was a newcomer who'd wandered haplessly into a hidden world, and all its inhabitants, alerted to my arrival, fell in line to initiate me. It was as though there was a secret that only mothers and infertile people knew: that all we are is our bodies, and what we are most meant to do is reproduce them. Our particular choices and interests and talents are incidental; all that matters is the thing that makes every woman exactly the same as every other. And completely different from men.

An invisible curtain had been drawn, and I was pulled in gently by my elbow. Here was where the gears of the world were turned; here was who, without anyone's taking note, were turning the gears: not just the women of the world, but the childbearing women, the women whose roundness hinted at their special affiliation.

One morning on my bike ride to work, I noticed that with every pedal, my thighs had begun to tap the hardness in my abdomen. That fullness felt good. Passing the flat-bellied students on their way to class, I felt physical and fully realized. Pregnancy was pure creative force; it put the late-night efforts of my fellow design students to shame. What was an architect's aspiration except to mimic that inventive mastery, to replicate the miraculous form? I was building something singularly amazing and I didn't even have to think about it.

When I arrived at work, my boss had left a message that he wouldn't be coming in until the afternoon. We were accustomed to his absence; he always had meetings, but he also seemed to be going through some kind of crisis, all his friends peaking in their careers while he worked for the poor and drove a station wagon. His single indulgence was having the very latest smartphone, and when he'd describe its brand-new features, I would roll my eyes and take comfort in my certainty that I would never own a PalmPilot.

That day, Zhang Ying was the only other person in the office, so at lunch I asked if she minded my eating an egg out in the open. I peeled it and held my nose, suppressing my gag reflex.

"That egg smells funny!" Zhang Ying said as she stood up.

"I know; that's why I asked. I'm sorry!"

She came over and inspected it. Having been a vegan my entire adult life, I didn't know that eggs were not perfectly sealed natural packages. That you could not boil two dozen at once and eat them, day by day, over the course of a month. The flavor was so repulsive from day one that I hadn't noticed them getting incrementally more repulsive, a bit more blue, a tad more slimy.

"Amy, it's rotten!" she said as she nearly slapped it out of my hand, the girl from the land of the thousand-year egg.

TEN

It felt like we were getting close to finding a family. Our 111 questions had generated thousands and thousands of answers. It was still February, still a month to decide, but we were focusing our attention on two couples. Jevn liked Jeff and Cindy best. They had, by far, the best profile cover photo. Three pairs of muddy boots lined up on a doorstep. Papa-, mama-, and baby-sized boots. They were a family who explored the dirty world and arrived happily home together.

"Robert and Deb are good, too," Jevn said. They lived in Colorado, where Robert was an architect and Deb was a banker. I wouldn't have liked the banker thing, except that she said she saw her career as a way to help people.

"Yeah, I really like them," I said. It turned out that Robert worked for an architecture firm where Jevn had been an intern for several years. They knew some of the same people, people who had directly influenced Jevn's decision to become an architect. But there was something I didn't like. In an e-mail referring to all the things we had in common, Robert said that the Japanese character for *crisis* was a combination of one character meaning danger and another meaning opportunity. Both pregnancy and infertility were, perhaps in our cases, crises, I thought, but the opportunity he was referring to was certainly his own. I ignored this, because we had so many significant things in common.

"What do you think of that Indiana couple?" Jevn asked. Paula and Erik were theologians who had a two-year-old adopted daughter. We had liked their letter because it was straightforward, without zany captions or margin art, but I had already put them in the *no* pile.

"They have the other birth mother they're talking to, and they said they're probably moving right around the time I'm due. And, remember? They wouldn't tell us what names they like." We'd sent them the 111 questions, but Paula didn't answer that one. If she withheld simple information from me, I thought, she couldn't really expect me to be forthcoming with my child.

But as rigorously as I was scrutinizing everyone, I had a pit in my stomach that made me wary I was in no state to make any judgment at all. The physical reality of pregnancy had finally taken hold; I was distracted and unfocused, exhausted and ambivalent—the last person who should be in charge of someone else's entire future.

We slid through the door and into class. As we settled onto the carpet, Nina turned and smiled at us. "Hi!" she whispered loudly, lifting her shoulders and waving fast. She was holding a diagram showing a happy cartoon face. "Don't go to the hospital as soon as you feel your first contractions. If you can smile, that's how you know you're not dilated enough; you'll be waiting there for hours, and they'll try to medicate you. If you're nervous and excited and you gotta go somewhere, go to the grocery store and stock up."

Emotional Signposts, she explained, were the predictable sequences of feelings and attitudes that mark a certain sequence of physical progressions in labor. The happy face becomes a serious face, and then a very unhappy face as a mother approaches pushing. You can read slight changes in your feelings, instead of fetal monitoring or exams, to know exactly where you are in the progress of labor.

"Dads, you know you're about to have a baby when she loses confidence and starts saying, 'I can't do it!'" That was when we wouldn't need confidence anymore, she told us, because the automatic processes within our bodies would have already taken over, and pushing would begin, with or without us.

Nina had us lie down and pretend we were getting ready to deliver a baby. She told the birth partners to make sure the mothers were breathing by repeating the words *Breathe, breathe, breathe,* interspersed with encouraging words like *You're doing great.*

"Breathe . . . ," Jevn whispered awkwardly above me. This was no special breathing, like the panting of Lamaze; it was a steady inhaling and exhaling at the frequency I accomplished involuntarily all the time. I closed my eyes, but I was concentrating on the mind game. What would it feel like to have a person inside me, and then what would it feel like for that person to come out all of a sudden?

"Are you breathing?" I felt Jevn above me, examining me from different angles. It was strange to be together in this context, to be asked to touch each other, or to simulate such intimate support, when we no longer had any physical contact in the real world. But we couldn't think about it. I kept my eyes closed. I felt him pause. He pressed his fingers to my wrist. He leaned in and put his ear to my mouth.

"What are you doing? That's not how you check my breathing!" I said.

"Oh!" he whispered. "You didn't look like you were breathing, so I thought you might be dead."

Of the many women who reached out to me after learning of my pregnancy, I was most surprised to hear from my history professor, who invited me over early one morning for breakfast. In class, she would stand at the front of the darkened auditorium beside images of Rome projected to twenty feet tall and make you feel like architecture was a worthwhile thing to study.

I stepped nervously onto her porch and knocked.

"Amy, hey!" She opened the door and stepped back to invite me in. We didn't hug. She guided me into the living room, and we sat down at a small table. And then she began to speak in that somber way that had become familiar to me. One mother speaking to another about the burden we by nature bear. She was ready for kids when she had them, and yet, ready as she was, she said she hadn't anticipated how radically her life would change, while her husband's life remained largely intact. She said she was the one who wasn't allowed to forget the kids needed to be picked up from school, she who always made sure they were fed, who left work immediately when they were sick. She'd hoped to share some kind of enlightened partnership, but the asymmetry was ingrained and inescapable. "And, all the more in your situation," she said, "it will probably appear that Jevn isn't an equal partner, and he can't be. You will just have to come to terms with that."

There it was again, I thought: the difference between men and women. The most self-evident thing, the least of my concerns, and yet women everywhere kept slipping me notes in secret, ones that said, In the end it is all about that difference, and in the end you are alone. But little did anyone know Jevn. I was always having to tell people that, no, I had not been abandoned by my boyfriend. Yes, astonishingly, he stuck around to help me with the adoption. I was offended for Jevn and myself that people were impressed with his behavior. He was doing exactly what a man should do. And I didn't see what I would gain by fixating on the difference.

My professor wasn't wearing her glasses, and without them I could make out the young person she'd once been, the one who traipsed around Rome and Greece taking the black-and-white photos I loved so much. She said that as happy as she was to be a mother, she felt her child's birth was an ending, the last day her husband really knew her. And what made it even harder: from his perspective, they'd only that day begun.

We hadn't touched the bagels, but I had to get to work. She led me to the door.

"You're going to have to keep in mind, you might be an A student under other circumstances, but you can't expect that of yourself next quarter."

I nodded, but I hoped being pregnant would in fact make me more intuitive, more decisive, extra creative, and that compared with everything else I was going through, school would seem simple.

"I'm teaching a studio; maybe you should think about taking it. Architecture and the Body. I'll keep in mind everything that's going on with you, you know? It might make things a little easier."

On my way home from work that night, I passed the architecture building, buzzing with fluorescent lights, perpetuating buildings illuminated by fluorescent lights. When I fell asleep, I dreamed that the baby was a cat. It came out of me slippery and wet and licked its paws and cleaned itself. I swaddled it carefully and loved it instantly. And I was relieved; I knew from experience that I could manage a cat. But I felt confident that in the end it would be a girl. If men were so deeply different from women, I couldn't imagine I'd be creating one in my sleep.

ELEVEN

A yellow rubber ducky teetered on the edge of the bathtub. A child's footstool stood by the sink, a bucketful of bath toys beside the toilet. The walls of the tub were decorated with colorful foam letters, and the shower curtain was a vibrant display of deep ocean life. It looked as though someone had just that morning lifted the baby out of the bath and, token of a life lived fully, neglected to put one last toy back in the bucket. When I went to use the bathroom, I felt I'd entered a secret chamber of their marriage. Sitting on the toilet, you would never believe that a baby didn't live there or hadn't disappeared that morning, moments before you arrived.

The nursery was painted light green, for a girl or a boy. The white slat crib was full of pillows, the shelves a clean display of classic infant toys, wooden blocks, a teddy bear, a pyramid of colored doughnuts. Between them, generous intervals of white space. Everything perfectly positioned, untouched. Books beautifully bound but unbroken. Was it a child's bedroom or a gallery, exhibiting precious artifacts of infancy, commemorating the fleetingness of childhood? It echoed with a deep stillness. I walked past it back to the kitchen, where Jevn was talking with Bob and Tami.

"It's so warm for February!" Tami exclaimed. "Bob and I thought we could sit out on the terrace."

Another alien world had opened itself to me. Bright and sterile, like the Neighborhood of Make Believe or a 7-Eleven at midnight. An imitation of regular life, shimmering with artificial color. All the evidences of normalcy, but barren and dormant, buzzing with man-made energy. I could hardly believe I was a part of it, the other half of an unnatural partnership.

We'd been communicating for a couple of weeks over e-mail, but the real reason we decided to meet them was simply that it was time to take the next step and start meeting people, and they lived close by. They gave us a tour of the house, and then we went outside to sit on the terrace. Tami scurried back and forth to the kitchen, bringing us refreshments on a tray. They hovered around us, chatting nervously and making sure we were comfortable.

"We use this table for parties sometimes in the summer . . . and I grow vegetables in the garden over there, beyond the hydrangea. Tomatoes, squash, just a few things. We just got this patio furniture last year."

I wondered how often that ducky got knocked over stepping into the shower. Whether visiting nieces and nephews were allowed to play with it. Was it put there in the hope the baby would somehow follow? Was it there for a home study, a subtle communication to a social worker that they were prepared to parent, down to the rubber ducky at bath time?

Or was it teetering there for me? Had they anticipated the moment when I'd find myself sitting alone in the bathroom? Was it there to help me more easily project the life of my child into this place, down its corridors and into its rooms? Imagine, as I sat peeing, its life unfolding, growing up within these walls, waking up every morning in the green room just around the corner, light combing through the clean white shutters with the sunrise? Did they put the ducky away when no one was coming or going? Was it braver to have a place where you stash your rubber ducky, or braver to face it every day, in the absence of the thing it stands for?

Bob was a pilot, and he guided us around the side of the house to show us the Cessna parked in the driveway. I told him that my father had his glider license, and I'd been flying since I was young. It was my dad's favorite thing to do and his single extravagance, experimenting with physics in an engineless plane. I might have mentioned it as a thing we had in common, a familiarity with small planes and airfields, an intimacy with flying. We could have smiled at the implication.

"Motorized planes seem really hefty compared with gliders!" I said, instead pointing out the difference. I was wary of anything that appeared to be a promise, or a decision, or a leaning toward a decision. I'd realized as soon as they greeted us that we wouldn't choose them, and it was something of a relief to tour their house knowing that nothing they said or showed us would ever touch my child.

We walked through the side door into the basement and sat down on the couch in the finished area, where there was a large television in the corner. Bob seemed anxious, impatient with our conversations about college, and planes, and neighborhoods. He took hold of my forearm.

"Amy, I hope you'll choose us. We are really interested in talking with you further." That hope went without saying; that was why they'd written to us. That was why we were here. His eyes began to swell.

"Sometimes at night I go into the nursery and sit in the rocker . . . I dream of the day I'll bring our little baby home, and our family will finally be complete." He clenched my arm heavily. "I long for the day when a child will put its little arms around my neck and call me Daddy."

I nodded like I understood, but I refused to accept the burden he was trying to give me. I couldn't rectify nature's injustice; I couldn't be responsible for making his dreams come true. And I could never give my child to a couple who thought they needed it. There wasn't such a thing as needing a child the way the starving kids in Africa need food. And, although I'd once thought that *need* was exactly what would make me feel good about giving my child away, now I wanted to find the opposite. A couple should want to have kids because of the abundance of curiosity, and passion, and love they had to give—not because of an absence the child would only fail to fill.

Couples we met expected to win us with charm and warmth they couldn't convey in a profile. We'd see how real their lives were, and it would be harder for us to reject them. But inside the actual house my child might grow up in, the smells and the light and the temperature provided immediate answers, and a few days later, we would have to let them know that their perfect house and natural wood toys and family and friends and pets and playgrounds were, for reasons we felt powerfully but couldn't explain, not enough.

But just days later as we drove to meet another couple, I reminded myself that no one would give my child the life I would have given. We needed to finish this process; we needed to rest. I told myself that might mean compromise. The new family would think differently. They would do things I wouldn't do. And, somehow, it would all be okay.

I could smell the bulk spices and home-cooked whole grains from Kaitlynn and Roger's doorstep. As we sat down in the living room, Kaitlynn explained what openness meant to them.

"We visit Elizabeth's birth grandmother four times a year. I guess we see Nikki about once a month, but we only see Jeremy once a year because he lives in Florida now. Jeremy is her birth father," Kaitlynn said as she stirred Jevn's tea and then handed it to him.

We'd sent them our list of questions, and what had been really impressive was how little they'd tried to impress us with their answers. They said they didn't spend much time outside and weren't *normally* happy. The last show they saw? It was last Sunday, but he couldn't remember what it was, and he didn't like it very much. Do you ever build a fire? *Nope, no reason to.* How is your family imperfect? *Let me count the ways! We don't have much money. We don't keep our house clean very well. We don't play enough games together. We eat out too much. We don't spend enough time together.* Holey socks? *Throw them away.* Do you drink Coke? *I prefer Pepsi products. And I love fast food.* What do you read? *Reader's Digest and not much other than that.* How do you celebrate your anniversary? *A night out at a local hotel.*

They hadn't skipped a single question, and they answered as though they were taking a polygraph. Their answers were so unapologetically wrong, I was intrigued. As people experienced in open adoption, they were perhaps boldly communicating that honesty is the key, the single thing needed to make an open adoption successful. They lived nearby, so we thought we'd give it a chance. But after just a few minutes in their living room, I could see that honesty alone wouldn't make this work. The consequence of being doted on by two parents and two birth parents, eleven grandparents and great-grandparents, ten half siblings, seventeen nieces and nephews, fifteen adoptive uncles and aunts, and countless other birth aunts and uncles, birth grandparents and great-grandparents, celebrating six Christmases and five Thanksgivings, was plain to see: their adopted daughter, Elizabeth, was spoiled.

Maybe they would have spoiled any child, biological or adopted, or maybe the radical openness was meant to compensate for adoption's built-in sorrows; they'd made adoption a better-than-biological childhood, and Elizabeth, spinning gleefully in the middle of the room while we watched, was ecstatic proof of it. But she was also a thing in the world with which my own child would have to deal.

"The sibling matters," I said to Jevn as we drove away.

"Definitely," he responded.

At my mid-February appointment, my midwife sent me home with a fuzzy photo of wild white clouds against an ominous black sky, tick marks along the frame and a dotted circle, placed in what seemed an arbitrary corner of the fog. The grainy image had moved on the monitor as they rolled the cold plate through the gel over my abdomen. They read my belly like a crystal ball, and the airy features of my future had a sex. It was advisable for me to know so I could tell the adoptive couples if they wanted to know. But when they handed me the photograph of a foggy penis and the callout "boy," I still could not believe it was a thing, still growing inevitably toward a moment when I would no longer be able to not believe it.

My sister and I decided to call him Liù, the Chinese word meaning six and pronounced as a single, downward syllable, "Lyeeoh." We liked the sound; the translation didn't matter. Why not name my indigestion the Chinese word meaning six? She told me her students named themselves all kinds of names, imitating the sound of English names: Banny, Fransquall, Denven, Dawie. They often got their names by looking in the dictionary: a girl named Rainbow, boys named Pal and Stiff, a girl named Purple—she knew two, in fact. There were girls named Phoenix, Irony, and Naive. She knew a guy named Pink, a girl named Tower, another girl named Siren, and a guy named Bank who had changed his name to Shell. Some named themselves after favorite foods; she taught two girls named Apple and one named Chocolate. There were normal names like Harry and Elvis, but those were girls, and Hannah was a guy.

Liu. *Leo.* LYO. I am so excited.

TWELVE

It was early March. It was time to start making decisions. This is about *the boy*, not you, Jevn would say. I was being selfish, he was saying by saying that. I wasn't focusing on what was good for our son; I was letting myself get hung up on my own feelings about the couples. Perhaps there was no way to give up a child without suppressing a certain uneasiness about it. And yet ignoring my instinct to protect my son made adoption feel exactly like abandonment.

His top choice was Jeff and Cindy, the couple with the mama, papa, and baby boots, and one afternoon we met at my apartment to speak with them. Jevn sat on my futon with the phone in his lap; I sat in my desk chair in front of him.

"Hey, guys! How's it going?" Jeff said.

"Hi, Jeff," I said.

"How's your Sunday?" Jevn asked.

"We just got back from an amazing ride, the Little Miami River watershed. Gorgeous day. I had DJ on the back of the bike the whole way. He fell asleep on the drive home. What's up with you guys?"

"We're doing well; I think we're just doing a lot of thinking about the adoption," Jevn understated. "I wanted to ask you and Cindy about how DJ's birth mother approached this process."

"Hi, you guys," Cindy joined in. "You know, I think she struggled a lot, too, but in the end she saw everything we had to offer, and she just knew we were the family for her son."

"I keep returning to my operating principle," Jevn said, "that this adoption is about the boy, not us."

He was always drawing this distinction between *the boy* and us, but I still couldn't think that way. I could only think *with* my son. My selfishness included him. But if my task was to ignore the alarms I experienced in my blood, beating through vessels that wrapped around him, I needed time to learn a new kind of discernment; I couldn't simply let go of thinking altogether.

"Well, it's about everyone—the child, the parents, the birth parents," Jeff responded. "You have to come to a decision that everyone can live with. We have a beautiful arrangement with DJ's birth mother. We're always sending her pictures or talking on the phone, and we meet up two or three times a year."

"Are there any negative aspects of open adoption, in your experience?" Jevn persisted. One negative aspect, Jevn probably thought, was the birth mother's freedom to reject even those couples who fit her own criteria perfectly. I looked at him angrily, and he averted his eyes.

"I think I'm the wrong one to ask about negative aspects of open adoption," Jeff answered. "As long as there's mutual respect, I don't see the problem."

Jevn stopped his line of questioning, but he'd substantiated my doubts. Jeff answered too breezily. He was a jock. That's why I didn't like him. They didn't just go for long hikes; they rode in three-hundred-mile bike races for which they'd had to have a helmet specially made to fit their infant son. I'd tried to tell myself: at least he'll take my son outside a lot. It wouldn't matter that he'd be ripping through energy goo as they sped past rivers and trees whose silences would be obliterated by cheering onlookers and blow horns. Jeff's being a competitive cyclist didn't in any way preclude quiet walks in the woods and good conversation on other days.

"There aren't any negative aspects," Cindy said definitively. "There's nothing different or special about it, as far as I'm concerned."

Cindy often reminded us about how comfortable she was with

adoption. She couldn't understand other people's hang-ups over infertility, and she insisted that there was no difference at all between adoption and biological means of having a child. But whether she felt comfortable or not, I thought, there *was* a difference, not the least of which, the arrangements I hoped we would make throughout my son's life to see each other. She said they kept all the things DJ's mother had given him in a box Cindy painted with an Indian motif, and I wondered if we would also be reduced to a box and stored away.

"I think we should meet them," I said anyway, after we hung up, because Jevn really liked them, and I wanted him to see I was trying. "We need to figure out our next steps with everyone we're still in touch with." We had begun sending out notes to certain couples we'd had significant contact with, saying we did not think we were a "match." It was scary to be dismantling bridges when we still didn't know if there'd be one that held. Couples usually wished us luck, but sometimes they responded angrily, as though we'd deliberately led them on.

"And Robert and Deb want us to come out for spring break," Jevn said, getting his things together to go back to studio. He was always leaving as soon as our immediate business was done. He showed so little curiosity about my body, erupting and stretching as we spoke, that I was embarrassed when my belly moved visibly in his presence. A vulgar reminder of my general unwieldiness. I could no more focus my mind to make a decision than I could discipline my body to sit still.

"Yeah, should we meet later today to talk about that?"

I didn't want him to leave. I wanted a break from being broken up. I wanted him to acknowledge the reality of what was happening in the space between us. I wanted Jevn's arms and mine holding our son together. But he was an arrow, shooting straight toward a target. He would help in every decidedly productive way, but my emotions and my rapidly evolving body were forbidden territories in the new world we inhabited together. He said we could talk about talking later, and he closed the door.

I was getting used to that, and it was getting easier. He no longer filled the frame the way he once had. I was grateful for his help, but some days I wished he was less involved so I could enjoy the single certainty of hating him.

When he left, I thought, no, it has to be Robert and Deb, the Colorado couple. Robert and Deb were great. I could imagine being proud to talk about them: that Deb's grandfather was a professor of philosophy; that her grandmother was the first woman in Poland to earn a Ph.D. Deb assured me she'd never *think* about drinking Coke; her father used Coke to remove rust from car parts. And they were resourceful—not so much with holey socks, but they said they'd decorated an avocado tree they grew from seed for Christmas.

That morning I'd gone to church, and someone I'd spoken to afterward had reminded me that trials were blessings to produce endurance. I wondered, endurance for what? What could be harder than this? Jevn sometimes said the same thing, that what doesn't kill us makes us stronger. But I hated my own strength. Every convincing appearance of it infuriated me. The pastor had read Ezekiel, and I preferred the comfort of its violence: I will tie you up with ropes so that you cannot turn from one side to the other until you have finished the days of your siege.

◎ ◎ ◎

In the morning, I tripped over a bag of coffee beans sitting on my stoop. Attached was a folded map with directions to the nearest coffee grinder. I followed it and shared a cup of coffee with my neighbor Andy. Sometimes Andy would knock on my door with groceries in his backpack and make me dinner. He wouldn't call or arrange it, he'd just come in and start cooking.

And I can't persuade the father of my baby to walk one pace slower to stay beside me, I thought later that morning, as I stepped into the elevator behind Jevn.

Molly showed us a sample of the Permanent Surrender of Child form. In addition to my name, age, and address, and my child's name, date and city of birth, there were three lines for me to fill out, stating why I was requesting Catholic Social Services to take custody of my child. Molly addressed me. "Here we'll give a summary of your reasons, that you're a full-time student and that you're not married."

I had never expressed it so straightforwardly, and I was surprised that those reasons were enough. If I did lose contact with my son, he might look up his records and think it was as simple as that.

The document outlined the items I would surrender with my signature: all my rights as parent, including visitation, communication, support, religious affiliation, and right to consent to my child's adoption.

"Technically, you'll give custody to the agency, not the adoptive couple, and then we place him in a home. Of course, since we've been working together, I'll advocate for the placement of your child with the family you've chosen, and I'm sure it will be approved. I've never seen that not work out."

I wasn't concerned about the legal details; I was only worried about finding a family. Since December, I'd been steadily approaching the day when I would have to be able to sign that form, but I had assumed that by now, I'd have taken all the steps, that they would have led to the couple, and then the Surrender would just feel like the next move forward. I was so much closer to the end, but I was as far from being able to imagine signing that form as I had been last January.

"You'll know, Amy. I can't speak from personal experience, but I have seen this happen so many times. Birth mothers have told me that when you meet the right one, you just know. You've done a lot of good work, and you still have time."

I tried to imagine what that *just knowing* would feel like. Whether it would mean I wouldn't have doubts. Or maybe there would be doubts, but they would be dwarfed by the certainties. Had I already met them? Was it possible to just know, and not know it?

It couldn't be Robert and Deb. We finally received their responses to the 111 questions, which Robert said he found "aggressive, overwhelming, and too personal." He said, "It seems like you're trying to give us a multiple choice test, rather than build a relationship." But we were building a relationship with every exchange, and with every exchange, we were getting the information we needed.

They wouldn't answer the question, How do you celebrate your anniversary? They said it *falls in the realm of private.* What would you do if your twenty-two-year-old daughter told you she was pregnant? *This sounds a little too close to your current situation for us to be hypothetically giving advice. Sorry.* How is your family imperfect? *All families are imperfect. We prefer to focus on the positive.* What is the most beautiful place in the world? *All places have their beauty.* For some questions, they referred us to newspaper articles they'd written, or to previous e-mails. They reduced our 111 questions to: spirituality, environment, parenting, and community and answered them broadly.

"Friendship has to develop naturally," Robert argued. "You can't rush it. To quote Gandhi, 'Love, which is a condition of the heart, cannot come by an appeal to the brain.'"

More clichéd words of wisdom that didn't apply! It was impossible to pretend that the "friendship" we were developing was a natural process. That it didn't have an immobile timeline and a definite end goal. And even as they thought we should just relax and let love grow, they pushed me to make a commitment to them.

"Between our interests, love of outdoors, being Christian," Robert said on the phone, "it sounds like we should talk further and see if your child is meant for our family." As far as they were concerned, we just had to work out the technicalities. "Our adoption agent, Sandra, knows our personal details, so she can answer any further questions about us and advise you on the legal issues involved in an out-of-state adoption." That is, they wanted us to work it out with their agency and leave them out of it.

"I was thinking, actually, that I could move to Colorado so that it wouldn't be an out-of-state adoption," I told them. I was ready to forget about my internship and about school. I just wanted to do the adoption right. I would lose my university insurance, but their agency would cover maternity costs. Being near them would help me to think of myself as a surrogate mother and to care for the baby without growing attached.

"If you were to move to Colorado," Deb responded, "I think you should look into Medicaid or COBRA. The costs you invoice to the agency are ultimately billed to me and Robert. But I'm not sure that you should leave Ohio, anyway. That's where all your support is!"

There was also a significant difference in the retraction periods of the two states. In Colorado, a birth mother had thirty days to change her mind after signing the papers. If I stayed in Ohio, I'd have only twenty-four hours.

"Do you think there are a lot more issues to get resolved?" Deb asked.

"Are you starting to get comfortable with the idea of us as the adoptive parents?" Robert added. "I hate to say it, but you are going to have to let go eventually."

They'd had five previous adoptions fall through; they'd attended one birth and they'd given money to two couples; they'd had one birth mother disappear completely; and so it wasn't surprising that they wanted a commitment. But I was tired of being reminded I'd have to let go, as though my instinct to guard my son was unreasonable, or unnatural, or stubborn. It was true, I had to accept the limits of what I could predetermine or control; I had to acknowledge there were things I couldn't know. But at this stage, that was all I would let go of. It would be my single achievement as a mother: to find the right family and to find the right moment—to let go of my son, himself, perfectly.

But it couldn't be Jeff and Cindy, either. We found out that they were Christian Scientists, and when I asked about it, Jeff said it wasn't a topic that was open for discussion. But I needed them to be able to talk about it. It was disturbing to think they'd avoided telling me. We met, but I don't remember it. I was copied on an e-mail to them from Jevn in which he apologized for my obstinacy and told them that their cover photo was our favorite. They responded that in their "fairy-tale world," we would get married and keep our child.

I couldn't bear the thought of more Dear Birth Mother letters. More first phone calls and meetings. More hard-to-find but inevitable flaws. More fights with Jevn about how impossible I was being.

Then I thought about Paula and Erik, the Indiana theologian couple who wouldn't tell us the names they had in mind for a son. We'd already had a few conversations, they lived close enough to us that we could meet them pretty easily, and I remembered liking some of their answers I'd skimmed through before. Paula said she was passionate about reaching out to people in need and *practical expressions of Christian love and justice*, as well as building lasting friendships. What do you use your basement for? *Paula is notorious for stocking up on tuna when it goes on sale.* Do you ever build a fire? *Rarely, but Erik grew up in a farmhouse with a wood-burning stove in the kitchen, so he's the expert.* Paula's favorite T-shirt said *Think for yourself,* and they both had T-shirts that said *I Miss Chicago,* where they lived before they were married. They kept the TV in the basement, and among their kitchen appliances: *a little thing that looks like a waffle-maker; you put slices of bread and filling in it, and it grills them into sealed little sandwiches (we never use it).*

We didn't have a lot in common. They didn't spend their free time outside, or riding bikes, or building things, and they had no special relationship with mountains; they hoped someday to move back to Chicago, the flattest city I knew of. Erik had played basketball in college, but they weren't physically active as a couple. They weren't architects or musicians or designers. But I had grown skeptical of coincidences and things in common.

I read their answers to the 111 questions, pages and pages of answers, in their entirety. So many couples had received them defensively, like a volley of tennis balls forcing them to angle a response. But Paula and Erik responded as though I were handing them a curiously shaped small fruit, graciously exploring its various qualities with spontaneous ease and pleasure. Their answers were generous but straightforward, unfolding without calculation; they gave specific and varied dimension to what I'd designated only as a general region of acceptable response. In some cases they rearranged my map altogether, so compellingly elaborating an answer that it was rezoned in my own mind: a territory with hidden resources I'd previously thought unworthy of exploration.

One such territory was Eating Out. I'd asked, "Do you eat out or cook?" and they might have guessed the response I was looking for. A home-cooked meal eaten around the table was the image of stability and security they'd want to guarantee they could provide. It was what I'd grown up with. My family sat down every night, said grace, and talked to one another. Mom made fresh vegetables she grew in the garden or bought from her little man at the fork in the road, always accompanied by salad in a wooden bowl, and after my sister and I became vegetarians, she worried about our health and practiced making lentil loafs and tofu cheesecakes until we all liked the way they tasted. She must have made a decision about it early on, because it was always that way; even when it meant Dad came home and then went back to work afterward, we rarely changed course. On the few occasions when we did, they were specially designated "Fend for Yourself" nights—rare and exciting exceptions when we were left like the uncivilized to scavenge for leftovers and eat them out of sync with everyone else, maybe even standing.

Most couples had taken my cue to describe the dinners they planned to have together at home. But Paula and Erik apologized that they couldn't eat out more. They explained that a meal out was for them an invaluable opportunity to see friends and set aside the preoccupations of their own lives. Because they couldn't afford to do it much, they compensated by eating out for breakfast or getting coffee with friends whenever possible.

Those few words of explanation made me turn back to my whole history and all the things I took for granted. I saw that while there was a kind of security in sticking tight around a table together, for Paula and Erik there was a different, more dynamic kind. The world extended far beyond their own home, and their investment in the families of other people was an important part of their own. Jevn had wooed me in much the same way. Not by saying what I wanted, but by sweetly pushing at walls in my world to show me the infinite expanse beyond them. It was frustrating and unsettling and uncomfortable at first, but it created space in me that filled up fast with affection.

I sent them an e-mail, and we began communicating more regularly. There was something I really liked about them. I liked how articulate and clear-thinking they were. I liked that so many of Paula's e-mails began, *Erik and I were talking about it, and* . . . Like every couple, they'd said they were best friends, but in various ways, they revealed that the fuel of that friendship was conversation bolstered by mutual respect and interest. Any issue might move and change and evolve through conversation; either one of them could shift the thinking of the other.

I even liked that they didn't have a lot of money. My son would benefit from having resourceful parents, but more than that, there would never be any confusion, in me, in them, in my son, about what was being exchanged in this transaction. Financial security could never make up for the destabilizing loss of his family bond. We would only attempt to compensate for that loss with things that could begin to measure up. He would lose priceless things, but he would gain other, absolutely incommensurate, impossible-to-measure things.

Near the middle of March, Paula e-mailed, saying that she and Erik would like to think seriously about working together on an adoption plan. *Above all*, she wrote, *we're sensing that you are the kind of person we would be very glad to have as part of our lives. Since we're interested in the possibility of future contact, that's especially important to us.*

They said they'd stopped corresponding with the other birth mother they'd been talking to. They still didn't know where they were going to move in the summer; it depended on where Paula was accepted to doctoral programs, but that seemed like a surmountable complication. There was just the problem of her unwillingness to tell me the name they had in mind for a boy. In an e-mail, she said she'd heard stories of birth parents changing their minds, leaving the adoptive family to deal with loss while having also sacrificed a cherished name. It wouldn't feel right to reuse the name with a future adoption. "Having said all that, let me defuse this issue a bit by telling you that the name we have in mind for a boy is Jonathan."

Jonathan. It fell like a velvet cloak over him, revealing him. When Jeff and Cindy had said they would name their son Jevn, it felt like false flattery. But the name Jonathan was somehow right, and despite all the Johns I'd known, it was the name of nothing else.

But the moment I felt I might have found them, my guard returned. What about how different we were? Even with Robert and Deb, with whom we had much more in common, we'd struggled to reconcile our differences. They'd told us they simply couldn't conform perfectly to our standards. We'd never achieve some kind of perfect eclipse, with them as parents giving our son exactly what we'd have given him. They warned us we would have to relinquish control when we relinquished the baby and "step aside" to let them move into the parenting role.

Paula and Erik addressed our differences in a similar way, but with an entirely different emphasis. They said they couldn't be held to our standards, standing in for us and performing as us. But they didn't see why they should have to—not when we could be there, standing in for ourselves, performing as ourselves, giving him all the things they knew we had to give him.

We continued to correspond and speak on the phone, unearthing not sameness, but sympathy. They were not the image of what Jevn and I might have become, ten years down the road. It seemed they spent most of their time drinking decaf coffee and reading theological texts from the thirteenth century, two things I'd never done. But they were in fact not like any image at all; they were constantly moving, thinking, and recalibrating—where they would live, how they would parent, where the money would come from. We couldn't know exactly what kind of life they would provide, and they didn't make promises. What mattered wasn't the shape of the movements, or where it took them. What mattered was that we had a good feeling about the place they originated.

They had adopted their daughter, Sarah, a few days after her birth and had initiated contact with her birth mother, who had planned to have a closed adoption. Over time, they'd developed a relationship. Even so, they wanted to avoid modeling our relationship on that one. Our relationship would, naturally, be unique, and we began practicing it. We practiced telling each other incidental stories from our days and sharing our biggest sadnesses and hopes. It felt like when I got my first lunchbox, before I started kindergarten. The only thing I knew about the whole world ahead was what I witnessed every morning, my older brother and sister leaving home with lunchboxes in hand. So I practiced that. I put an apple, a banana, inside, closed the clasps, and carried it into the living room, dreaming of the future. I sat down on the cold brick of the fireplace and opened it. I loved the security of those varied things carried safely within the simple turquoise box, and I toted it around to every room in the house. I knew I couldn't know anything about what the future held, but I knew I was somehow equipped for it.

And now, as then, I tested my relationship with Paula and Erik, experiencing the weights and movements of the interior stuff as I practice-carried things in it, into this and that space of my life, having no actual idea what open adoption would hold. I practiced calling them, practiced talking about them, practiced telling them hilarious stories, telling them sad ones, practiced imagining where they would fit—before the weights became real. Soon everything would depend on those dynamics, the sadness and loss and pain, the relationship with my unknown son, with Jevn, being able to fit within some new and clean and unfamiliar turquoise box, the confines of our relationship.

But we hadn't met them in person yet, and as we drove west toward Indiana over ever flatter terrain, I prepared myself to be disappointed. We had been in this place so many times before.

On our way, Jevn and I argued about our recycling project. We were still collecting cans and taking them to be recycled every few weeks. Jevn thought we should abandon it. Let kids who drink Coke deal with their own waste. We were busy enough as it was, and I shouldn't be carrying bags of cans up and down the stairs anymore. I totally disagreed. If we weren't willing to do it, who would be? And then what? Just let the aluminum go into the landfill? And figure out how not to care about it? And then what else might we teach ourselves not to care about? He thought my extrapolations were absurd.

We maneuvered around the tiny, flat, empty downtown of Fort Wayne to the restaurant where we'd agreed to meet for lunch. Just outside, we saw Erik standing on the sidewalk. We recognized him from the photos, and that early Sunday morning, our car was the only animate thing in what might have been a stage-set city. Erik turned toward us, and just like love, it happened in an instant: Erik's hand shooting skyward, honest as a rocket, to say hello, here we are, and to direct us where to park our car. Like falling in love, time was split in half in Fort Wayne, Indiana. It was a fine edge; I barely noticed it, but everything that followed fell to one side, and everything before fell to the other. One look, and somehow I knew he was my son's father.

We continued around the block and parked the car. We got out and approached him, and we walked together to the restaurant.

"Paula's inside, trying to persuade them to seat us. A small technical difficulty: the place we chose for lunch is a bar, and Sarah is, of course, a minor!"

We joined Paula, who was chatting with the staff. She was smiling, touching the hostess on the arm, both of them laughing, even as we were refused seats. A manager decided that we could be seated outside instead, and we arranged ourselves around a table on that sunny day that was not quite warm enough for sitting out there.

"Before you got here, we were talking about how not to have a second car," Erik said. He said they wanted to end up in a place where public transit would give their children freedom and independence and would allow them to remain a single-car family. Ideally somewhere like Chicago. They asked us if we had any ideas. It was a problem we couldn't imagine, but we thought it was great—public transit was great; living in a city was great; thinking about reducing your environmental impact was great. That they were talking about second cars instead of second babies was great.

After lunch, we walked around Fort Wayne, and Sarah wandered ahead or fell behind, inspecting things in the grass beside the sidewalk. Her eyes were dark under the canopy of her long eyebrows, which tilted at their ends in a smile. She was curious; she studied everything around her.

"Sarah loves animals—all animals!" Paula told me as we both watched her.

"I loved animals when I was little, too," I said, and I felt I wasn't just making conversation. I was giving Paula information I hoped she might someday share with my son. I told her how my dad would rescue turtles from busy roads, sometimes snakes and frogs, and he'd bring them home in a box and surprise us; we'd keep them for an afternoon before we'd hike over to the creek to find a home for them. Those rescue missions could have been the origin of everything I felt about justice, and love, and beauty.

"That was why I became a vegetarian, initially," I added, and Paula said she was a vegetarian, too.

As I watched Sarah crouching at the edge of the sidewalk, I realized I wanted her for my son's sister. And as Jevn pointed toward a cornice and told Erik something about the architecture here, I turned back to my conversation with Paula and realized I wasn't waiting to be disappointed.

Driving back to Cincinnati, Jevn and I were silent. I think we both felt something big had happened. Finally he spoke.

"I had such a strong instinct to trust them, if they did something I doubted—I think I would question myself."

I held still, as I sometimes did when Jevn spoke openly. Those moments felt precious and delicate. I wanted to preserve his fragile feeling and my own. It had been building slowly, as detail by detail we'd grown to trust them, and it happened fast, Erik's arm in the air. It happened as magically as I have ever fallen in love. And that I knew, though I couldn't know enough to know, was exactly what gave substance to my knowing. Erik's hand reaching unself-consciously skyward, generous and firm, loosed my imagination. An honest gesture that split the sky and freed me from my own formless and uncertain desires.

Jevn dropped me off at my apartment. Before he left, he reminded me once again of the river, and for the first time I could imagine letting go.

THIRTEEN

When I was little, I kept a list of the things I loved. I rewrote it every night. It included my pets and my family, but knowing that even the loss of a creature as insignificant as an ant would cause the world to collapse, I always ended by writing that I loved everything else, too, even those things I hadn't mentioned or didn't know about. Sometimes I thought it was knowing I was an accident that made me love everything so much. Every single thing was something I almost never got to see. But by remembering everything, I hoped to preserve it. This began when the world was very small and my list very short, as it was when I was eight and got my first diary and used it for this purpose. It was given to me by an elderly German man from church who had written on some of its pages already, in letters that all had square corners. He smelled bad and spit when he spoke: "You. Not. *Forget!*" His words hinted at that idea that consumed me, the certainty of loss.

The eventual disappearance of everything began with our cats, twelve of them, one by one, over the course of my childhood. Then it was the hills, which were leveled to make Walmarts and Kmarts and Targets and telemarketing centers. My dad would tell me those developments were going to help pay for my college education; my mom would refuse to shop there. Then it was the snow, which would often start to fall right on

Christmas Eve and linger in the hills through winter. Now it was almost hard to picture there.

Arriving home for spring break, I wanted to show my son all the things I'd loved. I took a bike out to ride my old loop through the hills, but my stomach got in the way. Instead, I drove the car with the windows down, inhaling every twist and turn. I wanted my son to taste them, to remember them deep in his cells. That night, I found the book I'd gotten in Italy, *Oh!*, and I packed it to take back with me.

School began again in April, and I put away the profiles. Nearing campus the first day, I braced myself. A whole new group of students would be back from their internships and surprised to see me like this. From a long distance away, I saw my friend Brian stop midstride and stare at me. I approached him, embarrassed. But this was only the beginning of the humiliation I would face, returning to school.

"You got your hair cut!" he said, not noticing my girth even as he hugged me. I'd chopped off my hair so I'd have less to think about. Bangs were, in fact, itchy and distracting, but I was glad they delayed the shock of my pregnancy, which came to Brian eventually.

Enormous as I felt, my stomach was the size of a small basketball, more like I was five, not seven, months along. Nina assured me I just carried differently. I gorged myself on raw tofu and raisins, along with eggs and milkshakes, and my midwives reminded me to keep eating more because now I was building his brain. Small as he was, I felt my rib cage was too narrow to contain him. Sometimes he braced himself against my spine and pushed my lower ribs outward or tried to raise them like a garage door. Sometimes, aggravated by his efforts, I tried to help, pulling at my ribs with my hands to stretch them open. Sometimes, when I saw Jevn talking to other girls, I wished my belly were bigger, so I could wield it like a weapon.

My environmental geography class was held on the other side of campus. I passed McMillan Lawn, where Sleepy Amy and I sometimes studied in the sun. It was where, in the moonlight as we walked, Jevn had asked, "Do you see the angels?" I had wanted to be game, so I said yes, but I searched the sky to pinpoint what he might mean. The glow around the street-lights, the fog at the surface of the asphalt from the rain, or the moon's illumination of the clouds? I was satisfied that among the visible things, I was seeing something you might call an angel.

"Yeah?" He laughed. "Where?"

As I passed that lawn, I tried to imagine being a regular student just walking to class to do doable work and then relax in the sun, like you were supposed to do in college. I entered an old, normal building, with big, heavy windows you could lift open on a beautiful spring day like that one, straight hallways, rooms in a row, numbered sequentially so you could find them, right angles at every intersection of floor and wall, wall and ceiling.

The professor was a woman in her forties who was naturally beautiful. She read through the syllabus, and I got that beginning-of-school feeling of academic decadence: a whole new field of study would be laid out for me, chapter by chapter. Population dynamics, ozone loss, resource depletion, food webs and energy flow in ecosystems—high-level, philosophically fascinating, and urgent issues. We were talking about the end of energy, and topsoil, and life as we know it. After the adoption, maybe I would quit architecture and become a climate scientist.

When class was over, several students crowded around the professor at the front of the room. Another class was starting when she finally got to me, so we stepped into the hallway. I told her that I was pregnant, that I was doing adoption, and because I might miss some classes for appointments, I thought she should know. She waited for people to pass. Her eyes were big and beautiful, and she gazed at me sympathetically. When the coast was clear, she told me that she was adopted, too. She said she'd never met her birth mother, but she thought adoption was an amazing and selfless thing to do for a child. I stepped back at that. I wasn't telling her to be congratulated, and it wasn't about being amazing—it was just about making a reasonable plan and doing it. It was for everyone's benefit. I explained that I wasn't doing the old kind of adoption. It was a new and improved kind. I would get to see my son.

"Oh, that's wonderful!" she said. "He will love you, Amy, believe me. He'll be so grateful for what you're doing for him."

There were so many significant moments still ahead of me that I couldn't imagine a time when that would be the reassurance I wanted. Right now I just hoped to have a healthy birth, to stay confident about Paula and Erik, and to get through school without incident.

I returned to the freezing-cold lecture auditorium of the architecture school. The professor showed us a documentary made in the 1970s about the simplest idea imaginable (and yet it had no bearing on the thermostat): people like to congregate in the sun. We watched black-and-white aerial time-lapse images of crowds of people in New York City plazas, moving at the pace of the earth on its axis within the irregular polygon of direct sunlight that inched across the plaza. The camera focused on two men talking. Every few seconds, one would step slightly, and the other would shift in response, and finally they anchored their conversation alongside a crack in the sidewalk. Subconsciously, they moored themselves against an almost imperceptible line and stayed.

Architecture was simply an elaboration of that impulse: to put yourself definitively in relationship to something outside yourself, because even if it is mobile, it's probably less fleeting than you are. These were the kinds of lessons that made me want to stay in architecture school; they felt as big and important as climate change.

I walked home from my first day back. I'd taken off my jacket and was wearing a bright red maternity shirt my professor had lent me. I felt a confidence I'd never had before, a joyful indigestion, and as I crossed the street, a car that had the right of way stepped on the brakes and waved me along, smiling. It was the same intersection where Sleepy Amy and I had once been hit by a car; it had been going at a slow speed, but we still ended up on the hood, hearts racing.

I began to notice it in other places. I felt I could have crossed a busy road, right in the middle, without looking, and everyone would have happily frozen in place to protect me. Somehow being two made everyone give way to me. People who bumped into me apologized profusely. My child had a ticket I'd never had. Somehow everyone knew this baby was meant to be here.

One evening, as I was working on my studio project from home, my father called to hear how school was going. "Amyseek! Fromtennessee!" he would always greet me. He didn't ask about my pregnancy. He asked about Paula and Erik, and I said that, yes, we were still thinking they were the ones. Mom was on the other line. As we talked I looked at my model in progress. My building was a theater, with layers and layers of walls and thresholds guarding a deep interior space, the stage.

"Would you like to hear a silly story about your mother?" my dad asked after he was satisfied things were going well. "I was pulling out of the driveway, and she came running over to the car, waving and flailing her arms. *Walterrrrrr!* She was so excited. I stopped the car and she came up to the window, and do you know what your dear old mummy said?"

". . . No?"

"She told me she'd just seen a robin." He laughed. "That's what she was so excited about! Flailing her arms!" He liked to tease her, but the way tiny, everyday things made her happy was not so secretly among his favorite things about her.

"It was *two* robins!" my mother exclaimed from the other line.

When I hung up the phone, my heart sank. I wanted my son to know my mother. I wanted my dad to take him for walks. I wanted my parents to want him.

I was thinking all the time about letting go. I only wanted to let go of my son in the way that all mothers eventually have to—with some certainty I'd provided everything he would need in my absence. It wasn't enough to entrust him to Paula and Erik; I wanted somehow to give him a deeper equipment, something he would keep with him inside. I began taking walks to Mount Storm, lifting my shirt to let him feel the orange warmth of the sunset on his surface. I wanted to plant that warm light in him like the smallest seed of desire for simple things: light, and wind, and shadows. His hunger for those things would lead him to every place I would have shown him. And then, I thought, I could let him go, like Moses in the woven basket.

One evening I was walking down the grand staircase on my way home for the night, and I recognized two boys I hadn't seen since fall coming from the other direction. As they got nearer, they saw my stomach.

"Whoa! You're pregnant?" They studied me with the earnestness of animals. "Can I touch it?" They each aimed a single index finger at my abdomen and slowly made contact.

"It's hard!?" one said gleefully to the other. And to me, as if I might make sense of the surprising firmness.

It was the kind of pure curiosity I wanted to find in Jevn, but he remained unmoved by my body and stoic in the face of my anger, which came in crashing waves he'd simply wait out, forgiving and forgetting. We'd done everything we could do to prepare for the adoption; there was nothing else I could demand from him. That loss of control left me unmoored, and I tried desperately to draw him back, picking fights to regain his attention, but he wouldn't indulge me. He returned to his own life and became a fresh mystery to me. While I was trying only to find adequate alternatives for the most basic and necessary tasks—bending to tie my shoes, leaning over a drafting board to draw—I wondered constantly where he was; I imagined him happily relieved of his responsibilities and free to focus on someone new. I wrote to Paula about it. She didn't mention Jevn in her response. She just said she thought I must be feeling alone in some very important ways.

Only sometimes Jevn would catch me off guard by reassuring me that the pain was real and that we were both feeling it. He called me from Colorado when he went for a weekend to visit his family and to collect some old photographs to give to our son.

"The sight of babies has sunk me," he said. "I'm looking for stuff to bring back to give him, but I wish I could share memories with him most of all."

Paula and Erik visited for Easter. We had a weekend of double dates, and when they dropped Jevn and me off at my apartment for the last time, it felt like something should happen. Every time we saw each other, our connection felt stronger. It called for some gesture, some expression of what was happening between us. But we just fumbled our goodbyes, as heartfelt and inadequate as a failed first goodnight kiss.

They sent frequent news from home. They'd started telling friends about the potential adoption, and the prospect had accelerated their decision to move to North Carolina, where Paula would begin her Ph.D.

*The update on us is: we have bought a house! And, on the topic of trust . . .
we bought it sight unseen!*

She said she'd heard a story about a Native American tribe who remembered a child's birthday as the day his mother first thought of him;
on that day, the mother would begin to compose a song, which remained
uniquely his throughout his life. *I suppose I'm finding myself humming a
little*, she said. I liked the feeling that we were pregnant together.

They assured me they would allow their child to be an atheist—
broad-mindedness was important to me. But they said that they would
have a lot of conversations about it. They said they thought of their spir-
itual life as always evolving, always deepening and changing. *We really
want our home to be a place where questions are asked and answers aren't
given out quickly. I guess we'd like Sarah to think of her life with God as an
adventure, not as a script for the right things to do or say.*

Paula wrote that she'd learned from her agency in North Carolina
that the baby must be given Jevn's or my last name and not theirs at
birth, *because there can be no official indication that you and Jevn and Erik
and I know each other! Isn't that bizarre? It is an officially "anti–open adoption state"!* Paula said that it felt right anyway, properly reflecting the reality of the situation. When he arrived, he would be ours, and only after
his adoption would his last name change and he'd become theirs. She
added that she didn't mean to assume anything, speaking about the adoption as though it were a certainty.

In those early stages, liking them didn't feel like losing my son. It
felt nothing like building a house together, intimately and over months,
that wouldn't in the end have room for me. Our relationship had a beautiful lightness, but it didn't feel like having my son lifted, gently, out of
my arms.

The school term ended uneventfully; I got a C for the first time in studio.
And for the first time, I had no feelings about my project. I returned to
my internship downtown, just as we began another session of birth classes.
Nina stood before the class, tugging at a piece of paper with both hands,
making a harsh clapping sound.

"See this? I can't pull it apart? Now . . ." She used scissors to make a tiny cut at one edge. She tugged once, and the paper ripped in half. "That's an episiotomy, people! The doctor is going to say your perineum isn't opening wide enough to allow the head to come out. He's going to say you just need a little cut, but that is going to weaken the whole surface, and you'll tear—I tore all the way to my anus! I was unrecognizable down there for weeks! But the line is nice and straight and clean, so your doctor can sew it up easily and get back to his golf game."

She showed us how we could press back on the head as it pushed at the perineum to allow the opening to work its way wider, stretching more gradually. Then you might not tear at all.

"You moms who have had babies vaginally before, you have what's called a proven pelvis. Don't let them tell you you need any of it— Cesarean, episiotomy, epidural. I'm telling you, they're going to look for every opportunity."

This class wasn't held in a basement. Nina had invited us to sit in for free on a regular birth class for married women who had planned their pregnancies. There were windows and chairs, and we pulled the blinds to watch childbirth videos that were no longer shocking to me.

These mothers were having more problems with their pregnancies than the teenage moms in my other class had had. One had feet so swollen she could no longer wear regular shoes. Another had acne and rashes all over her skin.

"I want to make sure you guys understand all the positions you can try. You don't have to lie down or stay in bed. Moms, let's sit down on a birth ball, and dads, you stand behind the moms and we'll practice lifting them as they have a contraction."

Jevn stood behind me and lifted me, stiffly, as if I were a heavy bookcase.

"Your pelvis is not one solid bone; it can move and open. Does anyone know how snake jaws work?"

In mid-June, Paula and Erik returned to Ohio for a meeting at the adoption agency. We introduced them to Molly and talked about planning an entrustment ceremony. Molly suggested that we lay out, in detail, how we hoped our future contact might work, but because we agreed we wanted a very family-like relationship, one that would grow and change naturally, we also agreed not to put anything down on paper.

I was proud to have Molly meet them. She caught my eye many times while we all talked, and I could tell she just knew, too.

One night, Jevn called me while he was moving out of his apartment with the ten-foot-deep closet. I was surprised to hear from him; there was no business we needed to attend to. I was determined to let go of him, let go of dreams of him and hopes for the future, let go of his music, his mountains, his way of drawing, but I told him I was glad about the baby, because it meant my feelings for him didn't have to end; they would get to have some kind of life, somewhere in the world without me. It was about 7:30 and the sun had just set; summer was coming. I was lying on my bed, listening to the bamboo with my windows open, and he told me he was lying on the only few pillows left in his apartment. He said he was waiting to understand why we couldn't be together. That the day we met, as much as this night, he wanted to know me.

My belly had become a stranger—like someone other than me entirely—but I'd suck it in and feel lithe and aerodynamic, surprised to look down and find it protruding just as unapologetically as before. One night I went into the studios to collect aluminum cans and found I couldn't bend over at all. Leaning sideways into the recycling containers we'd clearly marked *Aluminum Only*, I discovered plastic bottles and crumpled napkins, X-Acto blades and scrap chipboard. I threw a plastic bottle across the room, and Coke sprinkled the floor. Students working just paused to look at me.

At night, my belly slept on the bed beside me, more than in me, and I dreamed it was a greyhound, galloping away. I followed it, collecting my loose skin, returning it to the cavity below my ribs. Sometimes the bulge was lopsided and the movements it made had character; sometimes they made me smile. Telling Paula and Erik about it, seeing them accept it as reality, reality enough to call it Jonathan, made me think that inside my belly really was, maybe, Jonathan.

FOURTEEN

It was on the side of a road somewhere in Switzerland. My mother, flagging a car with French plates, thinking it was her friend, instead met my father. I'd pictured that road a certain way. A steep slope on one side, a valley on the other. I thought I would recognize it, instinctively. When I arrived in Grindelwald, I borrowed a bike from a cyclist I met near the station. "The Alps are easy," he said, "just once up, once down!" I followed him for a while, but he left me on the mountain with half a banana. I hadn't had anything to eat or drink since I left Italy the night before, but I didn't want to change money again.

Standing on the side of the road, I looked across the valley and wondered whether the wind had swept across the very same glacial ice and climbed up on the air, cutting through the heat of the sun all those years ago, when things aligned to make me possible. I stepped over a fence, pushed my hands deep into a trough of water, and drank. The chill in the air, in midsummer, was the fine edge along which I walked. What if my father had turned off to have a rest—what if she was behind him and took no note of his plates? I wouldn't be there, in the Alps, trying to give weight to the lightness of my origins. I would not be here at all, and no one would be grieving.

On the train leaving Switzerland that night, I'd written a letter to

Jevn. *I went biking in the countryside today. Remember the time I fell asleep at your place and you woke me with fruit? I will have missed you in so many different cities by the time I see you again.* He responded, *All those places seem closer to me because I have been thinking about you there. I'll call when I am in Denver. I'll know what to say when I call.* Just weeks later, I would try to break up with him, and days after that, I would find out I was pregnant.

◎ ◎ ◎

Tall trees surrounded the pool. I put my keys and shorts on a chair and stepped slowly into the water. I fell forward to my shoulders, and the heaviness floated up like a balloon. I didn't know until that moment how heavy it had become.

After spending so much time trying to persuade myself I was pregnant, I don't remember when it became impossible to imagine the opposite. Thin again, bendable, hollow. I swam back and forth across the kidney-shaped expanse, through leaves and insect casings, wearing the same swimming suit I'd had for years, stretched tight around my stomach. But in place of the weight, there was buoyancy, a feeling I didn't think I'd get to feel until I'd surmounted so many more hurdles.

When I got home, I lay on my bed, shedding the dry dust of chlorine-coated skin. I felt like I was ten again in my damp bathing suit, succumbing to that special swimming sleepiness, my skin radiating the day's heat. My surface was so perfectly acclimatized to the room temperature that a soft summer breeze made me pull the comforter around me the wrong way. I found peace in the warm stillness, knees nested one in front of the other, belly resting softly beside me. My body felt everywhere-worn. Outside, the row of thick bamboo filled the south window; as the sun set, the shadows on the wall shimmered, and I shut my eyes to sleep.

The questions returned to wake me, as they always did. I went out to the stoop to escape them. The sky was saturated, and the sun, already set, was still illuminating the rims of the clouds. I triangulated; those distant clouds, just above me, the approximate location of the sun beyond the crest of the earth, my life here in Cincinnati. How little this problem in fact was, whether I kept him, whether I gave him up.

The Nepali woman who lived next door passed by, slowly and heavily pushing her grocery cart, followed by her friend. She stopped to look at me. Her dark eyes squinted under her scarf.

"I think tomorrow you have much problem," she said, nodding once, unsmiling. Her friend stopped behind her.

"Yes . . . Pain. *Pain.*" Her friend shook her head sadly.

Jevn called to see if I wanted to go to a movie. He picked me up at my apartment and we walked down the hill. It was the end of the world, spaceships and space creatures, and some celebrity had to save us. I happily let those alien concerns displace my own; the cold air removed me entirely from the summer of the world outside. I savored the last seconds as the credits rolled, and then I felt my own forgotten and foggy concerns begin to crystallize and return to me. Jevn dropped me off at my apartment, and though my due date was just two days away, he didn't ask how I was feeling.

The next morning, I returned to the pool. Between laps, I sat on the side in a lounge chair, my hands behind my head, my skin covered by a soft summer oil. When I bleached dry and began to bake, I'd get back in. I swam like my mother, alone, on my side. Leaping out to my right with one arm, the other paddling short and softly in support. I'd roll to my back and look up at the sky. Back and forth, water filling my ears with silence. As I pulled myself out of the water, each rung of the ladder restored the burden.

I had been half-attentive to my internship. Our only project had me on my feet in a planned community north of Cincinnati, going door to door to survey residents about their neighborhood's successes and failures. Most people didn't want to take a survey, but one man answered the door and then stuck his head out to look up and down the street.

"What are you doing out here in the heat? How far along are you?"

I was embarrassed.

"Do you want some water? Do you need to sit down? Here, come in." I went inside. I was riding on the back of someone everyone wanted to protect.

In the middle of July, Paula and Erik came back to Ohio. They stayed an hour north in Dayton with family, and the four of us had meetings with

Molly and excursions in the city together. The evening before my due date, we packed a picnic for a concert on the banks of the Ohio. We spread out our blanket and picked at the fruit salad and the crackers. The sun was setting; the air was perfectly warm. I asked Paula if she didn't think Sting had aged remarkably well, but I stopped in the middle of what I was saying.

"I think I just peed in my pants," I said, stunned by the sudden wetness.

"Amy, I think your water broke. Let's take you to the restroom." She told Erik and Jevn to wait there, and we weaved across the lawn between the picnic blankets.

"I think she's in labor!" I heard someone say, in a kind of a panic. But Nina had taught me not to panic. It was only time to go grocery shopping. She made labor sound like another infinity, another stage of an endless process that would keep me safely removed from the decision.

Paula handed me wads of toilet paper under the door. I looked down and saw a little bit of blood on my underwear. Stall doors slammed as people moved in and out around me. I sat for a few moments, feeling the weight lower than before, then quickly got up, stuffed my pants with toilet paper, and suggested we should stay for the concert we'd paid to see. We made our way back to the blanket, and I sat down carefully, but the loss of fluids meant his elbows were no longer cushioned but sharp, and I started to experience his bones in my belly, a human being in my belly, where a human being doesn't belong.

I'd told Paula and Erik I wanted them to be there with me for the birth, and I'd submitted a form to the hospital giving them permission to be. I wanted to share the experience in the same spirit with which I would eventually share my son, but Paula thought I might change my mind. We drove home from the concert and they left me to spend the night in labor. The moon was full, hanging just above the treetops to the southwest, casting cool light through the bamboo. I sat on my low futon, beside Jevn's big blue duffel bag, beside Jevn, who tried to rest, and waited anxiously for the deep pull of the heavy door, the release into the unknown.

Labor wasn't painful like being dealt a blow—it felt like labor, like digging a ditch. I stood still to rest between each exertion. But before it started, no one would tell me that. Even Nina had shrugged her shoulders when I asked her what it would feel like, as if it were a peculiar place, its features so singularly elusive, no memory could clutch and keep it, much less escape with trinkets that might hint at its particular strangeness. Or a place like death that simply mutes the mouths of all its witnesses. Nina had assisted a hundred births and had four of her own, but when it came to that question, she just said that everyone's experience is different.

Over the phone, Nina advised us both to go to sleep. Sleep as much as possible, preserve your energy. We would need it tomorrow. Eat. She wouldn't describe the nature of the pain, but she insisted it was nothing to fear. She told us to call her when my contractions were regular and five to six minutes apart. My contractions were intense but erratic. My stomach clenched and I was comforted by familiarity: contractions were like period cramps—but cosmic. Each one a threshold. And between them were intermittent phases of complete relief, when I could fall asleep. When a contraction came, it would shock me awake—a hand inside squeezing, pounding, pulling some interior and intricately connected flesh with sudden certainty, into an abyss even deeper inside. And this pain had real purpose: each contraction was a passage to a place where there were no words, only work.

Jevn lay quietly beside me in the dark. The crickets were chirping, and the loneliness was sweet, like a sleepless night camping. I already longed for the fullness, the perched expectancy, the before-everything of pregnancy. Speechless, Jevn turned and touched me, and, wildly, his hands explored the still-evolving terrain. They seemed to have a hundred questions, and as he broke the silence of eight months, he answered my own. He held me. We kissed. But a powerful aloofness had silenced me. My body was moving ahead. His touch grasped a skin I was shedding, and I could only mourn the glimmer of desire as it receded. I felt him let go, as if he'd given up, and then he settled and went to sleep.

I sat for hours watching the moon. It was the only orienting thing in a night that seemed to wrap itself around me. While the world slept, I worked, turning its gears with calm concentration. Waiting, perplexed. What was happening was the biggest and yet most natural thing in the world; I didn't know what to do, and yet, as though I had been specially trained for it, I had no doubt. I didn't think about what Nina had taught me; I just remembered she'd said not to be afraid. I pushed forward blindly through the night, trusting myself at every step. The animal darkness, the bamboo waving, the thin panes of glass, the cranks that opened the windows north and south, the little strap of metal Jevn had wedged between the window frame and the brick to hold the bird feeder, the vast park, all its trees, the insects. Everything seemed to be gathered, knowing something most real, most meant to be.

I imagined my son doing his work from the inside, so close and so far from me. But even as we approached each other, on either side of the thin surface of my skin, I couldn't translate the feeling into a person who would have his own name. Jonathan. I was not laboring for someone else. I had the blinders of an insect, performing its clicking, repetitive, buzzing task, deep under the surface of the bark, deep within the nest. My rhythms were the unself-conscious habits of the living soil. I did a woman's work, the invisible nighttime work of turning a heavy world slowly on its axis.

Time was a deep black landscape whose boundaries surged and plummeted, condensed and sailed. Time was no longer a string that could be traced, step by step, from here to there; time was infinite textures of darkness. *Yesterday*, I thought, trying to pin time down. Yesterday was so beautiful you could really see that once this wasn't a city. That day, a cloud of a world floating far away, it seemed the ground had forgiven the way we'd unsettled it.

Yesterday—I tried to remember it. I'd sat in the shadow of dusk and spotted the sun still shining on the top floors of the apartment building across the street. I could measure a movement as monumental as the planet on a scale as minute as the floors of a high-rise, as shadow swallowed the building, floor by floor, and the upper levels peeked over the arc of the earth, as it turned away from the sun. Here, on the steaming asphalt, releasing its warm breath, it was dusk, but on the eighth floor they were having a spectacular sunset. The windows of the airplane that passed above had a view, too, and they flashed in recognition.

In another world, I thought, I would bend and ride a bike. That thought was another cloud that crested and broke across the sky. Before it disappeared, I'd forgotten its shape altogether. I was detached from all my thoughts and history and hopes. The night had taken shape and developed topography. Night wasn't comprised of simple laminations that securely lapped the day. It felt like a land we could live in forever.

But morning came, dimly. It pushed cruelly forward, and night's dimensions, its chambers and secret passages, dissipated. Morning cast the same brash light on everything, on the students racing to their classes, on the park across the street, on me. By sunrise, the contractions were four minutes apart. Nina arrived angry that I'd progressed so far without calling her. But I'd been lost, or busy. I hadn't been timing my contractions; they were worlds I'd entered without duration. Jevn had fallen asleep, as she'd advised us to do. And I hadn't felt like I needed anything.

She was upset that I hadn't eaten or slept. She shook me alert and made me remember the things I was supposed to do. She put grapes and ice in my mouth. She cleaned my house hastily, as though someone were arriving for dinner. She touched my back as I leaned through contractions. My forearms rested on my light blue wingback chair, and I bowed forward, letting the weight hang down. I'd been laboring for hours, and I could feel Nina reading my Signposts. I was still in the earliest stages of labor; I could still smile and speak. Her examination shifted to the sunburns in my armpits, where I'd neglected to put sunscreen when I went swimming. I was flushed and swollen and rashed and burned, like a many-layered watercolor, all shades and textures of pink.

My contractions were so strong that Nina thought the baby would arrive by late morning. But twelve hours came and went, and I was still able to smile. I thought my son and I had our own pact; I'd let him feel the orange warmth of so many sunsets that he would want to arrive at the end of day. Jevn did his job; he told me I was doing well, he massaged me and stayed close. He and Nina behaved like a team, bustling around me, making work. I was a giant parade balloon bulldozing clumsily forward as my drivers scurried far below, tending the strings that bound me loosely to the ground.

This was as intimately as I would ever know my son. From the tiny seed he was to a thing with ankles and fingerprints, he moved through me, and as he did I would take an impression. I would linger on every moment, feel everything and hold it like I wanted helplessly to hold the sunset. But I didn't want Nina to see me turn reflective. She'd know I'd reached full dilation when I started to fall silent, and then I would say I don't think I can do it, and that would be when I would start to push, and then it would all be over. I resolved to smile, to stop time and keep this closeness to my son.

By two in the afternoon, I was no longer progressing and my contractions became short and erratic. We decided I needed food and a walk. We went to the park across the street, but by the time we got there I couldn't put one foot fully in front of the other, and the contractions stopped me in my tracks. I managed to smile as I ate a baked potato Nina or Jevn had bought somewhere, sitting by the pond in the park overgrown with summer. I made it only halfway around before Nina suggested it was time to head to the hospital. We wanted to get there no more than three hours before the birth. My birth plan specified that I wanted a natural birth, but we would wait until I was dilated enough to ensure they wouldn't medicate me and, if for some reason they did, the impact on the baby would be minimal; his systems would have already begun detaching from my own.

Park staff, trimming trees along the pond, asked, cheerfully, "How far along is she?" Somehow they knew not to address me, but I was surprised to be seen at all.

"She's having contractions now!" Nina held my arm, but she sounded far away. Something had changed. The sun had shifted and it wasn't anymore the white light of early afternoon that has no trace of melancholy, the short shadows of noon skies, the blared-out blues, the flaccid clouds, the time of day that doesn't ask to be remembered. Now oranges were emerging and the thistles could be distinguished among the taller grasses as the shadows lengthened. Nina said, "It's time to go."

I felt myself retreating, hiding from needles, and medicines, the intrusion that threatened to alleviate the pain and diminish my experience. Nina wanted me to deliver at home for exactly this reason, but my insurance wouldn't allow it, so we had written a birth plan, signed weeks ago by the hospital; only under extreme circumstances would medical intervention be allowed. Nina would be there to enforce the contract. The hospital had a hundred methods to make the process more efficient and to mitigate the thousand pains of childbirth, every one of them a critical step in the transformation to motherhood.

I was not to be confined to bed but allowed to move freely and assume different positions as I felt the need, standing, squatting, perching on a birth ball. I was to be allowed to drink water freely; please provide crushed ice. Vaginal exams during labor only when absolutely necessary. No internal fetal monitor. No enema. No stirrups. No removal of pubic hair. No amniotomy. No heparin lock. No catheter. Low light and quiet throughout labor.

IV allowed only if absolutely necessary, and then only into the arm, allowing maximum mobility—not into the back of the hand. Do not induce labor or accelerate contractions; no Pitocin. No stripping of membranes. Thumb-sucking and nipple stimulation only to induce/regulate contractions. Do not break water. If membranes rupture early, allow maximum time (twenty-four hours) before discussing antibiotics. Heat for pain relief: allow use of shower. Narcotic pain relief only, if necessary (Nubain, Demerol). Only local anesthesia, only if necessary; please use Stadol. These to be used before epidural; no epidural unless critical. If critical, back off of epidural toward the pushing stage to allow the natural instinct to push.

Mother allowed to push when she feels it's necessary, but given direction for the protection of the perineum. Perineum to stay intact using compresses and support. If breech baby, still attempt vaginal delivery. No episiotomy. No forceps or vacuum extractors. Allow baby to come straight to breast after birth; no cleaning or weighing. Fundus massage for placenta delivery. Mother will hold baby through delivery of the placenta and during any tissue repairs. Please make a blanket available during repairs. If emergency C-section is required, mother to remain conscious and screen to be lowered before delivery. If no distress, son to be given to mother immediately at C-section delivery.

Allow umbilical cord to stop pulsing before disconnecting it. Father will cut the cord. Allow baby to cough to expel its own mucus; do not suction baby's mouth. Use cloth if necessary. All tests and procedures on baby to be done while in mother's arms. Oral vitamin K only. Use colostrum in baby's eyes instead of eye ointment and delay eye treatment for one hour. No PKU/glucose testing. PKU after forty-eight hours. No circumcision.

No hepatitis B testing. Father will accompany baby for any procedures required outside of delivery room. No heat lamps.

Private room for postpartum. Baby will "room in" with mother. Mother will breast-feed. No bottle feeding, no pacifiers; if necessary, feed supplements using a dropper, feeding syringe, or cup.

The hospital would be a battleground, and these were the terms of engagement. I was grateful for Nina, there to fight for them so that I could concentrate on every centimeter of his shifting: every tremor would be a script I would study to understand what this was, to create a son. We were carving and crafting each other and there would be no loss of consciousness. I wouldn't leave him, or slip away. Every feeling I felt, I was meant to feel.

Nina shut me in the back of her minivan and we drove home to pick up the blue duffel bag, packed with my blue and white nightgown and a bandana to hold back my bangs. I wanted to stay, but I said goodbye to everything I knew, and we drove to the hospital less than one mile away. All the incubating, considering, dreaming would soon be over, and my son would confront me with the question of what I was going to do.

Jevn must have been updating Paula and Erik, but I don't remember overhearing it. I don't remember saying anything about them, but I must have told Jevn I wanted to be alone, though it no longer seemed like a request I had to make. We arrived at the hospital and went directly to the third floor, the labor and delivery wing I'd toured just a week before; I'd seen nurses rushing in and out, a waiting room full of families, a vending machine. I'd seen women in various stages of labor then, but I couldn't have imagined the faraway worlds they were inhabiting right before my eyes. Now I saw it through a fog, and I heard Nina say there were no rooms available. We'd be admitted according to medical necessity.

"That's what I'm telling you. Her contractions are regular, two minutes apart, a minute and a half long. It can't be more than an hour."

The nurses in reception didn't know I'd enjoyed a concert, spent a night gazing at the moon, had a day in the park, a long walk and a potato by the pond, all before making my way to the hospital. I wandered slowly in the hallway for an hour with Jevn holding me steady, his arm wrapped tightly around my shoulder, while Nina went to war. Finally a crowd of nurses surrounded me, escorting me to a room and preparing me to receive antibiotics because my water had broken almost twenty-four hours ago. Nina told them to wait.

My Signposts read: deep labor, dilated, on the cusp of pushing, but once I was perched on sterile sheets made frigid by air-conditioning, labor ground to a halt. The birth was suddenly as far away as the city, visible only at a distance through the small window. The lights in my room were low and incandescent, but the white light of the hallway, illuminating the floor in a glossy line below the door, brightened the whole room like a slow flash every time someone came or left.

The sun retreated, and I found myself alone again in the dusk and approaching night. Nina and Jevn were somewhere in the dim corners of the room, enlarging and appearing, then evaporating again. Then the darkness arrived at the window like a ghostly compatriot and deepened the thresholds that divided me from the world I'd known. Words from outside me crept in, distant voices speaking; the loss of sterility of the womb environment, of infection, Cesarean, antibiotics. Voices I couldn't locate in the darkness, words that didn't recognize how far away I was and how unreachable.

Nina pointed the shower hose at my swollen lower back. I leaned against the tiles and closed my eyes. She had explained that pain and heat travel on the same nerve pathways, and so if you fill up the highway with heat, then pain won't have any room to deliver messages to the brain. Relief comes by tricking the brain into thinking all it feels is *hot*. The water was scorching, and the room was a cloud of steam. Spit and tears and all kinds of wetness mixed; heat condensed on the tiles. The world was wet and undifferentiated. I was somehow naked. I was a monster, my body transformed, a lizard expanding its frill, parietal eye pulling me places no one else could see.

It could have been that the pain was simply not the point, when Nina had been unable to describe it. I wouldn't have called it pain, even after so many hours, with progress completely stalled. I was in hard labor, but the arc of his skull had nested in the curve of my sacrum, and the contractions were thrusting him hard against my tailbone, which began to protrude like the dorsal plates of a reptile. But even as I clenched through ineffective contractions, I couldn't measure that feeling against any prior pain.

I reached back to touch my spine, and the grotesque and bony swelling gave me a surge of vigor and certainty to push past the limits of my strength. My center moved south from my heart toward the pit of my stomach. I leaned on the head of the bed and swayed my hips like a cow loping across an uneven field, weight swinging heavily from hip to hip. But all the while we were not making progress. The emotional signposts were no longer legible. I wasn't moving in the proper sequence. I was holding on.

And about then a bell clanged with sudden news. At any other moment I would have recognized it. It was the ring of a phone, the kind that had spiral cords that tangled. People had heard I was in labor, and some were calling to find out how it was going. They wanted to know, specifically, do I want a milkshake? I couldn't understand: milkshake. I couldn't understand someone piercing the darkness, offering a milkshake to help. Vanilla or strawberry? Jevn would have vanilla. His gentle voice penetrated my corridors, asking what kind I would like. And in no time whatsoever, there were milkshakes. I opened my eyes and saw flashes from the places outside my darkness where the sunset had just swept across everything, dragging everything's shadow across the world. From where birds had cried the end of another day, and maybe someone had turned off the lawn mower and produced solid silence. I saw a world where milkshakes were made, constantly, for a million reasons, in a place with blaring lights 24/7. The milkshakes had arrived in pink and red cups.

Jevn told me I was doing well; he told me to breathe, breathe; he told me I would be okay. He perched behind me as I balanced on the ball—lifting me from behind for each contraction. He cradled my head. He said words he had been told to say, words he had been told would reach me, words he meant. I was comforted by his presence, that he wanted to fight this fight with me, but it felt more like he was clinging to me as I fought it. Nina asked me what I wanted to do; she was beginning to falter. She was thinking I might need the antibiotics. She suggested I kneel on the bed, my forearms resting on the elevated head of it. Swaying my hips, still trying to loosen his cranium out of my tailbone. I was beginning to feel it was my fault. I kept changing positions: kneeling on the bed, sitting on the ball, pressing my face against the wall of the shower. All amid warm, dim, infinite light.

—And then something happened; a crowd appeared. I was told to rest on my back, the head was beginning to bulge at my perineum. It wasn't safe anymore to sit, even if Jevn lifted me for contractions. I was supposed to lie down and look in a mirror and see. I opened my eyes and surfaced for a moment. So many faces assembled around me, smiling, moving their mouths. Flashes of light. I didn't want to see the head; I didn't want to watch; I wanted to stay inside. I didn't want to arrive at this moment. I reached down and touched his head. And then I felt an irresistible urge to push. My body gripped and folded me without mercy upon myself. I wasn't dilated enough; they told me not to push. I pushed. The silence inside me broke, as though the doors were torn open, my ears breaking through the surface of the water, and I could hear everyone. Five, seven hands handing me a boy, all lips, swollen and red. Falling on me like a bodily organ, like a blind bloody seal. I kissed him; I might have eaten him. The work had been done, and I had become a mother.

There was activity all around me, and the crowd spoke to me as if resuming a conversation from before. They looked in my eyes and couldn't see that I didn't recognize them. There were things outside me to tend to; I was to nurse; I was to hold him, like this, like that. The perineal massage, the afterbirth, holding still for stitching me up. I had ripped messily, the way that makes it hard to sew, and the nurse pulled at me with a hook-shaped needle. Nina making sure they didn't suction his mouth or eyes. It was all a blur, but I joined in, with words. Jevn told me I said something about Thomas Jefferson and something else about cheese.

It was, inconceivably, over. I would be moved to a postpartum recovery room. I would need to get cleaned up, the nurses would be there in a minute, and I would be rolled out to another room. I didn't care when I would finally sleep. In the world, reordered, there were new imperatives. In my arms, he was smacking new lips, testing a face. He wanted to see what straight up feels like, relief to his long-curled spine, stretching feet and toes, but he found default again in a lump that approximated the bulge of my belly just twenty-seven hours ago. I felt my soul had stepped out and sat beside me. I was propped by pillows in the hospital bed, looking deeply into the eyes of my newborn son, quietly completing the arc between my chest and knees. He would break from nursing, bobbly head, to look at me, the only person who did not make me doubt myself.

A vague memory began to return to me, that I'd been part of things before, on the planet in a certain place, with seasons, and a location that mattered to me so much. The sun had set hours ago, falling across the city whose name I couldn't remember. I was roused in the middle of the night by sudden, jerky tests of new physical boundaries. He snapped at air in his mouth and smacked his chops for my breast. A blur: rest, darkness, love, and waking to find the best things in the world are true.

FIFTEEN

They're here, Jevn whispered. Paula and Erik tapped lightly at the door, and Jevn was tiptoeing over to let them in. I lay on clean sheets in postpartum, where I fell in and out of sleep, holding Jonathan in the still deep darkness of early morning. Staff came and went quietly, and Jevn and Nina spoke to each other outside of my range of vision.

I opened my eyes for Paula and Erik, who planted their feet at a distance and leaned in brightly to congratulate me. They took Jonathan carefully in their arms and, as they chatted to Jevn and Nina, continuously returned their gaze to him. I didn't feel anything then, not jealousy or anger or fear or happiness. At that moment, anyone might have come in and held him. Everyone else was extra; their feeling for him incidental and minuscule. I experienced a peaceful amnesia as I blankly accepted their comings and goings, meeting and forgetting them all at once. Paula pulled him close and smiled; Erik opened his mouth in pretend surprise. They lay their hands gently on his tiny, soft chest and whispered, Hello! Hello, little boy! I didn't mind at all. I didn't have to say hello.

They must have stayed for only a few minutes, because that's all I remember before they were gone. Then I saw Jevn had Jonathan, but the distance between his joints was too great and our son too little; he couldn't mold himself around Jonathan to cradle him tightly. He held him in a nest of tangled elbows and wrists, bending acutely. He spoke softly to Jonathan at close range, frozen in place, as if the father's job was to hold his son completely still until the glue dried. As if his nose was securing Jonathan's. Or maybe he thought the father's job was to supply his son's first breaths.

It wasn't until morning that I remembered the plans we'd made. The thought didn't come naturally to me, but because Jevn was sitting in the chair facing me when I woke.

"What time should I tell Paula and Erik to come?" he asked, and I must have answered, but I only remember that we spent the early morning passing Jonathan back and forth, laughing at the jolts of his body as he learned to hold himself still and at his spontaneous and triumphant stretches. Still exhausted from labor, I took short naps with Jonathan pressed against me. I woke when nurses would knock at the door and push him onto my breast, and when midwives made their rounds, *How's Mama today?* They examined my stitches and gave me a hemorrhoid pillow to sit on. Other nurses stopped by with lunch. I was protected within a swarm of services and constant interruptions, perpetual reminders that I was a patient, and you couldn't ask much of me. I welcomed everyone who entered, and I was happy to look out the window when they left. I was happy to recall, with a distant fondness, that I'd once been an architecture student in a city whose name I just then remembered.

We had entered the state-mandated seventy-two-hour waiting period: three days and nights to adjust to motherhood before I could legally sign papers. Ohio's official acknowledgment that birth is a transformation for both mother and child, one powerful enough to undermine any decisions made prior to it. A last opportunity to change your mind, it was still not enough time to put together a new plan if you did, but it was a painfully long time to spend with a child you felt certain about giving up. Before the birth, Molly suggested giving him right away to family or friends, to foster care, or even to Paula and Erik—my signature would just make it official, three days later.

Our workbook had other suggestions for avoiding unnecessary pain.

Do not have a natural childbirth. Do not breast-feed. Don't "room in" at the hospital. Have your adoption plan and the reasons for it written out and handy in the hospital, for reference after the birth. I had ignored all of it, and as I lay in the hospital bed, nursing my son, those seventy-two hours no longer seemed a needless formality. They were the measure of my motherhood. They were walls built in the absence of my own to protect it. I had seventy-two hours to sleep next to my son and smell him. To show him the sunset and the view over the treetops in the park across the street. To swaddle him close and watch him discover his length. Seventy-two hours to be a mother. I wanted all of them.

Jevn went home to take a shower, and I called my parents to give them the news. They congratulated me and said they planned to drive up in the next couple of days to meet everyone. I looked at Jonathan as I described him to them; seven pounds twelve ounces seemed such an incomplete appraisal, and I laughed, looking at him, reducing him to those things, ten fingers and ten toes, knowing he was hearing me, knowing he knew it was not a good description. When I hung up, I turned back to him. Our conversations were captivating but mostly wordless, mostly smiles and looking, reading each other's faces. But soon I felt someone at the door, and I saw that my architecture theory professor was waiting at a distance for me to invite him in. He was a big black man, but I'd never seen him outside of school, and without its aura he seemed smaller. He took all the time in the world to look at me.

"You look ten years older." He smiled from the far end of my bed. I could tell he meant it in a good way.

He sat down gently on the bed, thick reading glasses and a clean black beard streaked with gray. He had a way of watching concepts formulate, gazing up at them in the air, reaching out gently to touch them and responding to their feel. He speculated about design without authority, except the authority of his reserve and modesty. I held my son and listened to him.

He marveled at my transformation to motherhood, pausing occasionally to examine me. He said he hadn't become a father so easily. For months after his daughter was born, he couldn't really believe that he had a biological connection to her. It was only after she was several months old and he was left alone to care for her for a weekend that he began to feel their bond. He was telling me not to expect Jevn to have the same experience I had. And reminding me that, even among mothers, I was on my own.

He smiled at me gently, but the fat folds of his face kept it slack, tinged with sadness, as though he could see something over the horizon I couldn't. He had never hesitated to talk about his personal life, or God, or death, as a way of talking about architecture. Or maybe what I liked so much about him was that he talked about architecture only as a way of getting at those things.

Jevn returned in the afternoon, just before another professor stopped by with a gift, a toy that was black-and-white-striped with a few splashes of color, a product, he explained, of the latest research in newborn visual development. Jevn was very close to this professor, but I didn't like him. He entered awkwardly, not suited to social visits, not scaled for intimacy, and then he sat on the edge of the bed and grinned as though it was all very amusing.

Paula and Erik didn't arrive until later in the afternoon, and I recall only that Jevn and Erik went together to the solarium. It seemed they had more in common at that moment than Paula and I did. My motherhood was engulfing and absolute, while hers was contained and in question. But Erik and Jevn could perhaps share the same disbelief about fatherhood, that same tentative and abstract connection my theory professor had described. Jevn said they'd talked about something of the sort; Erik suggested that all fathers were, in a way, adoptive fathers.

When they left, Jevn told me he enjoyed conversation with Erik. It often seemed that the things Jevn felt most deeply, he expressed with the least elaboration. He would point to only the most self-evident reality, and you'd know that the entire, infinitely more complex truth was still hiding in the bushes; this was just its tail. I knew he was telling me he wanted them to have Jonathan. That he trusted them, and that even after so recently meeting his son and having enjoyed his fatherhood for so few hours, he was ready. The world may be reconfigured, but that feeling about them hadn't changed. I didn't respond.

But then, visiting hours were over, and we were alone. I walked around our room in only my hemorrhoid pad and panties. I'd been sponged clean, but I was still caked with spit and vomit and residual blood, my son's and my own, the humble regalia of motherhood. I came out of the bathroom, breasts first, pelvis proven, and Jevn cringed and asked me *please* to put on clothes. I argued that both the nurses and my son needed constant access to my body. And my boundaries had been redrawn; I was inside out, my precious interiors could now be passed around the room. Any gesture of modesty would have to extend outward to enclose him. Jevn sighed. In clothes, I walked to and from the solarium to gauge my injuries and to try to move at the speed of real life. Sometimes I practiced carrying my son, like my turquoise lunchbox, to see if I could imagine carrying that weight forever, and to see if I could let it go.

Women are *built* to bear babies—that was what Nina told me to reassure me that the pains of labor would be bearable. Our bodies contain ancient wisdom and animal strength; when labor begins, she promised, I would know just what to do. But my next step had fewer precedents in nature. Were women built to give babies away? What ageless detachment, what primitive reserves of indifference, could I count on in a moment like this? What could I find in the pages of my workbook to persuade me it could be done—what so many people had told me, with certainty, they could never do? What did Molly, what did anyone, really know about that?

I wanted thunder to clap and the mouth of the world to devour me before I could sign papers if it wasn't right. I wanted my own body, still bleeding, to tremble the pen out of my hand before it could renounce my motherhood. But there was no question what I would do. My mother was proud of how carefully I'd prepared. My father called it an unmitigated disaster, mitigated. Molly had never seen a couple work so hard to find the right family, and my professors were impressed that I did it all while keeping up with school. My boss didn't mind that I hadn't come in to work since Monday; he told me from his PalmPilot he knew this would take some time.

As I went to sleep that night, Jevn in the chair beside me, I tried to imagine the pain of giving up a child—a pain more mysterious than childbirth, one no one could reassure me about. I tried to feel it. The magnitudes and velocities and shapes and frequencies of the sorrow— as I'd experience it the next day, and then, years later, after the loss had weaved and wound its way through all the fibers of my life. But I could only imagine it as a lump sum. A single impact. A loss of oxygen. Falling off a cliff. Pushing my head through a windshield. Things that made me flinch at night as I fell asleep thinking that soon I would sign the papers. I woke up breathless, the air knocked out of me. In my mind I had taken one step too far toward an unimaginable future—and I fled back, waking with a start—to return myself to the fork in the road that was still accessible to me in the early light of morning.

Sometimes it wasn't my imagination that woke me. Sometimes it was my son, shifting slightly. Aroused by the gentle first contractions of hunger, pressing his tongue lightly to the roof of his mouth in the tender beginnings of his strongest reflex. And I was like a tool calibrated to register the early tremors of an earthquake; I was ripping through the surface of my sleep before his still semiexploratory movements had organized themselves into want.

I understood the risks associated with the intimate bonding of breast-feeding and sleeping together. Lying there beside my son as he smacked his jaw in the darkness, I was reminded powerfully of the warnings detailed in my workbook. But what more reasonable first test of whether you should let go than whether you can? Natural childbirth, breast-feeding, "rooming in" were not, after all, responsible for creating the dangerous bond. The dangerous bond was already present.

Forty-eight hours in, the hospital began to prepare our discharge. It was the natural moment to give my son to his new parents. I could return to the only life I knew, and my son would never touch the things of my world and rearrange them. But while Jevn filled out paperwork, I found myself clinging to the letter of the law. I had seventy-two hours; that meant twenty-four left. I wandered the hallways while he worked, looking in at the other mothers. There were mothers eating Doritos and receiving cards and balloons and flowers. Motherhood was perhaps no less brand-new and mysterious for them, but they had their lifetimes to make sense of it. How could I make a decision when I'd had only a glimpse of motherhood? How could I know if it was a thing I could live without? What was the meaning of wanting such things—your own heart, your own cells? Are these desires we should have to defend?

I'd become another kind of creature, and for all I knew my child was some new and necessary subsistence. The smell of his head could comprise my new universe. My food was the way he blinked his eyes; my breath was when his elbows straightened. What we had was not yet even a relationship. I could see that he was a person outside me, but I was unable to experience for him those things we experience for other people: sympathy, concern, interest. He was a satellite creature of myself. His return gaze closed our systems. He folded easily into my new hollow. What was the meaning of giving him away? Who thought now was a good time to do that?

There was something I still needed to know. I couldn't possibly know what. Giving him away wasn't possible, it wasn't possible, it wasn't possible. But I couldn't tell anyone this, that I was rethinking the whole plan. I would make enemies of everyone who had supported me; my entire scaffolding would be ripped away. I just wanted seventy-two hours, that was all.

We had to leave the hospital, but we couldn't take him home because if we did, Molly and our workbook had warned us, it was unlikely we'd go through with an adoption. Instead, one of my friends arranged for us to stay overnight in the hotel where she worked. Jevn glanced angrily at me as he helped me pack our things, including a car seat lent to us by a crisis pregnancy center. He rolled me in the wheelchair, my son in my arms, to the discharge area. Someone admired Jonathan in passing and asked, inexplicably, if Jevn and I were siblings. We both smiled, confused. But I tried at that moment to imagine what it was we were, having had a baby we were going to give up. Our relationship cut short by the thing that is supposed to be binding. I could just see the light of actual day, through the vestibule and the automatic exit doors, admitting measured breaths of warm air into the refrigerated hospital lobby. It was sunset. I would become a real mother, and I would know what we were, when that light fell on us in the real world.

We were stopped before we passed the threshold. The discharge hadn't been fully processed. We returned to our room, where the nurse told us, reprovingly, that we'd missed dinner. No one seemed to care about my insurance, which wouldn't cover another night in the hospital without medical necessity. I sat back down on the bed, and Jevn took the chair beside me. Dusk fell, and trays of food were brought in. Nurses picked up where they had left off, each one teaching a different trade, touching me as though motherhood was a thing that was everyone's to grab and adjust.

I'd been warned that once the staff knew about the adoption plan, they might not be willing to give me attention, but in my few days in the hospital, I'd experienced only the opposite. They'd given me a full introduction to my body's new functions. Nurses showed me how to pull him onto my nipple when his jaw was relaxed to get a nice, open latch. One stuck her hand into my abdomen, all the way to my spine, to demonstrate that my muscles had split with pregnancy and I'd need exercise to restore them. They taught me how spraying myself with warm water out of a bottle would ease the initial pain of peeing. They showed me how to re-create with a blanket the tightness and comfort of the womb. When I had arrived two days ago, I didn't know how to change a diaper, but everything I had to learn had been mastered already, and the nurses shared their secrets generously. They smiled at my son as though he were the only baby in the postpartum wing, and I the only mother.

A nurse arrived with my discharge just as we'd begun to think we'd have to stay another night in the hospital. She was joined by several other nurses carrying blankets and diapers, which they stuffed into Jevn's blue duffel bag. They brought plastic bags for a few things that wouldn't fit: a spray bottle, some extra nursing pads and diapers, a small manual breast pump. Then there was no more packing to do; they just stood there, lingering. Finally, one of them asked if she could say a prayer for us. They put their hands on my shoulders and asked God to give me the courage to keep my son.

When we pulled out of the hospital parking lot, I watched everything go past—things that had once been familiar. We passed the university and the park. The studio lights in the architecture building glowed brightly. The rich grain of the world I'd been so enmeshed in was smooth and small, like I was high above it, still in the upper levels of the hospital. Like my new world was bound by bigger and smaller things.

And soon I was sitting in a heavy chair nursing my son while Jevn stood, and sat, and paced. He was frustrated. In no version of the plans we'd so carefully made were we ever camped out at a hotel in the suburbs with Jonathan. I ignored him. I was entranced, watching Jonathan at my breast. It surprised me to find it so beautiful; breast-feeding had always seemed somehow vulgar or incestuous to me. But then none of my maternal instincts were speakable; I wanted to swallow him, to squish him, to kiss his mouth. My motherhood was so staggering and strong, it searched every avenue to express something superlative.

I asked Jevn to take a picture. If I could document that special angle, his tiny chin bending toward his sternum, his fingers curled in pause, I thought I would have all I wanted. And then we could move on with our plans. Jevn sighed forcefully but took out his camera.

"Can you hold him like you want him?" he asked as he aimed the lens. "Is it his profile you want? Just, like, the top of his head?"

"Yeah, the head, it doesn't have to be perfect. Are you getting his nose?"

"Just his nose?"

"Sort of like his head, and his chin, and his nose."

"Do you want his eyes?"

Jevn liked watching Jonathan, but he had closed a door. He did exactly what I asked; he clicked the camera, but he couldn't capture it. It was something you could really only see from where I was sitting.

I don't think he was surprised when, the next morning, seventy-two hours had passed, and I still wasn't ready. My legal protections expired, I had only my own boundaries. I was accountable for every step. I leaned heavily on one excuse: that I wanted to nurse Jonathan through to the end of the colostrum. The colostrum, a fatty substance that precedes the arrival of breast milk and lasts for several days, carries antibodies, their exact balance naturally calibrated to the needs of the child. Nina told me that people who receive the whole colostrum as babies will have stronger immune systems throughout their lives.

I don't know if anyone believed me. All I know is that I ended up in my apartment with my son. No crib, no rattles, no baby clothes, and no car seat.

SIXTEEN

My parents and Jevn's mother had arrived. My sister, too, from China. They were all staying at the same hotel nearby. Paula and Erik were making short visits every day from Dayton, an hour's drive away. I was in constant conversation with them, telling them, *I think I will sign tomorrow.* I spent most of my time sitting on my low futon, my son lying on his back on my thighs. I looked at him intently, searching for conviction. During one of these moments, my sister paused to admire me from a distance, leaning on the wall in my bedroom. She had knitted a hat for Jonathan in China. It made us laugh when she put it on his head—it was at least three sizes too big. It was amazing to see how small he was compared with the smallest head she could imagine from the other side of the world. She was still offering to move back to help raise him, but I didn't take her seriously. She called him Lìu, even though his name was now official: *Jonathan*—followed by my last name, and then Jevn's.

Jonathan looked blankly back at me, squirming lazily, squeezing his fists, marching slowly with his legs, and I dropped tears on his chest.

"This is such a good experience for you," she said.

Jevn's mother and my parents came over; our families filled my apart-

ment, someone sat in my light blue wingback chair, people squatted on
the edge of my futon. Nina joined us with photographs of the birth. One
in which the three of us—Jevn cradling my head, my mouth fallen open
to take a breath and my son bloody at my chest—look like we've fled a
brutal battle and collapsed in the first safe place we could find.

Jevn's mother wanted to hold Jonathan. She asked if she could take
him away to spend time with him, maybe keep him for a night, just
grandma and grandson; Jonathan was her first grandchild. I told her no.
Every day I thought I would sign the papers. Every night I thought would
be my last.

But for all the activity around us, the question hanging heavily over our
heads, it was a period of strange pause. Jevn and I were parents, and our son
was watching us. There were moments we forgot everything else.

"What time is it, Jon? What time is it?" Jevn asked Jonathan, who
was lying on his back on my bed one afternoon, looking, vaguely curious, back at Jevn. "Is it time . . . for . . . kisses? *Mwhamwahmwha!*" Jevn
attacked from above, and Jonathan wriggled. Then he turned to me.
"Erik told me when Jonathan gets older, they'd feel comfortable enough
to let us take him for the summer. That'd be really good. To show him
Colorado."

I didn't want to talk about it. I was looking at Jonathan, worried
about how little he cried. I thought babies were supposed to cry; it made
you know they were working properly: breathing, and desiring, and responding to disappointment.

"I want to see if we can get him to cry," I said, taking his bear away
from him. He looked at me. "Are we being mean, boy? Aren't you going
to cry?" It was fun to tease him, to play as if there could be any reality
other than my insatiable drive to protect him.

"I bet if we tickle you, you'll do something!" Jevn said, wriggling a
finger at the folds of Jonathan's neck. "It's sneeze time! Sneeze for us!"
Jonathan had a series of faces, and gestures, and stretches, and sneezes
that we wanted, somehow, to capture. We put a tape recorder on the bed
beside him, but most of the things weren't audible, and he wouldn't do
any of them on command. He opened his mouth blankly like he might

yawn or sneeze. His head fell side to side slowly, as he gained and lost control of his neck muscles.

"He's just looking for something to eat," I said, recognizing the particular slackness in his jaw. "Is that what you'd do if you were in the wild, boy? Just open your mouth and hope something you can eat goes in it?"

"Are we torturing him?" Jevn asked, but I didn't know.

"Here you go, love, here you go . . ." I lifted him off his back, cradled him, and positioned him to nurse. Behind me the bamboo was waving in the window. It had grown overcast in that inviting summer way, when weather is a momentary drama and it leaves the whole world steaming and smelling like earth. Jon began to nurse. I felt a stream of water dripping down my arm. "Oh! I thought it was raining," I said. "He's just drooling on me!"

"What did you think was raining? Inside?" Jevn laughed.

"I thought the fan was somehow bringing rain in."

"You didn't think you had a drooling baby in your arms?"

We sang the "Tennessee Waltz," and "Puff, the Magic Dragon," and "Wild Montana Skies," and every song we could think of any words to. I sang "Rocky Top," and Jevn would overlap me with "Rocky Mountain High"—the unending battle of our rival mountain homes.

"Do you like our singing, Jon?" Jevn asked. Jonathan had stopped nursing and was looking at us. "I think he's just tolerating it."

"He *has* to like it," I argued. "We're his parents!"

"Let's sing a John Denver song."

"Good morning, America, how are ya? Don't you know me; I'm your native son! I'm the car they call the Cutlass Ciera Gold—"

"He doesn't want to know a car commercial song!" Jevn exclaimed. "Don't you know songs?"

We returned Jonathan to his back on my futon as we both crouched over him, watching him closely. As we sang, I told myself that he was not the most beautiful child in the world, that I just saw it that way because I was chemically predisposed to. In the afternoon, Jevn fell asleep next to him, both of them resting their arms above their heads, like they were floating aimlessly among the clouds. Or like they'd lifted their feet to let the river carry them.

I welcomed the unnecessary pain in all its forms. Cradling my son, kissing him, putting my finger in his tiny mouth to touch his soft gums—I invited grief in. It did not feel unnecessary at all. In fact, I thought, the pain was invaluable. It was bound to arrive after I signed, and then it would tell me with certainty whether my signature was a mistake. Why not bring the grief closer, faster, fuller, sooner, to make that future sadness a single blow and invite it to strike now, to test my resilience like concrete or steel to see if I would break? Why not invite that augur grief to this side of the signature and give it power to change things?

I wanted to feel it all. I wanted to feel it all at once. I would hold my head underwater to see how I fared. There would be no second-guessing. And if I couldn't bear the pain, I wouldn't sign anything. If only I could get grief to operate in this way.

We decided to let Paula and Erik take Jonathan overnight. If I could spend one night without him, then maybe I could survive two. And then, possibly, three. And then, perhaps our lifetimes. They were hesitant to take him, but that made me remember how much I trusted them. When they arrived in Dayton, Paula called and asked whether I wanted her to bring him back. She was willing to turn around and make the trip again to return him to me; she wasn't sure I could survive, either. But I wanted them to have him; I wanted his life to start.

I went into the world and looked for the place it had left off. I played darts in a bar. I tried to get better at balancing the tiny weight and casting it through the air. I tried to think about architecture, or milkshakes. The little things that comprise real happiness or the bigger things that make our individual lives seem small and light. I prayed for direction.

I tried to bridge back to myself: I knew exactly what it was like to not have a son. But I couldn't make my son's absence at that moment touch his absence for the twenty-three years prior. I couldn't find that familiar old place, so very like this moment, when I didn't have a son, and I wasn't a mother. But then I felt a flush of excitement as I tried to own an amazing prospect, what must have appeared to be the case: I was just a twenty-three-year-old college student, without a care in the world.

When I got home, I pumped breast milk to keep it flowing and put it in the refrigerator to feed him when he returned. We met in the park across the street from my apartment the next day. They handed him to me, along with his things, and my heart raced with fear and excitement. I don't remember that we said anything about the adoption, but maybe I mentioned the colostrum. Their daughter, Sarah, was angry and said Jonathan was *her* baby. My blood curdled; was I allowed to say that?

My son slept in bed with me because I hadn't prepared anything like a nursery, with a ducks-and-rattles border. I had met so many hopeful couples, I knew well what a "forever home" should look like and exactly how ill-equipped I was. I had no crib to lay him in, but as deeply as my body devoured rest, still I slept lightly enough to temper my pressure against him. My body lay in wait for the moment I was needed, my place on earth validated by seven pounds and a beating heart. He fell asleep again as he nursed, and I was the sea, incubating its salty life, regulating the temperature of the world around him as we shared the tiny pocket of air between us.

Early one afternoon, more than a week after his birth, I was sitting on my futon, searching my son's face and wondering what damage I was doing, dropping so many tears on his chest. There was a knock at the door and my mother came in as I'd never seen her, like a sudden summer storm, simultaneous lightning and thunder. She'd been talking to Jevn's mother, and their worry and speculation and fear had worked to unhinge her. The next step was clear to everyone, and that I wasn't taking it made her doubt all the details of the story she thought she knew. She began to question everything. She wanted to know whether Jevn was really the father. She'd heard about our fighting and wanted to know whether it was safe to leave Jonathan alone with me. She tested every possibility. Why would I turn against such a well-made plan—had I never intended to give up my son? When had the lies started? Did she know me at all? She stood stiffly before me, bracing herself, begging for reassurance that I was still the person she knew.

But I was unwilling to give it to her. As I sat watching her, my son watching me, I almost welcomed concerns so far from my own, from a land so foreign I remembered the comfort of other kinds of troubles, real problems, in other places. I knew I'd overstepped everyone's tolerance for my indecision, but my mother's doubt gave me confidence. I asked her to leave, and I didn't explain, and I didn't care about the consequence; I would have no family but my son, and I would have time with him that I wouldn't apologize for.

And for the first moment, I was alone with Jonathan. My friend Andy came over at sunset with a backpack full of food; he ignored my swollen eyes and fried squash in the big iron skillet my mother had sent me off to college with, reminding me never to wash it with soap. He played guitar, and I sat my delicate bottom on the concrete stoop with my son in my lap. In my mind I considered my many friends who had become like family to me and had so much to give my son.

As I washed the dishes afterward, I put Jonathan in the other room and left him. It was the first time someone hadn't been there to take him from me. I enjoyed the play between having him close and then having him just far enough away, over there in the bouncy seat someone had lent me, where, if I took a step back from the sink, I could see him. That moment felt like motherhood. For the rest of his life he would see things I wouldn't see, love different things; we would explore the space between us. But we would be anchors for each other, perpetual reference points. I would peek around the threshold of the door, and when he spotted me, he would smile.

The natural thing was to keep him. I wanted a hundred more days like this. A thousand. I wished I hadn't made such good plans, so perfectly.

But my son's life needed to start. He was ten days old. He needed the alphabet and shots and things I couldn't even think of. It was too late for me to figure those things out now. Paula and Erik took him for another night, and I moved faster than my fears; fresh hot water channeled down the salty surface of my face. My eyes were endless springs, my swollen lips like features of a sultry summer landscape. Thick streams bent at the corners of my mouth and leapt off my chin. I scrubbed myself hard, halting at the edges of new hollows and sensitivities; I was rashed and sunburned and still bleeding. I drove down to the agency alone.

Papers were assembled on the conference table; a tape recorder lay in the center. Proceedings began like a liturgy. People moved about the table and settled into chairs. Forms were pushed in front of me. People looked gravely into my eyes. Someone pressed a button and explained that what I said would be recorded. There was written a sequence of words I was meant to say. Everything happened with order and intention, as if it wasn't against nature at all.

I looked at the page. I'd read those words on the Surrender before. *Voluntary* meant that it was my will, my unencumbered desire, but I could think of few things more malleable than desire. And still nothing I desired more resolutely than my son. The words were certain and concrete and cold. *I agree and understand that under Ohio law, signing this document means that all my rights as parent to the above named child will end.* I wanted to be able to say, on record, words that felt more precise. Words I wouldn't mind my son someday hearing me say on tape.

Molly and the other social service workers waited.

"I feel like the only thing in the world I know anymore is that I'm my son's mother." There was no longer room within me for other knowledge, like knowing I want to give him up, or even knowing what being a mother means.

Molly sent me into the side room, to see if I could cry myself dry, to reach that barren desert in which I could use the cold, legal language the state required. Those infinitely deceptive words that would brush like sandstorms across all the complexities, wear them smooth and make a decision seem like one solid, eternal, changeless thing. How could I put on record that that was how things were? That the world does not turn and churn and change?

In the counseling rooms there were tissue boxes on every side table. Everything was staged for my performance. I cried for half an hour before I got back in my car and went home. But everyone was still perched in wait; Paula and Erik were still poised to take him home to North Carolina. Jevn wouldn't sign until I did, because his signature would give me full custody of our son and the freedom to make my decision without him.

Adoption was not a real plan, it was just a resting place for the unthinkable: having a son, giving up a son; both had been unimaginable to me. I had thought that somewhere along the way it would become clear to me what I should do and that one path would come to a natural end. I didn't dream that the one I abandoned would survive, powerfully and viscerally, in my imagination. Or that he would stretch, and smile, and yawn.

One afternoon, I got a call from my history professor. She was on vacation in Cape Cod, she had heard I was struggling, and she wanted to reiterate that she thought I should give my son up. I had a bright future ahead of me as an architect. The only certainties were other people's desires: Paula and Erik and Sarah wanted to have him. My family, Jevn's family, Jevn wanted me to give him up. Everyone I'd convinced about open adoption remained convinced. The agency was a mile away, ready to take my signature. I was a ripple in a swelling tide.

Paula called me to ask me what I did to get him to stop crying. I couldn't tell her because I had never seen him cry. I had put him under cold water in the shower because I worried he didn't cry enough. But even then he just looked at me incredulously.

She brought him back and sat in the wingback chair I leaned on during contractions. She was impressing me with games she had already taught him. The games tested his memory and challenged his ability to recognize patterns. I didn't even know you could play games with a baby as young as my son. She counted to three and blew on his tummy. One, two, three, and blew on his tummy. If she stopped at three and didn't blow, he still wrinkled his face and squeezed his fists anyway. I left the room to get a glass of water in the kitchen. Returning, I passed by her and said something. Jonathan's head jerked toward me.

"He recognizes his mother's voice," she said, fearlessly.

Paula said she didn't want to take my son away from me. One afternoon we sat together on my futon and cried, knowing we were crying for our own exclusive concerns, and out of compassion for each other. We were tragically enmeshed; each the source of the other's pain, each the threshold of the other's future. We stood like tired boxers, clinging to each other to stop the beating. I could end her suffering, some of it, but only at my own expense. She was the only one who could see the magnitude of what was happening. She wasn't telling me it was somehow good for me. She knew what was at stake; she was weighing it every moment. We were two pieces in a puzzle that were negotiating the exact shape of the cut that would at once connect and divide us. We were pressing at each other through a curtain to establish the precise profile of our grief.

Returning to Dayton with Jonathan for the third time, Paula called to ask if I walked a lot while I was pregnant; she figured out if she walked with him, taking big strides, he sometimes stopped crying. My sister told me they may be good parents, but she couldn't imagine anyone loved him the way I did. But did I love him? I couldn't understand that. Love, or anything, standing between me and my son.

I needed to buy groceries, but I didn't have anything to carry him in. I had to hold him in my arms. I set out gingerly, taking small, careful steps down the hill to the store. I was hypnotized by the cracks and irregularities in the sidewalk, determined not to fall. I held him tight, his head, his tiny bottom. He didn't make a sound. He was still collapsing back into me, and I couldn't rely on him to hold himself up. He took me for granted, and I felt dangerous; there was no one I would not destroy to keep him safe. In the aisles, I had to carry him because he was too small and floppy for the hard metal kid seat at the front of the grocery cart. I couldn't believe anyone could be too small for those.

I needed one circumstance to be different. I needed one word of support from one person I could trust, and it would give me all I needed to know. I needed one of the barriers to give, just a little bit. Why hadn't I thought about all this before? I called the University Child Care Center. They told me they charged $155 tuition per week for an infant and $135 per week for a toddler. With my discount as a university student, the rates would be $150 and $130 per week. They didn't have any openings, but they could put me on a waiting list. There was a $30 charge for being added to the waiting list. They asked if I'd like them to mail me their brochure.

I don't think I spoke to Jevn in those last days. He doubted my intentions and glared at me with suspicion, but I was angry that I'd let him have any say at all in what felt so entirely like my burden. And yet, seeing his distrust made me distrust myself. I was angry at myself for being indecisive, for indulging my motherhood. I wondered whether I'd been lying to everyone the whole time.

Paula proved herself again and again. She reminded me that the decision was mine, that it really was a decision, and that I would be a perfectly capable parent. She didn't want me to feel obligated to her just because we had come this far. She said that either way she would be grateful for having gotten to know us. I am not sure I believed her. Was she not weighing the loss the way I was? Was she not waking in the night, breathless, imagining her own life without my son?

One day, two weeks after my son's birth, she called to tell me that she, Erik, and Sarah were getting ready to return to North Carolina. She didn't say that she had finally come to terms with what was at that point obvious.

But I couldn't let them go.

Several days later, I called my midwife to find out how much I had to eat to continue producing breast milk. She told me it would take 450 calories a day. I'm sure now she meant 450 *additional* calories, a total of 2,450 calories in a day for a nursing mother, but then I wasn't thinking straight. I held fast to that number. I could barely eat at all, but I made sure to consume 450 calories every day. I managed half a peanut butter and jelly sandwich, or a bagel with cream cheese. Or two apples and a handful of nuts. I ate in a day what I thought I had to in order to produce breast milk. And several times a day, I plugged into a rolling machine that made noise like fast ocean waves, drawing milk from both sides at once. My friend Andy listened at the door before knocking; he would come back later if he heard my machine running, and he knew not to open my freezer, where the milk was stored. When the freezer was full, I put the milk in a special box, and I arranged for it to be shipped to my son in North Carolina.

SEVENTEEN

My breasts swelled over the Rockies. Across Nevada, they pushed against the limits of my fitted cotton dress. Boarding the plane for California, I abandoned the wasteland of my decision. I couldn't read; I couldn't think. I could barely remember signing the papers. I just looked hard out the windows of the plane and watched the ground get farther and farther away. But as we lifted off, there was nothing as heavy as my chest, weighted with milk. I wore the green checkered dress that had been tailored for my sister in China. She lent it to me in Nanchang when I had taken a detour from my European travels to visit her, along with the silver sapphire ring we exchanged once a year. I'd worn it in Italy, and then she wore it in China. It turned our skin green and itchy, but its promise was to guarantee we would see each other again, no matter where we had to travel to do it.

By the time I reached the hotel, I was swelling out of the straps. I pulled the dress halfway over my head and my sister tugged vigorously to get the tight waist over my chest, all the while exposing my postpartum belly and saggy underwear, stuffed with padding. She pulled and pulled. We laughed until I peed in my pants. When we finally got it off, I sat down with my little portable device, wincing at the first pump, till my breasts, hard as bricks, softened.

My sister had left Ohio for Los Angeles to take a class for her ESL degree. She'd be leaving L.A. in a few days to return to China, and so, a week after I signed the Surrender, my whole family decided to meet for a Seek Family Wave-Off. It used to mean getting off the couch and gathering in the driveway to watch my sister or brother pull out on their ways to college. Now we had to travel far and wide to be together, just to wave goodbye, and now we were waving away greater distances.

I changed my clothes and joined my family to see California for the first time in my life. The Third Street Promenade, Venice Beach, the hills near Malibu. We didn't talk about my son or my summer; it was the same as every time I emerged from my room after being sent there as a child; they welcomed me back without mentioning what I'd done, happy that everything was back to normal.

We weaved our way through Los Angeles and found everything beautiful. We rode bikes along the ocean, and a shiny statue person lurched out at me on the promenade and made us laugh. We danced beneath the bougainvillea in a parking lot, just because the day was so perfectly warm. Dad joked that we should try to wake up on East Coast time and go to sleep on West Coast time; there was so much to see and do. I would slip into the bathroom periodically to pump, but I wasn't saving milk for Jonathan anymore; it was just to relieve the pain as I let my milk dry up.

On our way back from the Getty, Dad pulled the rental car over to inspect a bridge that was apparently designed for significant seismic loading. Cars passed at inhuman speeds, each one tugging ours with it for just a second. We followed him in a line along the shoulder of the road, as we'd been doing on road trips since we were little.

"See anything unusual?" he would ask, squinting as if the underside of the bridge were a text. We would all have to guess. What single member should be added to keep the bridge from twisting, or shearing, or buckling? Or what single member, if removed, would cause instantaneous collapse?

We followed a trailhead west into the foothills. I felt I had awoken to reality. Embodied, dusty, mountainous reality. My body felt fully extracted, and still the sunset mined my depths, puncturing a remnant vein of joy that surged and filled me. My tears joined the world's waters. I was an entire planet, with deserts and oceans and infinite black cavities, every moment a different surface barreling into darkness just as the sun began to rise across another. I have a son; I don't have a son; it is all the same dusty, difficult reality.

◉ ◉ ◉

My signature on the line of a million credit card receipts. My signature on my driver's license, at the ends of letters I still wrote by hand. My signature floated lightly all around the world, doing its little work. I'd written my name as I had a thousand times before, and the horizon didn't bend, and sound didn't somehow gather, extracted from every corner of the earth, and fly formlessly off the face of the planet, leaving a noiseless vacuum pounding in its place. The microscopic fibers of the paper received it, held the ink suspended, and didn't crash under its weight or drink it up. The world was the same at 3:55, when I pressed the pen to paper, as it was when I returned my eyes to Molly, to the room, to the window, to my sister.

I held still; I didn't want anyone to read my emotional signposts or think they knew what was happening within me. My sister's face was red and swollen. Tears streamed from her eyes, but she held my gaze with a desperate urgency despite them. And yet she didn't say a word. Everyone had trusted me to do what was best. Trusted me, somehow, to know what was best.

In those days before the Surrender, everything was the same as it had always been. The swings were squeaking in the park across the street; the sunlight was still kind and warm on my stoop. At the grocery store, people squeezed by me; no one made room for my heavy thinking. Not a soul at the bar where I threw darts looked sideways at me. Five times I'd showered and dressed myself. A sleeveless dress with tiny flowers that went all the way down to my ankles, my bangs held back with a single bobby pin. Five times I drove downtown. Nothing was registering the magnitude of what I was about to do. I thought I could absorb the impact, and there would be no evidence of what I'd done. But I was approaching a chasm, and only from a distance would the two lands, before and after, appear to be connected. And all of those times I didn't do it.

Then that one morning. Rain was falling lightly, but there was warmth on the wind. I held on to the stillness before everything. Suddenly, I thought: I want this trouble. I am ready for anything, the force of any blow—but there were never any signs. No indication anywhere of right or wrong, no answer that could provide a station point. In the cold room on that hot day in August, there was just the synchronicity of my hand, holding that pen, and a moment, one of a few, when I thought it was my only choice.

Paula brought Jonathan, but I only remember that because in the lobby outside the conference room, she took pictures of my sister and me holding him.

Molly tried, months before, to walk me through the hours just after the signature. What would I do when I got home? I imagined my son having his first end-of-summer in North Carolina. He'd arrive at the height of heat and be incubated by the humidity. Everything past its bloom, the loud insect drone, blue jays screaming that it would all soon be over. Night would fall after a long dusk and he'd wake to wet grass and wet windshields and wonder for a long time before he'd know where that water came from.

She kept reminding me: *me*. What would *I* do after the signature? It was very important to be able to visualize: Two hours later. Four. The next morning. I had filled out the lines in the workbook. And now, so much later, it provided a script. I did what it said in my little workbook I would do. It was a process, with steps, and I took them. I signed my name, got in my car and drove home. I parked beside the Dumpster and entered through the side door. I picked things up off the floor. Registered for classes. Packed for California. Movements unworthy of being written, as mundane as any summer Saturday's afternoon of chores.

Molly told Jevn that I signed, but I don't know when exactly. I wasn't talking to him for some period right before the signature, and I didn't call him after. I knew he'd sign as soon as he heard I had—he had no doubt about what we should do. He had already spoken it in that room with Molly, and he'd held true to his name, true to his word, and proven me weak and faltering by comparison. But I didn't know he'd do what he did then. He left town without a word.

The spotlight was turned off, its burning urgency now just the diffuse smell of heat. No one was watching me closely anymore; everyone's questions were answered. I went home and walked numbly around the pond in the woods where I'd labored, but I remember nothing more about those first four days of August.

Soon after I got back from California, I received a letter from my father. His letters were always scribbled, written when he couldn't sleep because I was facing a big or expensive decision. *You've got some proud parents back in Tennessee,* he wrote. *Your mom and I couldn't imagine how difficult your decision must have been. I'm sure you made the right decision, and not because you wouldn't have been an excellent mother.* He said as a single mother I wouldn't have been able to give my son my best. He said that now Jonathan would have two mothers who love him.

Over the phone, Paula told me that she'd gotten a nice note from my father, too. She said that Sarah was adjusting well to having a brother, that the other day Sarah had kept Jonathan entertained by singing to him so that Paula could take a shower. It was a relief to talk to her; she listened as no one else could bear to listen. I told her I was excited about Jonathan's life; I couldn't wait to see him grow. But I missed being pregnant. I missed the very few things about motherhood I knew. I missed choosing a radio station based on what I wanted him to hear. I missed him kicking and hiccuping. I missed eating to feed him. I told her everything would be much harder if I didn't feel confident about her and Erik as his parents. She said she was grateful that I felt good about them, that she was immensely grateful for me and Jevn and Jonathan in her life.

One afternoon, I walked down the hill to meet my geography professor for lunch, swinging my arms and enjoying the end-of-summer heat. It's not hard to not have a son, I thought. No one had to sing to my son so I could take a shower or watch him so I could go to lunch. But what was hard was that I'd just had a baby, but no one could see what there was to be excited about. No one could see what was hard. My thoughts would cycle back to Jevn in search of recognition, a place to land, but they would ricochet into the void. An ache overtook me like a river with its own desire and direction; I wondered when he'd return from Colorado and whether we'd ever speak again.

Standing in the line to order, I told my professor that I was doing well. We took our sandwiches outside to sit in the sun. I found I didn't want to say much. I was ecstatic and devastated, but I couldn't explain it.

"So in the end did you name him or did they?" she asked.

"It was their idea, but we liked it." I hated the implication that one of us was in control, the other subjected to it. But then I also didn't want to imply that everything was easy just because we agreed on so many things.

"It's amazing to have seen what you've gone through. It makes me think of what my mother must have gone through," she said. "But your son is going to be able to know you and see how much you care about him, and really understand what you did for him." She had been consoling me since the moment I told her I was pregnant, but things were too close to measure against her experience; I didn't want to give her the comfort of comforting me.

"I just want to go back out west, back to California or to Montana or somewhere," I said. Anywhere, far away from everything, somewhere I'd never been before. I loved it out there, where there was only enough water to keep things on just this side of mortality. I was restless. I wasn't ready to revisit what had just happened and decide what it meant. I wanted to keep moving.

"Well, you know I'm going to Montana, right?" She smiled, surprised.

I didn't know. She told me she was leaving the following week to do research in Yellowstone; another professor had dropped out so there was an extra space, and she invited me to join her. The timing suited my internship, as we'd lost funding for the project I'd been working on before Jonathan's birth.

It really was a big sky in Montana, and big air, and long roads leading to infinity between the grasses that inched golden all the way to the razor-sharp mountains. We listened to lectures about grizzlies and geology and the ecological impact of the rapid development encroaching on the periphery of the park. Sometimes we were in the geyser fields or the backcountry, with a moose or a bear in sight, and sometimes we were in conference rooms, which still felt like out west because there were exposed wood beams and windows looking into the forest.

We stayed for a few days on a ranch in Wyoming, where we went horseback riding, the kind of horseback riding people do when they don't really know how to ride horses. It was a slow Disney World ride through the scenery, and the horses were so bored they bumped their noses into each other's rumps. I used to take riding lessons at a tiny stable in Tennessee. I'd go every day for a week in the summer and learn how to post and barrel race. Once one of the trainers asked me, didn't I know I had a beautiful smile? I was always sad, for no reason I remember. And I was always hiding the space between my teeth. At the end of the day in the ring, our teachers would let us ride in the pasture. One horse would start to run, and then we'd all run as a herd, all the way to the farthest corner of the field. The bouncy trot would swing into a gallop in a magical moment when the animal realized we weren't pulling back on the reins. Its ears would fall back as it found its frequency, half wheel rolling on a four-point arc, and half bird as it caught air: roll, fly, roll, fly. It was a special gift the trainers gave us, to let us experience what felt like those horses' deepest desire.

After our group ride and after dinner in Wyoming, I made my way down to the barn to ask the ranch hand if I could ride one of the horses out in the field. He brought out a massive black stallion and told me to squeeze my knees in and pull back low and taut on the reins. When I did, the horse tucked its chin and the whole left side dropped low, and then the right as it pranced forward. For all my summers on horseback in Tennessee, I'd never ridden a Tennessee Walker. After that, we wandered into the field, and in the cool shade of the canyon just past sunset, I dug in my heels and clung tight.

Over the next week, we were guided through the backcountry by a man who'd lived in the park for thirty-five years in a mobile home full of books. He walked us across a geyser field, where hot sulfuric oceans lay beneath thick plates of crust. Geysers were those openings that revealed the world's watery nature all the way to its core. The cracks were soft and inviting, edged with rainbow salts, revealing bulbous yellow voids and turquoise chambers just beyond the darkness.

"Everyone talks about the balance of nature," he said, standing in front of one of them, "as though nature would find some kind of peaceful stasis if we humans just left it alone. But look at this place—the grizzlies, the geysers; nature is violent. It's precarious and schizophrenic, devouring itself ruthlessly, destroying in moments what it has taken millenia to create." Everyone's efforts to comfort me didn't comfort me, but listening to him did. Around the fire that night, I felt an animal part of it all, my losses just residue from the world's habit of destruction.

It was also easy in Montana to pretend the whole thing had never happened. I could no longer really imagine being pregnant. Even my milk was dry. I could take my heart out of it and tell myself that Paula and Erik were simply a young family with a new son, and it had nothing to do with me. But the morning of the last day, conversation among my professor's colleagues at breakfast turned to the subject of children, and it felt disingenuous to listen as though I wasn't a mother.

"I had a baby in July," I said finally, to let them know I was a mother, too.

"Oh! Really?" one of the professors said. They all looked at me.

I didn't know what to say next. I had a baby in July, but I gave him up in August? I couldn't really talk about my newborn son without explaining his absence. I couldn't describe his delicate features without admitting I hadn't seen him since his adoption. Why mention my motherhood at all, just to undo it?

I explained everything quickly. I had to—I was making everyone confused. I hoped by describing my diligence about his adoption I'd gain back ground so I could join the conversation as a fellow mother, but the more I spoke, the more it seemed as if I was changing the subject. And breezing through such a weighty story made me seem like only the most heartless kind of mother. The more comfortable I tried to make everyone, the less like a mother I seemed.

I returned from Montana and called Paula and Erik in North Carolina. I wanted to hear the sound of their voices and for all of us to remember that this really happened, I really did have a son, we were all part of it, and we were all going to get through it. There was no world without this experience, but I wasn't alone in it. They'd witnessed my motherhood. They understood it.

They didn't pick up. Their answering machine said that I had reached Erik, Paula, Sarah, "and the newest member of the family—*Jonathan!*"

EIGHTEEN

I turned to the life I'd chosen. Students returned to school as always in September, a hundred new costumes, a hundred reinventions. We piled into the large auditorium in the architecture building.

"Did anyone see the report in *U.S. News*? We ranked second in the country among design schools and first in interior design! Good going, guys!" Our director shook his tiny fists.

The faculty assembled on the stage, and everyone found seats as the cold vanquished all our steamy memories of summer. Students greeted one another and braced themselves for another year. We sat down and shivered and, if we'd thought ahead, put sweaters over our knees.

I was excited; I couldn't help it. The impulse to reinvent yourself at the start of school was like a natural instinct. Summer was a chance for a set change, and this crowd of students wasn't just coming back tan from the beach; they'd sublet flats and held design internships in fashion-forward cities around the world. They were coming back with professional confidence and clothes you couldn't buy in Ohio.

"This year we're saying goodbye to someone who's been here longer than almost anyone on staff. After twenty years, Professor Collins has announced his retirement. Congratulations, Professor, and we'd like to present you with something to remember us by—"

The director looked to the back of the auditorium and we began to turn our heads, and then there was commotion at the rear doors. One opened, and Jevn came running down the side aisle stairs with a prize of some kind, while everyone laughed and cheered. I watched the scene, stunned. He did not appear to be the father of a baby he'd just given up for adoption.

I was always looking for him, always afraid I'd find him. I'd seen him one other time, right before school started; he was across the street near the little cinema and our favorite restaurant, but he ignored me, grimacing strangely at no one, to tell me that he saw me but that there were no words to say about it. I'd sent e-mails when he was in Colorado, and he responded by assuring me he was thinking often of Jonathan and me. I said I was angry with him, but he said he had never done anything to hurt me and never would. His composure made my anger feral. It seemed as though while I'd been pregnant, speaking to him daily, relying on him at every turn, he had somehow managed, in the midst of it all, to heal, apart. I was left with the loss of him—but then I couldn't distinguish the losses: Jevn, my son, myself.

We were like the number eleven, he had said. Between us there was another, invisible one, made of space and air. I looked for him, hoping our proximity would sharpen the features of the absent third, and the hollows in his cheeks would tell me how to feel about it. When I saw him in the auditorium, I wondered what I could learn about the shape of my son in this vast divide: Jevn, leaping fast down the stairs in front of the whole cheering school, and Jevn, three months ago, lifting me gently off the birth ball for another contraction.

I stared, frozen, toward the stage, one of the many reinvented faces in the crowd, and watched Professor Collins graciously receive his gift.

When the assembly ended, someone grabbed me by the arm. It was a professor who'd taught at the school I attended in Copenhagen. He'd squatted with me on the grass in front of Grundtvigs Kirke, a church with dramatic stepped gables at its westwork, and advised me not to abandon the things I drew until I'd really tested them. He said it was always easier to start over, a new major, a new design, but at some point you have to understand that everything is in the details, the *how*. Not the *what*.

As I turned toward his grasp, I saw he was already holding Jevn in the same kindhearted but merciless old man clutch. He sat us both down on a leather bench in the hallway. He spoke soberly to the floor and under his breath.

"I know it was hard. I know it was, but do you know what I think about how you handled the situation, with finding a family and arranging for the adoption? And keeping track of your schoolwork and supporting each other? And making it possible for that boy to grow up in a stable home and still get to know you both?"

He tilted his face back to look down at us sternly through his glasses, his jaw clenched in a proud professorial underbite.

"A. *Plus*."

What I should have been doing that September: tracing the delicate fur of my son's cheeks and chin over his pounding heart and down his bulbous belly, to the scar of a belly button at the healing cord. I should have been exploring my child like a new country. And even more than a summer away, that new place would have changed me.

Nina hosted a pizza party for our birth class reunion after everyone's babies were born. Those mothers emerged as if from cocoons, fresh and wise, fed on long days in the new land. They sipped some of their first glasses of wine in months, those who were not breast-feeding. Sparkling cider for those who were. They wore their motherhood as comfortably as their babies as they chatted over them in their frontpacks. Nina had made prizes, and each was awarded, one by one. Karen got the award for the biggest baby, at nine pounds, three ounces. There was an award for the longest labor, thirty-six hours, and the best effort at a natural birth went to Rachel, who had had to deliver by Cesarean. I got the prize for the mom who made a good decision but didn't get to hold her baby every day. It was an empty picture frame.

I should have had no time to think about what being a mother or loving a child looks like. I should have been too busy doing it: nursing, and changing, and burping, and cleaning up. But my motherhood was like a flash of light in the eyes of an animal that disappears in the darkness. I looked for vestiges of it in the pressed-down grass where he lay and branches broken where he'd passed through. And I had nothing to do but wonder what loving him, that unknown hollow, should look like.

I'd moved into the attic of a house shared by design students who came and went, alternating between internships out of the city and school. Fall was approaching, and the early dark and the weight of the sloped ceiling was always pushing me toward the floor; everyone's boxes and bikes surrounded me as though I were occupying the back recesses of someone's memory. I had three roommates, but my interactions with them were limited: waiting outside the bathroom while one of them and her new boyfriend showered together. Fighting over cupboard space. Dirty dishes in the sink. Whose turn to buy toilet paper. My new walk to studio took me along a different side of the park, and, from the sidewalk, a clearing in the trees and a long lowland meadow framed a surreal, distant vignette: the short stone wall that wrapped around the pond where I'd eaten a baked potato in labor.

I turned to the life I'd chosen, and the whole point was now Architecture. Everything I had been through was so that I could realize Architecture. I wanted to see the place, Architecture, that had seemed so worth what it took to get there to everyone who'd given me advice. The thing that had competed with my son for space in my life and won. Maybe I needed my summer's experience so that I could access unknown reserves of creativity: ingenious lines, inspired organizational principles, buildings that admitted light and air and attested to a depth of humanity that all the kids who were just playing around in the mud pies of their fertility could never have conceived. Maybe God would give me creative skill to fill the void, and I would possess Architecture as no mother can possess a son; I would give the world good lines, and we would all understand why it had to happen.

We inhabited a Disney World of Starchitecture; no building looked like another, because our dean had had a mission to fill the campus with buildings designed by signature architects. Built of Styrofoam and Spray-Crete, the architecture building was in rapid decay, an invaluable lesson for architecture students prone to thinking there were ambitions higher than Stay Standing for a building to aspire to. One afternoon, our Environmental Technology class went outside to look for thermal bridges, breaches in the building envelope where outside temperatures entered in, a result of deterioration or a failure of design. My group found a place where the screen skin that secured the Spray-Crete was exposed; it looked like someone had kicked the corner out of frustration.

While we waited for our professor to come see what we'd found, people in my group started talking about their internships. Jennifer was wearing an asymmetrical black T-shirt, its V off-center. She had been in London, working for a firm that designed skyscrapers and transportation centers all over the world. She sighed heavily as she spoke about redlines and construction sets, as though among the things she'd learned about architecture was that you are supposed to sigh about redlines and construction sets.

"Didn't you stay here, in Cincinnati?" Seth turned to me. I wondered if he meant for my internship. Or was he hinting at the bigger experience I'd had, afraid to ask directly? "At the Design Center, I thought I heard?"

I'd come back to school with some amount of confidence, because what I'd done had been so big it seemed it had to be in some way adequate, but I realized then that it wasn't. I had nothing to say about my slow days in the office, waiting for tasks, waiting for the end of day. But I couldn't respond by describing labor and my son's adoption, either. I wasn't a mother, and I wasn't a proper architecture student, either.

"I think you've been away from school for a long time," Jevn had said months ago when I suggested our classmates were capable of being supportive and understanding. He didn't expect any sympathy from them at all. He certainly hadn't sent an e-mail to his entire class telling them about the birth, as I'd done. I had hoped to maintain control of the story and to ask for sensitivity. Jevn intended only to finish school and to move on.

He stuck close to the wall and avoided my eyes as we passed between studio and seminar, carrying drawings or models or slide reels or lumber. I searched him for scars; if he was still breathing, then I could still breathe; if he was getting work done and moving on, then I should be able to do the same. He would never say hi or stop to talk. One evening, riding my bike down the lawn in the dark, I almost hit him lying in the grass with someone I guessed was his new girlfriend.

It seemed Architecture should welcome me back, given my sacrifice, but as I stepped into my new studio, it felt like an ancient enemy. It was the same as always: a field of drafting tables, a latent tension, students arriving early and claiming their desks. The studio was trapezoidal in plan, and there was a single small window at floor level located in the most acute corner. You had to bend over to see out to the courtyard and across to the old part of the building, where windows were expansive and kindly placed at eye level. Still, someone shoved his desk as far as it would go toward the shard of light, monopolizing the single evidence of a world outside.

I found myself slipping into my headphones. Everyone wore them; they kept you from hearing the frenzied sounds of your studiomates tearing through trace paper on the trail of some inspired design. The music provided momentum; it elevated the beauty of the things you drew and helped keep you going. In studio, the biggest enemy was the blank page. We were coached not to fear it, but to strike fast: draw, draw, draw. Keep moving. Bad lines tell you something that no lines can't. Get the billion bad lines out of your system, so you can get to the good one. You can make something beautiful out of any starting point. It's the *how*, not the what.

I'd done that. I had faced a blank page and cast out a line. I wasn't stalled on the decision anymore. All that mattered was moving forward. I was going to build something out of what I had to work with. But inside my headphones I maintained a foothold in grief; I listened to songs we'd sung to Jonathan and songs we'd sung before him. I had to draw and keep drawing. I couldn't think about the possibility that we had given him up so Jevn alone could arrive at Architecture.

In the first week of the quarter, before studio was in full swing, you could leave school early in the evening. I took advantage of that to go home at sunset one night to call Paula. We talked about when I might come down to visit, and she let me listen to Jonathan's infant grunts. I hung up the phone unable to cry. It felt like my lungs were caving in, and my body couldn't coordinate the process: shake my shoulders, release the tears, think of my son, all simultaneously. I just sat, stunned.

I loved my son so much I let him go, I thought. A lot of the songs I listened to in studio suggested that, that real love doesn't depend on being together; it doesn't demand to be realized in any particular form. Letting go so that the one you love can have everything he needs was the most generous and wholehearted and noble kind of love. What better thing to offer than that best kind of love? But I couldn't figure out what my love should look like, or what it should do. I didn't know my son in the way that makes missing cinematic and colorful. I had no memories to cherish, no stories to relive in his absence. He had no space in my life I could leave exactly the way he left it. My love hung emptily suspended, without a trajectory.

My structures professor's wife called to invite me over for dinner, and I was grateful to get out of my attic room. I'd tagged along with Jevn on other occasions when they invited him over, like the time we'd all gone sledding, and then I borrowed her dry socks and danced in the kitchen with their children. They wanted to hear the whole story. They asked me careful questions with their brows furrowed, not believing I was okay, afraid I was just downplaying things. But by the end, they were relieved.

"We spoke to Jevn a few weeks ago," she said, "and we were a little worried—"

I reassured them that everything had worked out. I could give no life to their fears. I told them I'd just spoken to Paula, just heard my son's voice on the phone. I'd already made plans to visit. They were constantly sending e-mails and photographs, not just to me and Jevn, but to our extended families. All those good things were true.

"Well, this is such a relief to hear. You look so good. We'd been worried about you. We were worried about Jevn, too, but it's just different for the mother." She pressed her lips together in a flat smile, and the kids began taking dishes off the table. "I'm so glad it's all worked out." She held my eyes for a moment. "We'd been talking about renovating the attic, actually. We were thinking it might work for you—we weren't sure how definite the adoption was, or what other options you had, so we just didn't know, but we thought you might need a place where you could have the

baby and finish school. I thought I might be able to help a little, but—"
She smiled and shrugged, and I must have smiled back. My body had
become an infinite receptacle for grief. "I'm glad to know you wouldn't
have needed it. We might have just confused things if we'd mentioned
it. And it wouldn't have solved everything, of course, it was just a gesture, but we just wanted you to know we were here to support you how-
ever we could."

I walked home around the outside of the park. I walked fast. I could
not think about what she'd said. I didn't want to have such a clear picture of how it might have worked. I didn't want to think about how I
would have kissed him goodbye in the morning and handed him to her,
leapt down those five porch steps and walked up the hill to class. How
I'd have returned for lunch and to breast-feed. How their kids might have
sung to him so I could take a shower, and I'd have done my studio work
at the drafting table in their attic, trying hard to tear my eyes away from
him. How I'd have told all my professors, and, recognizing the kind of
motherhood they could easily make space for, they would have understood why I couldn't work as late into the night as the other students. I'd
have had a million school loans and gotten all Cs, and it wouldn't have
mattered. No other possibility would have even occurred to me.

I would never think about it. I only noticed the air was getting cooler,
that summer was really over.

That night in my attic I collected songs for a mix tape to send to my son.
I added "Wild Montana Skies," the John Denver song we'd sung driving
to the sand dunes in Colorado before I was pregnant. When we could see
them on the horizon, just below the peaks of the Rockies, I wanted to
jump out of the car and run for them.

"Guess how long that would take," Jevn said.

"It feels like twenty minutes? I don't know, it doesn't matter!"

Mountains had an energy all their own; I felt propelled by them.
When we finally got there, a couple of hours later, an enormous, shallow
body of water was moving across the plain in front of the dunes. It was
no more than an inch deep but it spread, searching for a container, and
we walked across it like giants across an ocean. Jevn warned me to stay
hydrated as we started up the face of the first dune. From a distance they

looked like a single range of small mountains running in a row right in front of the Rockies, but it would take half a day to get to the top, and then you'd see that they extended far into the distance—infinite, disorienting piles of moving sand and shadows—to the base of the Rockies. You could easily lose your bearings once you lost sight of the parking lot.

Driving back, he read to me from *Einstein's Dreams*. He read like someone unaccustomed to his own voice, gentle on account of it. Laughing, he told me about how he used to soak his saxophone reeds in Kool-Aid so he could suck on them during band practice. That night, sunburned and exhausted, we stayed in a Wild West, one-story, cheap hotel, the sole thing standing in the desert. I remember thin, dirty walls and the sun setting long and late, unhindered by any obstruction, pouring through the windows till infinity. We were very young but our spirits were aligned. Driving home the next day, we sang along to John Denver. It was a prayer to the landscape to raise an orphan child, to give him a drive and a passion to carry him in the absence of a family. Now it had real meaning to me. I couldn't know for sure that Paula and Erik would provide my son with everything I wanted for him, but the beauty of the world was a teacher I could trust. The sky and the wind and the sunset would be his most important guides, even if I'd kept him. I comforted myself that giving him up and keeping him were exactly the same.

I added "Kan Guo Lai," a song about unrequited teenage love that was popular in China when I was there with my sister. We had wandered the campus of her university and recorded ten or fifteen versions, sung by college students reluctant to admit they knew the words.

I added the song Sting was singing when my water broke and a version of "You Are My Sunshine," the song I thought my mother would sing while washing the dishes, by Gene Autry.

But I couldn't decide on a Patsy Cline song. My favorite had beautiful, bird's-eye images of travel, the pyramids on the Nile, sunrise over the tropics, the market in Algiers. And it evoked the bittersweet conundrum: that to go anywhere, you have to say goodbye to somewhere else. I'd fallen in love with so many landscapes; I longed for everyplace I wasn't. I wanted my son to travel and fall in love, and have his heart broken by beautiful places, too.

But for all that, the song said the wrong thing. *Just remember when you're home again, you belong to me.* I didn't want to even hint at that less noble kind of love. Love that longs, and clings tight, and possesses. But without the refrain, the poetry of travel was just an endless stream of images. What made it a love song was that the love found its way back. That's what love does. Even Moses, released to the river, returned to his mother's embrace. Without the return, love was aimless, loosed like a balloon till it floats away and disappears. Was there any difference at all between love like that and forgetting altogether? No, a mother might let go of her child, but that couldn't be the end of the story. There was always that moment—when she dries her hands and peeks around the wall, and, seeing her, he smiles.

Without it, love was aimless. Love released like a balloon till it floats away and disappears. There seemed to be little difference between love like that and forgetting altogether.

I'd use "Walkin' After Midnight" instead.

NINETEEN

I arrived in Durham Saturday afternoon. I knew the house I was looking for, because Paula had sent me photographs right after they purchased it. There was a tiny stoop flanked by hydrangeas someone else had planted years ago. Tall pines made a light forest ceiling, and beneath it was an uneven lawn, littered with pine needles and occasional rhododendrons growing wild, with hostas and azaleas fading into the bare earth. A push toy sat in the driveway, where it had been deserted. There were no curbs because it wasn't a proper neighborhood, just a little lane through the woods off of a busy road that connected Raleigh and Durham. It looked like a home.

"Welcome!" Paula sang as she let the screen door slam and stepped off the stoop to greet me. She hugged me with one arm; Sarah smiled at me from within the other.

"Jonathan's asleep, come in! This is our house!" She laughed as she led me inside. She was so at ease that the question didn't occur to me, how do we do this thing, open adoption.

"Hello!" Erik emerged from the kitchen and hugged me. "How were the directions? Are you getting the tour?" His manner was more reserved than Paula's.

I'd been to several homes of prospective families, but because of their distance in Indiana, and then the move to North Carolina, we'd never seen Paula and Erik's home. It hadn't occurred to me until that moment— if things smelled wrong, it was too late. The living room had hardwood floors and a big window looking out to the front yard. There was a couch with a slipcover in front of the window and a couple of unmatched recliners. It felt recently moved into, not fully occupied yet. There were stacks of books that didn't have places. Move-in clutter. Down the hallway were a master bedroom and a small bedroom for Sarah and Jonathan to share. We walked through the kitchen, where Erik was refilling his coffee, to the very large playroom that had been added on to the back.

"And these are our luxurious guest accommodations!" Paula indicated the futon, which had been unfolded and made up for me in the playroom. "We had it in Indiana and, actually, according to previous guests, it's supposed to be quite comfortable!" Between the playroom and the kitchen, there was just an open threshold and a large window over the kitchen sink. Curtain rods had been installed in both openings.

Paula opened a door from the playroom onto a covered terrace. We stepped outside, and she pointed to the corner of the backyard, where there was a small storage shed.

"And *that* is where we'll keep the television!"

Just then, Erik stepped out through the screen door, holding Jonathan, squinting and blinking. I was surprised to see him in physical form. I'd almost forgotten he had a shape.

"Hello, Amy!" Erik spoke for Jonathan. "Can you say hello?" He brought Jonathan close to me. His head bobbed, and with his chin still low in Erik's chest, he caught my eye. I do not know what I expected in that moment.

"Hi, Jonathan!" I smiled at him and touched his hand. "How are you?" He looked back blankly, furrowing his brow at the sunlight.

Erik handed him to me, and as I took him I realized I'd forgotten his weight, how elbowy and hard he was underneath the coating of soft flesh. He was difficult to manage, bendy and rubbery, full of will, looking this way and that. But whatever my expectations—maybe that we would merge like liquids the moment we touched, maybe that everything I'd wondered about him would have some kind of fleshy answer, or perhaps that the seven pounds of deep mechanics removed from me a month ago would click into place and I'd operate normally again—I forgot them in that instant. I didn't feel anything more powerfully than Erik standing twenty-four inches away, observing us. He and Paula were both smiling as they watched me greet him, and their presence produced an almost physical constraint. I stiffened from the outside, and at the same time my interior weakened, emptied of conviction. I felt loosely confined, like a boat in a log flume, free floating till it bumps an edge and is dumbly realigned to the direction of travel.

Molly had wanted us to lay out our expectations in detail, but I don't think we would have been able to address the fine grain of this moment, when, taking him in my arms, all my impulses went to war: my motherhood against their Entitlement, my hunger to enjoy our old intimacy against the costs they might bear to see it. But I didn't allow the battle to rage on for a second. I had an instinct even stronger than all the others: to protect their newborn family. I shut everything down, turned myself off, and simply drove myself numbly like a vehicle from within.

"Wow, he's gotten bigger! He has so much color!" I said, my heart hollow. Jonathan blinked his eyes at me, and then at the sunlight. He arched his back and jerked his head to look over his shoulder. His whole body reverberated with every motion, muscles in his abdomen called into action by surprise to counterbalance the movement of his head. He was getting ready to cry.

"We're still dealing with the colic," Paula said. I didn't want to think about what that might mean. Paula took him from me. "But I think the problem here is that he's extremely sensitive to transitions. Waking up, going to sleep, moving from one space to another, having someone new enter the room." Paula touched her forehead to his. "It's all very difficult, isn't it?"

Paula had dissertation work to do, and so Erik suggested that we take the kids to a park about a mile down the road. I felt myself detached from desire, instinctively reducing myself to avoid those edges. I had no idea whether I wanted to go to a park about a mile down the road with a family that wasn't mine, but I knew that the answer was, of course, "Yes! That would be great!" Erik buckled the kids in the car, and we pulled out of the driveway.

"The nice thing about our location," he explained as we drove, "is that we're just a ten-minute drive from the university, and there's a nursery school—that's it there—we think we'll put Sarah in next year. It's within walking distance of the house." Erik pointed to the school on the corner with a pine-needle-covered playground, and we crossed the intersection. "So even though we're not in the university neighborhood per se, several of our colleagues live in this area, and there are a number of places we can get to on foot."

We arrived at the park, and as Erik was unbuckling Jonathan, a woman with short black hair standing on the edge of the parking lot seemed to recognize us. Erik waved.

"I thought that was your car!" she said as she walked quickly up to us, crouching a bit to acknowledge the kids through the windows. Erik handed Jonathan to me and unbuckled Sarah from her car seat. Jonathan started squirming.

"Heather, this is Amy. Amy, Heather is in our department; we went to college together." He took Jonathan back from me and turned to Heather. "I was just telling Amy that we have a few colleagues who live near here. Heather and her husband had a not-so-small influence on our decision to move to North Carolina. In fact, they were the ones who helped us find the house; I'm not sure if Paula told you about that."

"Hi, yes, thank you very much." Heather nodded. "I credit myself with bringing them here!" She paused, looking at me to tell her who I was.

"Hi!" I said, unsure of what to say. We hadn't had a single conversation about what we should do in this situation.

"Amy is—well, is Jonathan's birth mother!" Erik laughed. "She came down from Ohio to visit for a couple of days! Amy is studying architecture there!" He said it as though each one of those facts surprised him.

"Oh, wow." Heather glanced quickly at Jonathan and stepped in to shake my hand. "It's so good to meet you."

Wow, I thought, myself. I would have understood if he had called me a friend or distant cousin or a babysitter or an incoming theology under-graduate who wanted a tour of the parks in Durham. But of course, the truth. Why wouldn't we just tell people the truth?

"It's so amazing you're here. Jonathan is such a beautiful baby!" Then she turned to Erik. "Did you guys meet in Indiana?"

"Well, you know Amy contacted us through the agency in Indiana, but they have offices here as well, so the transfer wasn't difficult." Erik elaborated the story, and we shared it like newlyweds, realizing it was fun to tell together. The improbability of our finding each other made everything seem meant to be. It was also easier to tell about it than it was to live inside it, and I found our conversation a welcome break from the alien new order of things.

As we talked, we strolled toward the swing sets. I helped Sarah into a swing and pushed her.

"Putt . . . putt . . . putt . . . !" as my dad would say when he'd pull the swing back, holding it suspended above his head for a moment, your heels dangling at his forehead as you barely held your seat, wondering when that moment of free fall was going to—"*Poooom!*" He would charge forward, pushing the swing until it was high above the reach of his arms.

It was a relief to play with Sarah. I could grab and squeeze and hold her tight, and even as she laughed and listened closely to me, there was no reason to fear I would swallow her whole to return her to my insides. Periodically, I would hear Erik and Heather laugh, but I couldn't tell what they were talking about. Maybe Paula's program, or Erik's research. Erik came over and handed Jonathan to me. He laughed as he realized he was focused on his conversation and hadn't asked. "I'm sorry, would you like to take him?"

I took him in my arms, my certainties about him reduced to a single fact: you have to cradle the wobbly head on the neck.

"Want to see something, Jonathan?" Sarah had her own curiosity about him, and she bridged the gap between us. I crouched down with him, but soon he was stretching with all his arms and legs. He was the kind of baby that arches its back and pushes against everything.

Paula told me he'd been crying a lot. We were calling it colic, but he was doing what any animal taken away from its mother would do. Cry-ing his eyes out, screaming until he had no voice. I had a secret hope that when we saw each other, some sublime peace would overtake him. I wanted to see our connection in his sudden silence. I had that hope, and I had its opposite. I hoped, for the sake of all our futures, that he wasn't crying for me. And from what I could tell, he wasn't. Not for me, not for anyone. He was just broken. Between my letting go and his family taking hold, there was a fracture, and now there was no one who could give him comfort.

Erik suggested we go home; Jonathan was probably hungry. I carried him, blind with crying, to the car.

On the drive back, Jonathan fell asleep, and I reached around and felt for Sarah's feet. When I caught one, I turned around and smiled at her. She was smiling already, waiting to see what I was going to do next.

"So, Amy, I'd meant to ask, how does it feel to be back in school? Paula said you're applying for internships for the winter?" Erik didn't talk about himself, except when asked, and then he was keenly attuned to the precise intent of the question. The things he shared had already been processed and organized, and he retrieved them generously on request. I could imagine him having been very popular in high school, an athlete and an intellectual with a military demeanor. A genuine good kid, accustomed to early-morning chores on his family's farm. I felt especially sloppy, immature, and female next to him.

He receded to the background around Paula, who was both more outgoing and more laid-back than he was. She was the oldest of her siblings. She reminded me of the girl in my neighborhood growing up who was at least three years older than the other kids we'd play with. She would inform us of such things as: *Today we will play cosmetology school in the basement.* She was the accepted leader, and we didn't think to supplant her or resent her bossiness; without her we had no idea how to have such intricate and involved forms of fun. I looked forward to spending time with Paula. I fell into a familiar role, listening and responding to her, following her cues.

When we got home, Paula asked if I'd like to feed Jonathan. She handed me a bottle and I positioned him on my lap. I wasn't sure if I was helping them as they prepared dinner, or if they were helping me, offering me a moment of closeness with my son. I held the bottle to his mouth, and the angles of his chin against his chest, of his forehead and nose, bore no relationship to the view of him I'd had when I was filling him up with my own milk. I remembered the sharp pull in my chest when he would get a good latch, the way he'd draw me toward him as he nursed, tugging at a deep seam that wound and tangled through my entire body; I would sit stunned and silent, hypnotized, captured in an interior net. It had seemed then that our closeness was inextinguishable; it extended forever in all directions. But now touching him felt forced. Like being introduced to each other by friends who didn't know our intimate past, and because of decency, we shook hands like strangers. I held the bottle like a writing implement, and he drank as though it were the only thing he knew.

We had a small dinner, after which Erik washed the dishes and Paula and I sat in the living room and finished our wine.

"I have to tell you, Amy, that you look very good for someone who just had a baby this summer! I have so many friends who complain about their baby weight. Is there a secret?"

We both laughed. My secret was that I hadn't been able to eat very much; my own hunger alone wasn't enough to motivate me. I'd grown accustomed to swallowing an egg and imagining it like a marble drop game, the channels and funnels and gears it would pass through to somehow reach my son. Now I dropped things into an infinite void.

"It's funny you say that," I said, "because I was in the computer lab the other day, and someone I hadn't seen since last quarter came in, and he sat down next to me and asked me when I was going to have the baby!"

"What would that make you now, eleven months pregnant?" Paula exclaimed. "But, you know, people see what they expect to see. I can't tell you how many times we've been walking together, Erik, the kids, and I, and someone will say they can tell we're all related. It's Sarah's eyebrows, or maybe it's just that Erik and Jonathan are both bald. I don't know! I'm of course thinking about how little we look like a family, but I guess when you put us all together—"

Erik refilled my glass of wine.

"Well, it seems like Sarah is really good with Jonathan," I said. "I was watching her with him at the park."

"She's a natural caretaker," Paula said, holding her glass out for Erik.

"Sometimes when Jonathan's asleep I'll remind her not to wake him. She'll watch him quietly and then pet him so, so gently."

"Does she see her birth mother much?" I asked. Her birth mother was now a kind of sister to me.

"Yes, we make sure she sees her at least once a year. It's a long trip; we go there. And unfortunately, at least for now, we don't see her birth father."

"We're off to bed; Amy, do you want to say goodnight?" Erik returned with Jonathan and lowered him gently into my lap. I held him and tried to think of what to say in front of everyone, realizing at that moment that my son would always be handed to me, and I'd forever be watched.

"Goodnight, Jonathan!" I said, straining. Paralyzed by self-consciousness. If motherhood was so powerful, my instincts should be kicking in. I shouldn't have to practice—I should be ready to perform on the spot. I should cradle him naturally, as if I could protect him from all present and future pains.

But I'd already exposed him to the very real unknown. I'd dealt his first blow. So what now? What was I supposed to say?

"I'll see you in the morning," I said, retrieving a toy truck from the inside edge of my chair. I would distract him with a truck, rolling over the surface of his belly, from the things I couldn't share with him.

I couldn't see them looking at me; I only felt them smiling. I don't know if they noticed my awkwardness or whether they derived any satisfaction from it. Maybe they were surprised to see I'd lost my touch so completely, so soon. My motherhood was a brief fog. How could they help but enjoy this evidence it had all but dissipated?

I held him limply, my wrists loosening from my heart the way they used to during piano recitals, when I'd find myself overwhelmed by the keys' impenetrable code. He began to cry. My body bowed. I handed him to Paula. The wound was already healing in a manner that excluded me, and I could want nothing more than for him to learn her shape and adapt to it. Soft and pink would be his comfort.

She held him firmly; we were erasing my motherhood from both ends. She knew exactly how hard to pat his back, like I knew with dogs. The limit. Too soft and they remain a distant mystery. Too hard is of course mean. But just under too hard is a kind of acknowledgment of exact material limits. It is being known. And dogs turn and smile at you like you've cracked them, the species barrier and their own. Paula knew the precise physics of swinging Jonathan over her shoulder without over-protecting his head. She could communicate in her body that this high-speed lift up into the air was a kind of joke, and it would make him smile and stare at her, full of suspense. He knew very little about the world, but he knew the next good thing would come from her. Perhaps I was really the audience, and Paula and Erik who felt watched.

I watched and smiled as she showed me the things my son liked to do, how he liked to be held, what made him laugh. I already trusted them as his parents. But still, I didn't want to be shown—as though there were information to know about my son that I didn't already know by filling him up with blood and causing his heart to pound.

⊙ ⊙ ⊙

Closing the curtain in the playroom that night, it seemed silly, what I had expected. There was no way to return the amputated limb to the body and expect coherent action. The thing I'd somehow confused with my own extracted and wandering soul was a helpless, tiny baby who reached only for miscellaneous things: dangling hair, a filthy toy, those trinkets in the margins of the Dear Birth Mother letters. He wasn't sub-stantially different from all the other babies in the world I'd never taken interest in, and he evidently hadn't been spending our time apart thinking about me. His life in the last few weeks hadn't been about discovering his sonhood. There was in fact no secret between us, no wholeness to return to.

And we were only at the very beginning of doing adoption. I could see clearly that he would need a long, long time to build muscle, and learn to talk, and learn what dogs are and what adoption is, and build forts and learn to read, and have his first tablet of lined paper, and meet his cousins, and have a crush, and scrape his shins on asphalt, and go to summer camp, and step hard on the edge of a shovel, and push it into the ground, and touch sharp things with his toes in the ocean, and learn arithmetic and algebra and geometry and trigonometry and calculus, and learn to dive, and practice piano, and quit piano, and slam doors, and move houses with his family probably several times, and make friends, and switch cereals, and get in trouble at school, and figure out that he likes physics but not chemistry, and learn to drive, and study for the SATs, and fall in love, and long for summers not to end, and lie sleepless at Christmas, and throw away his old favorite things, and throw water balloons, and fight with his sister, and find a temporary truce, and mourn his dog's death, and fly twenty times in a plane, and taste alcohol, and score a hundred baskets—before I might ever get a chance to ask him how he felt about this whole thing. I would have to let him live an entire life, and we wouldn't know the results of the experiment until it was over. There would be no opportunity to discover an error in the formula and begin again. Years would pass, so much would happen, and we might think about the life we missed, but we wouldn't really be able to miss it.

And it wasn't right to want him to save space for me. He would celebrate his birthday and not think of the moon that night we labored. He wouldn't even know that the moon had been there to remember. He would take his birthday and run, and I would have to let him have it. But that was motherhood for any mother: it's being happy that the ten fingers and ten toes you take such careful stock of will grasp and curl around the things of the world, will propel him forward and away, knowing that he will never look back into your eyes and feel what you feel.

I didn't wake up when they did to feed him. I awoke only when I felt Sarah watching me early in the morning from the side of the bed. Then I heard someone in the kitchen making coffee. There was an awkward intimacy when Erik asked me through the curtain if I'd like a cup. Paula brought Jonathan in to say good morning, and Sarah asked if I was going to get up. The performance resumed: playing, chasing, tickling. All the while, I felt the weight of constraints no one was imposing. I stopped every gesture short of its full realization. I did not bury my face in Jonathan's belly, or tell him that I loved him. It made me tired the entire day. I played with blocks and dolls and planes and held my eyes, heavily, from falling asleep. I would take every instant I could, a moment on the toilet, a minute running to the car to get my sweater, every chance I had, to rest my eyes against the exhaustion.

⊚ ⊚ ⊚

Construction on I-75 funneled traffic into a shoulderless two-lane road that ran for a moment diagonally across the old orientation of the road, still visible as a palimpsest of a grain, from so many thousands of cars running parallel to one another. You don't realize the different depths of a road, the thickness of the striping, the heave of the centerline, until you're forced to drive the wrong way across it. Hulking masses of concrete were placed just on the edge of the temporary striping. Driving on 75 was in these construction zones like threading an electrified needle.

I was aggressively embracing the good in everything. Squeezing it hard. Like I did my cats when I was little, so hard that the force cast a shadow over the sentiment. I'd squeeze those cats till the last bit of air in their lungs squeaked out, and I knew I'd achieved maximum affection. I liked Paula. I liked Erik. I loved Sarah. They were good at being my son's family, and I'd told Paula I thought so. There was no one else I could have given my son to. They were doing everything right.

As I crossed the border into Kentucky, exhausted, the mountains fell away, and I had the comforting sensation that my car might soon ascend into the ether and disappear. Nothing weighted the horizon; my body flew across the surface of the earth at an inhuman rate. The most natural thing in the world would be to lift off into the sky. Failing that, as I threaded the concrete barriers, I considered the impact of small gestures. My structures professor's wife's generous offer. Sarah reaching out softly to pet my son. Kissing him goodbye in the foyer. My signature on the line. The impact, if I turned the wheel just a little.

TWENTY

It was easier to be away from him. Away from him, I could love him as much as I wanted. I felt a pull and a devotion to him that I can only compare to my drive toward other untouchable things; beauty, poetry, justice. Things without definite contours that sit quietly filling your heart, wobbling your compass, giving general direction but no image and no precise destination. I felt closer to him when we were far apart; the needle stabilized. There were days when just because I could feel my affection for him, a visceral fullness like pregnancy, I felt I'd captured him—the same way I would watch a sunset and declare it mine.

"So which are you? An angel? Or a slut?"

I was very far away from him that October, in northern Michigan. Twenty-five of us sat in a sort-of-circle, an assemblage of wooden-armed chairs and couches. We were gathered in the main room of a breezy log cabin, designed extra-large and open-plan for conferences such as this one. The heat occupied the vast space above the rafters, while we sat wrapped in blankets below, hugging our knees or lounging back with our feet propped on the mismatched coffee tables in the center.

"Most people see birth mothers as one or the other. We are angels for giving up our children. People say they could never do something so courageous! Or, it's the opposite. We got what was coming to us. If we didn't want kids, we shouldn't have been sleeping around in the first place, right?" Laura was a birth mother of about fifteen years and the retreat organizer. She was an expert at open adoption. "Obviously neither of these extremes really describes us. It's important not to let other people's ideas about us influence the way we see ourselves. Reality is complicated."

Paula had told me about this retreat for birth mothers, in open and closed adoptions, a weekend of training on issues like handling conflict with adoptive parents, having children after adoption, talking to friends and colleagues about adoption. But I decided initially not to go. My grief existed parallel with the rest of my life, inside my headphones, within the lines I drew; while I was applying for internships, or designing buildings, or stopping by the conservatory to play the piano—but I didn't give it real time or space. If I didn't have time for a son, I definitely didn't have time to mope about not having one. I had to work harder so that I could accomplish all I'd given him up to accomplish.

But the grief would grow invisibly. It behaved like a tangle that develops at the end of your knitting yarn (when you are not the knitter your sheepherding aunts and uncles and sister and cousins are), building its own chaotic structures in a loose and inverse mockery of your aspiration toward a scarf, until it has gradually inched itself into your hands, where it stops all progress. You set things aside to untangle it, but as soon as you're back to work, it starts to build again. The faster you move forward, the faster its return. The more intricate your patterning, the more complex its configuration.

I would wake up at night gasping for air, but I wasn't just dreaming about giving up my son. I'd wake to find I'd done it.

I didn't care about workshops, but I decided to go to the retreat because I was curious about other birth mothers. I couldn't imagine birth motherdom as a permanent condition, only a sadness to outrun. What did women look like after a year, or ten, if they couldn't? I sent off ten applications to internships for the following term in Seattle, Charlottesville, Boston, Chicago. And then I made my way to the flatlands of northern Michigan to a foreign woodland drained of color, with trees like standing skeletons.

But it wasn't complicated at all to understand whether I was an angel or a slut. It was easy to be both and neither of those simple things. What was complicated was to understand whether or not we were mothers. I tried to see the motherhood in the women seated around the circle. I'd become attuned to the ways motherhood was represented in magazines and in movies, or in conversations I overheard. I measured my own motherhood against every reference. Before I'd left, I'd watched an opera on television in which a weeping soprano bellowed to a police officer: *We do not recognize your sovereignty; we are lionesses, we kill for our cubs.* Yes, I'd thought. That's how you know you're a mother. You don't abandon your child; you kill to protect it.

I studied the girls around the room. They were in their twenties and thirties, but they looked older. Mature and hardened. Several girls who were not wearing glasses at the welcome pizza party the night before were wearing glasses now. Most of us had cried our makeup off or hadn't put any on. Some of them knew each other from attending the retreat in previous years. They were sharing quilts or resting a head on a shoulder. I was wearing the retreat sweatshirt, having not brought warm-enough clothes. Actually, most of us were wearing it. Birth mothers together in forest green or red, united by the experiment we'd each entered blindly for our own inadequate reasons. Women as many as ten years down the road I'd just set out on, all still working hard on the project of living with ourselves afterward.

"We're going to go around the room, and each of us will tell the story of our adoption, wherever we are in it, whatever feels most important to share. When did you place your child? What is the adoptive family like? What's the hardest thing for you right now? What's the happiest thing? Who wants to start?"

A girl with short blond hair began. Her story was that her adoption had been closed because the adoptive parents said her visits were upsetting to her child.

"So after five years, they're telling me that it's suddenly confusing, and I don't get it. There's never been a problem before, but suddenly now they don't want contact." She said she didn't know what she'd done, and the adoptive parents didn't want to talk about it. "I can see wrinkles—

literally wrinkles!—on my forehead that I know wouldn't be there if I hadn't gone through all this. I used to have smooth skin, and it started in the first year after his adoption. And now it's permanent. Sometimes when I'm in my car I scream at God. Or I just scream. I'm sure I look crazy to the other cars!"

Seeing the child; not seeing the child. Both were complicated scenarios arising from the real problem: we were lionesses who gave up our cubs.

"I think the hardest thing for me, though," she continued, "is just not being able to talk about it with anyone."

Several of us nodded. There was no one to talk to and nothing to talk about; we had *done* adoption. My parents didn't ask about Jonathan; they asked, "How was North Carolina?" As far as they were concerned, Paula and Erik and Jonathan and Sarah were just straightforward new facts of the universe. They'd get pictures Paula sent, and they'd talk about what a great photographer she was or how cute the kids looked together. They sent birthday cards and packages of fair trade coffee. They embraced the whole family, but they would never talk with me specifically about my son. Definitely not how it felt to see him.

Only my grandmother's reaction was equal to the magnitude of what I'd done. She was furious. *He's a Seek child! Seek children belong with the Seeks!* But even she calmed down when the terms of the adoption were explained to her. "Well, you certainly did drop a bombshell," she said when she finally called me, "but I'm tickled to death that you're going to be able to have some contact with the baby. And if it should extend— heavens be praised if it does—very good to have the baby for a week to see me. I can't think of anything I'd like more, and Tunie would, too, and Aunt Mary would, too. And we're all deeply involved in it with you." She said she and my aunt Tunie were going to Pennsylvania to get some especially small knitting needles, as Tunie couldn't finish the sleeves of the sweater she was making for Jonathan without them.

When the first girl finished speaking, we moved counterclockwise to the next, a tiny girl with thick brown hair, holding her mug with both hands for warmth. She had regular contact with her daughter, but it sounded very formal: they'd meet in a neutral location, an ice cream place or a park, for an afternoon every six months or so. In some ways it sounded appealing to have the boundaries so clearly defined.

"Everything's fine; it's great to see her. She's in second grade now!" she said. "It's just, for those first seven years, I really thought I was happy about it! And then all of a sudden it hit me!" A girl at the end of the couch handed her a tissue from the box on the side table. "I usually try to think of the good things that have come from the adoption. One of the few good things is that everyone who knows me says I'm a much nicer person." She laughed. "I wish God could have done it some other way, but I guess I have to resist the urge to second-guess the big plan."

We were all crying and wrapping our arms over one another's shoulders. We had all softened since the first night, when we were introduced, and we chatted over pizza. We hadn't talked so much about our children then. Mostly we had talked about men. Men are assholes, we seemed to agree: the fathers of our babies and our current asshole boyfriends alike. Everyone got into it; it was fun. I listened quietly, feeling I wanted to stand up for Jevn, but I didn't say anything. There was too much pleasure in the consensus; too much consensus to interject. And some part of me was taking notes: don't express bitterness about men, and you will never become a birth mother.

But then, I was also highly attuned to references to fatherhood in the world, and that fall I'd watched *Stealing Beauty*, the Bertolucci film in which a father finds out only when his daughter is a teenager that he has a daughter at all. The difference between men and mothers. Whether or not they were all assholes, there was certainly no circle of birth fathers gathered on soft couches in another flat forest, eating goody bags of chocolate, weaving dream catchers by the fire, sharing their stories of loss and counting the number of marshmallows they could stuff into their mouths because they couldn't fill the void.

"I think you have to just remember your child is in the best possible place. I know that my daughter is with a very loving family," another girl said. "Her happiness is more important than mine, and I think that's why we're very special people."

Angels, I guess, was our conclusion.

"Yes, as selfishly as I would have liked to have raised my son, I think it takes much more courage to put aside your feelings for those of your child. That is the definition of a mother to me."

Our motherhoods undermined by adoption, we sought every proof of our love. We embraced a paradoxical idea of motherhood; we were the best kind of mother because we gave our children away. We told ourselves it was the right thing to do. That our children were better off with someone else. That it was God's plan. That our own feelings don't matter. That our children are happy. That that happiness makes up for every other kind of loss, our child's and our own. That men are assholes.

But didn't openness mean we didn't have to lie anymore? Instead of stories about their mother's disappearance, our children could take comfort in the truth—that we loved them. They could witness it firsthand. And yet it seemed the lies had only retreated; we still bore them in plain sight. We accepted that we were collateral damage of our child's adoption and took on an invisibility more complex than absence. We made our desires, our regrets, and our grief invisible, even to ourselves.

When the circle came to me, I only remember that I wanted to use the word *regret*, because it seemed like we weren't saying it for some reason, even though it was part of every story. Even though it brought those ideas—being a mother and not being a mother—together in a way that could endure the test of time: the way I am most fully a mother is that I regret giving up my son. Regret felt like a bridge back to my son, one that could stand because it was true.

Everyone was surprised at how new my adoption was, and they consoled me: *Your son is beautiful! His parents sound amazing!* Those things seemed to sit beside my regret, but they didn't elbow it or erase it.

I didn't want it to go away. Admitting my regret felt forward-looking. It felt like progress. It brushed away all the lies that were so tempting to believe, exposing the real project. Which, like Laura said, had to do with not reconciling those realities, but somehow living them fully. Angel and slut. Mother and not a mother at all.

But regret was also terrifying, and as soon as I said the word, I understood why they hadn't. I abandoned that forest in Michigan, as I had my son's house. As though it were birth motherhood itself. I wanted to wipe every surface of myself clean. I felt disoriented, like I'd been driving the wrong way on a highway for hours, and when I realized it, the whole world appeared suddenly freakish and foreign.

I wrote to my sister. I tried to express it. The alienation of regret. Regret undid things. It stole the oxygen out of the delicate universe I'd agreed to live in—I needed to know, can a mother *live* without her child? It was a straightforward but urgent, physiological question. She responded, *don't look back—look at the future!—that is what you wanted—don't ask yourself "what if"—it is not profitable speculation—amounts to nothing useful—cut it out :)*

◎ ◎ ◎

In January, I moved into an unfurnished three-bedroom apartment in Boston with five people from my program. I slept on a mattress made of two summer-smelling pool floats stacked one on top of the other and bound together with bungee cords. In the middle of the night I'd find myself on the hard floor, my hip dull with pain, and had to find the energy in my sleep to blow them up again. The pipes banged and clanged, like someone was beating them erratically with a hammer. The winter wind came right through the window I slept beneath and brushed me longwise from shoulder to toes. I waited at the bus stop with my roommates in the morning, but we parted at South Station; I walked across a long, cold, windy expanse onto land made of rubble to my internship at an architecture firm. My internship task was to find the right red for the interior of the lobby of a building that was well under way, and, like the leafless trees and the barren landscape, I concentrated my energies on essential pursuits. By my desk, I kept a picture of my son and a passage by Gabriel García Márquez about gratitude that Jevn had given me. Gratitude was many people's paradoxical solution to regret.

I would not tell myself lies. But I wanted to be able to commit to a certain way of feeling. I wanted to be steady like Jevn, and moving to a new city meant I could do that—put the story down and make it stick. I bought a serious, calf-length, black wool coat and wrapped myself in it like a vestment. I decided I wouldn't mention my son at all; my motherhood a vow of silence. I didn't, after all, have a son to go home to.

After work, I walked four miles back to my apartment. I set a straight trajectory on the sidewalk of the city I didn't know, keeping my head down and aligning myself with the right-hand edge. When someone crossed my path, I assured myself that I had the right-of-way within the narrow and unmarked sidewalk lane. Someone would swing his arms too wide and nearly hit me, or step out of a shop and merge into my path, not seeing me. Invariably, he wouldn't notice he'd cut me off. I tried not to react; I could be so easily overcome with grief. I told myself I belonged here—and yet, what was the Surrender but an official agreement, signed by all of us, that I didn't? I tried to think about red. The Right Red. Near the Common, I passed by bumpy graveyards, where freeze-thaws had shuffled and unsettled headstones. Bodies and bones mixed with soil; old chambers of lungs and coffins buckled and cratered the frozen ground. It seemed even the grave was a restless place. And mine was a cratered and unsettled motherhood. I couldn't keep it buried. I studied the faces of new friends I met as I told them the story for the first time. I wanted to see whether they thought mine was a livable condition. Their faces would reveal what they wouldn't say, but they seemed to share my question, studying me for answers as they looked back.

I couldn't deny my motherhood, and I couldn't claim it honestly. I couldn't do anything simple or consistent; I couldn't even stay sad. Sometimes, bracing myself against the cold wind as I walked along the Charles, I found myself smiling.

One of my new friends told me about dances held almost every night at different locations, and, knowing little else about Boston, I started going. I'd learned to dance when I was young, in a barn filled with old car and bus seats planted right into the sloped dirt floor. Everyone wore taps on their shoes, and they danced alone without partners, as good Christians do. A kind of clogging called flatfoot, it looked simple, so I'd tried it. I tapped and leapt and bounced to the music, but an old man pulled me off the dance floor and escorted me outside. He went back inside, and a few minutes later a little boy fell out the door and looked up at me, perplexed. He'd been told to teach me to dance, but he didn't seem to understand not knowing how to dance. He did a fast wagon wheel and some ornamented basics and looked up at me to replicate them, but try as he might he couldn't slow them down or explain them. What I could see was the gravity. Unlike tap dancing or ballet, which

aspire like the cathedrals to weightlessness and height, flatfoot was low
to the ground and heavy. You were always lifting yourself up from a bur-
densome weight.

I danced almost every night. Dances with set steps, old contra dances
and clogging that connected me back to the South. The structure and
constraint of fixed movements established for centuries, the wild release
of the whole history of myself, gains and losses, contained in my spinning mass.

And sometimes on Sunday mornings, I went to church and confronted
God the father. I had never been in a better position to hear him, reduced
by my loss to a state more primal than motherhood, more detached from
desire than a monk. But now it seemed absurd to ask why. Why had it all
happened, what good was in store because of it? God seemed to me very
much a man, casting generative potential into the void without turning
back to see what got fertilized. His creative prowess was a heartless force,
and his reasons couldn't be known by me.

The only thing I felt was the holy difference. That the Big Plan had
very little to do with me. God's ways had never been mine. People at
church said I should be grateful about the adoption, but I liked facing
that cold hardness blankly; it elevated God and made me turn on him.

We sang the Our Father and raised our fists in aggressive submission.

I took a weekend off in February and flew to North Carolina to see my
son. He was locomoting, backward, mostly. He drooled so much they
had to change his shirt several times a day. When Erik disappeared into
the woods to help Sarah find her shoes, I ran with Jonathan, threw him
upward and caught him, and he smiled at me. The morning I left, he lay
on his stomach, on my stomach, the way he had when he was first born
and they piled him, slippery, on top of me. He searched my face with all
his senses. Put his hands in my mouth, gummed at my nose. Pulled my
hair. When I left, my throat felt scratchy and sore, and I marveled that
my son had an independent biology, and that he had made me sick.

When I got back to Boston, a boy I'd met at a dance said that he
admired and respected me, but he'd been thinking about it, and if I was
able to give up my own son, he couldn't help but wonder what else I

was capable of. He didn't want to see me anymore, but it was just in time. My ten-week internship was almost over, and I was already packing to go. The weekend before I left, in one of the oldest churches in Boston, I was baptized into an incongruous understanding of God, the only thing certain that I often thought of him. In a strange union that embraced my body, its history and its denial, I was baptized under three cupfuls of water in the name of the Father, the image of the detached; the Son, my tragic loss; and the Holy Spirit. I left town without having found the Right Red, and in my internship evaluation, my supervisor said it would be a shame if I didn't pursue my love of dancing.

TWENTY-ONE

In April, Jonathan was nine months old. The colic had subsided, and he was practicing language that Paula described as "the funniest little combination of mumbling and humming." She said his voice was very much a little boy's voice. He was beginning to balance on wobbly legs and had a full head of bright white hair and a mouthful of baby teeth. She sent pictures of him proudly pouring a pitcher of water over Sarah's head in the tub, Sarah's eyes shut tight, laughing. *He smiles like the sun*, I thought—*like the happiness is coming from within him*. I realized I had thought of him like the moon.

Paula said that when Sarah turned nine months old, she realized she'd been Sarah's mother for as long as her birth mother had, and that felt significant. People would sometimes ask about Sarah's *real* mother, and although comments like that bothered her, having had her own nine-month gestation she found herself feeling a little more like a *real* mother. Now that Jonathan was nine months old, I hoped she'd feel more like his real mother, too, and that I might experience some kind of positive inverse: my son would feel to me more hers, and my loss, less.

We talked about these things like we weren't right in the middle of them. We were always lightening our relationship by exposing it to air: the fraught and complex aspects of our joint/mutual/exclusive motherhoods. She was the person who came closest to being able to understand. I'd tell her really hard things—like the feelings of regret I'd unearthed at the birth mothers' retreat—and she'd describe her own ambivalence as an adoptive mother. She said because she'd seen the strength of my bond with Jonathan, her motherhood could never be simple. Openness didn't make anything easier, but she said it at least gave her the assurance I was busy with school and not plotting to steal my son back. I laughed at that, but it was important—being able to share some of what we were each going through was heartening. Whatever the animal complexity of what we'd done, ethically and intellectually, we were solidly on the same side.

And at nine months, Jonathan was doing his own kind of sophisticated thinking. Paula said he was now able to recognize and remember people. When he saw someone he knew, he'd smile and his face would light up. But I didn't expect him to remember me. I might not even recognize him, he was growing so fast. On my way to see him, I reminded myself that much as he might have grown, he was still just a baby; I'd try not to expect anything at all. When I arrived, he crawled furtively behind a chair, and when Paula picked him up, he buried himself in her chest, glancing at me from the safety of her arms. Sarah made it easier by leaping into mine, but squeezing her I wondered, *If he does recognize me, what does he see?*

Paula would probably have prepared him for this visit by explaining that I was his mother in some simple way a nine-month-old could understand. This was important data he'd now be able to store and use, and maybe next time, and from then on, he'd recognize me and know something about how important our visits together were. But how could she not at the same time explain that I'd given him up? Those two facts were inseparable. Could he love me for one without hating me for the other? I touched his hand to say hello, and he drew it back as if he were afraid of me. And I realized I was afraid of him, too.

That question consumed me as I carried him to the park that afternoon. He had warmed to me after spending the morning watching Sarah climb on me, and run away squealing, and return all over again, and Paula suggested I try taking him for a walk. But it was the first time we'd been alone together since his adoption, and I was nervous. I pushed him gently on an infant swing, grabbing his toes every time he returned to me. I felt lucky when he smiled, arriving at my collarbone. But watching him watch me, I wondered what image he was now taking in to store. I told myself his furrowed brow meant he wanted off the swing, but I was afraid it meant more. I lifted him up, chatting continuously, adding stories, songs, spins in a circle—in a race with his growing consciousness. The more experiences we shared as his understanding took shape, perhaps the less he would see me through the stark circumstances of his birth and adoption. His affection for me might stand a chance against his anger. He studied me at close range, and it seemed urgent: I could not let him cry. His tears at that moment would seem decisive.

Rain suddenly began falling hard, lightning and thunder; real and outside of us. We stepped into a gazebo for shelter and watched it pour. I loved storms. They bent the rules of the day; people came alive and abandoned plans and ran for cover. The rain made our strange relationship feel real. Our relationship could get wet. It invigorated me. I stepped into the storm, holding him. Me and him and the pummeling rain, the only important facts of the gray and watery world. He wrinkled his face and looked at me, and I remembered putting him in the shower as a newborn to make him cry. I tried to own the confidence in our connection I'd had then.

When the sky began to clear, the world was a steaming memory, puddles everywhere reflecting a sky that had forgotten it made them. He pointed at one, and I dropped down to a squat. I leaned forward, and he held one hand around my neck while he splashed in the puddle with the other. Our heads were smashed together to give him leverage for the splashing hand, and he would turn, his nose nearly touching mine, and smile and scream. I stood back up, we found another, squat, splash, scream.

I had forgotten how magical puddles were. They reordered the known universe of my neighborhood when I was little; we knew exactly where to go for shallow ones and deep Barbie bathtubs; oceanic ones that spread across the street. We'd pick up earthworms along the way, returning them to the grass before they dried up or got run over. We called that activity STEW: Save The Earth Worms. I put Jonathan down and rolled up his pant legs. He steadied himself on me with wet hands, earnestly, as if our splashing was serious business. When I was finished with his cuffs, I lifted him and put him down at the edge of a shallow pothole. He kicked it and laughed. Then he crouched to touch it. I felt I'd found something real between us. Not my motherhood, but some simpler alliance.

After dinner Paula surprised me by putting on the mix tape I'd sent in the fall. Sarah danced, and she even sang along to some of the songs. Jonathan joined in, bouncing on his rubbery legs, and Erik bounced on his own legs a few times as he passed through clearing dishes. Washing the dishes was one of his jobs. Paula grocery shopped and cooked; Erik did dishes and laundry. They both cleaned, and, because their teaching schedules were flexible, they shared child care without needing much additional help. Paula seemed to savor the after-dinner social time, when her chores were done. We were drinking wine out of big, round glasses, watching the kids, and when my mix tape ended, she surprised me more by playing a mix tape my mother had sent, filled with children's songs she'd taught her students in France and Germany. *"Sur le pont, d'Avignon, on y danse, on y danse!"* I was impressed that my mother had sent such a record, or knew how to make one, or had the same impulse I did, to share music with my son.

"I was starting to tell you before about Jevn's visit, because it's just—so funny how these things happen with adoption." Paula sank into the couch, one leg folded underneath her, like it was a slumber party at midnight. I was a little sister, completely under her spell. "There's this little bagel shop we discovered; we can walk to it just down the street. Maybe Erik showed it to you; it's one of our favorite little places to go in the morning."

"I don't think so," I said, shrugging. I liked hearing about Jevn from them; Paula spoke of him like he was ours.

"Well, when Jevn was here, he and I took Jonathan there. We were sitting at a little table, eating our bagels. And one of my colleagues comes in. This is someone we know through school, and you know we just can't tell everyone the whole story, how the kids were adopted, what an open adoption is—most people know, but sometimes it's just easier not to get into it. And sometimes we forget who knows what. Anyway, so Jevn is sitting there with Jonathan on his lap, and I see this colleague taking a good look at them while she's in line. I wave hello, and I see the gears turning. She's looking from Jonathan to Jevn, who is of course like a perfect adult version of him, and I see what she's thinking." She laughed and leaned forward. "I'm having a secret rendezvous with my child's real father! At the bagel shop down the street!"

She laughed. I laughed; the foibles of open adoption.

I told her my own story, about a woman I'd met at a dance who, after hearing about Jonathan's adoption, asked me if I might consider being a surrogate for her. I had a proven pelvis and a proven ability to give up my babies.

"Amy, no. You have got to be kidding me!" Paula laughed.

That night I passed the bedrooms on my way to brush my teeth. I wanted to say goodnight to Jonathan, but the bond we'd built in the afternoon felt tenuous. And he was so sensitive. Paula said his sensitivity was sometimes so extreme, he'd get upset when her coffee cup wasn't centered on the microwave turntable. I feared what that might mean—was he trying in vain to right a world that had wronged him? But Paula took it in stride. Part of his personality. I imitated her, taking things simply, and after I brushed my teeth, I peeked in. Paula was laying him down on the bed to change him, and he had already started to cry. I could kiss him then, because then no one would know whether he was crying because of me or because of the changing. Paula stood back as I kissed his forehead, and he paused to look at me. His eyes blinked to focus through his tears. And then he started to laugh.

The next morning, my parents arrived to pick me up. I'd flown down from Boston after my internship, and they'd be taking me back to Tennessee to retrieve my car and drive back to school. While my mother and I talked to Paula in the living room, my father took Sarah for a walk; he found a construction site, crossed the No Trespassing signs, and let Sarah climb on piles of sand and gravel between backhoes and construction debris. Sarah returned quietly smitten, with dangerous new knowledge of the world within walking distance.

We said goodbye, and I settled into the hard cushions of the backseat, the soft seal of the doors as they closed dividing this family from that one more cleanly than I knew how to. As we drove through the mountains into Tennessee, my parents talked about what good parents Paula and Erik seemed to be. My mother said she sort of felt she hadn't lost a grandson so much as she'd gained a son- and daughter-in-law in Paula and Erik. But after Mass the next morning, when one of her friends pulled out a photograph of her beautiful newborn grandchild, she said nothing about her own.

It was nice to be home, where family was easy. Family had always meant: eating supper together and going for hikes. It meant knowing exactly what one another will think is funny, what words make us cringe (*panties, chuckle, nibble, snack*); it was conversations that begin when you can't really talk because you're brushing your teeth and the recognizable weight of each person's feet going down the steps in the morning. It was knowing exactly what part of the creek has the most crawdads and hiking through the tall grass to get there. It was turnip parties in the garden, when we'd take a slice right off the edge of Dad's knife, still warm from the ground and the sun, and spicy. It was Dad making us gag by calling those sweet moments *togetherness*. Above all, it was being able to take one another for granted and taking the greatest imaginable comfort in that.

But with my son it was the opposite. I second-guessed every word; I doubted every touch. He changed radically every time I saw him, and I couldn't even assume he would know who I was, or what he would see in me if he did. I'd created a whole different kind of family, one that would never be able to take anything for granted. It was only through our loss that we would know each other, and knowing each other would require intention, and care, and effort. Time together wouldn't be easy and obvious; it would always be a kind of tending to our wounds.

My father cracked peanut shells in his pockets as we walked through the neighborhood, talking about my good time in Boston, the good parents I found for Jonathan, and the exciting things coming up for me in school. It was just like when I was little; sometimes I'd have trouble sleeping and he'd lie down beside me and set happy things afloat in my imagination, with no narrative to connect them.

Remember Prince? The horse across the field by the gas station? He loved those apples we brought him, even the wormy ones from the trees. And Topsy, she was your favorite horse to ride, wasn't she?

It was as though the mere existence of such good things around me meant their goodness somehow extended to me. But they always seemed alien, horses floating across the groundlessness of night, while the crickets and cicadas and buzzing insects gave volume to the darkness.

Ebony jumped the fence that day! She must have been very hot! But she just went back to her stall, didn't she?

Surf Song, and Sugar Foot, and every other horse in the stable.

TWENTY-TWO

It was almost Jevn's birthday when I got back to school. I hadn't seen him in months, but he had been present everywhere all the same: Jonathan was growing to look just like him, and Paula and Erik spoke of him easily and often. We were always going to be in each other's lives, and on good days I thought things could be simple with us. So that Saturday I mixed up nuts and flour and salt and cinnamon, my mother's recipe, and then I mushed the bananas, cooked and cooled everything, and I took it to his house. A loaf of banana bread to say that I was sorry for everything, or everything was forgiven, and I still cared about him and always would. Simple. I stood on the stoop, heart pounding.

He opened the door and slipped out, pulling it closed behind him so I wouldn't see or be seen or be inadvertently invited into the gathering of people inside. I said, "Happy birthday!" and handed him the banana bread wrapped in aluminum foil. He narrowed his eyes and exhaled sharply through his mouth. He took the loaf in one hand but did not receive it; he held it away from his body as though I'd asked him to carry it for me, and he continued to observe me, smiling skeptically, as if, given enough time, I might do something else absurd. "Thanks," he said, as if to say, *It could never be simple with us.*

Years ago, during that phase of our relationship when we were deep in but still discovering so much about each other, Jevn told me about his father. He said when his father used to drink, he would look out the car window to see how swervy the lines on the road were getting, to gauge whether he might need to jump out. And he measured people like that; if they wavered, he fled. I wanted him to embrace the new me, who had come so far to get here, on his doorstep, saying, "Happy birthday!" but I had been so many things by then, so many unforeseen storms of rage, so many pitch-black midnights. How could he trust this system to stay? He put one hand behind him on the doorknob and stood, silent, letting the stillness expand between us.

I turned away and told myself I would never step on this sidewalk, walk turn down the street where he lived, ever again. What was wrong with making banana bread for someone's birthday?

I stormed home, abandoning my innocently contrived plans for peace; now I was fuming and felt ready for war. This bridge could not be built. He had always been my enemy. Why had I aligned myself with him for even a moment? Why had I let him weigh in on my pregnancy, as if he had as much to lose as I did? As if he had anything to do with me at all? I couldn't believe I'd let him make me feel guilty for my indecision about signing the papers. It was easy for him—there was no metamorphosis in fatherhood! No bloody extraction, no heartbreaking soul-splitting, no wrenching in two that might account for some duplicity. I emerged broken and torn, while he remained faultless, steady, and true. I couldn't help it if motherhood was messy, and I didn't care if he couldn't help it, either—I couldn't forgive him for being a father.

But then what was that moment, the labor and birth? A magical truce when we forgot our grievances. Jevn had been so present there, trusting my pain and leaping to help me, but he wasn't in focus for me, then. He was just a comforting figure on the distant horizon. When it was over and Jonathan was born, we'd been through something together that was bigger than both of us and our complicated relationship. It seemed it should change everything. Maybe I hoped he would ask me again, and, all our walls torn down, that I would find a way to say yes. It was days later, I was dropping tears on Jonathan's chest, when I realized that that distant figure had always, at least since last December, been walking away.

Seeing Jevn's distinctive features in Jonathan—in his eyes, in his smile, in his beginnings of a posture—made me hope there were other good things already built in, like Jevn's intelligence and care. But it wasn't fair that I had to let go of Jevn while experiencing a brand-new fascination for someone who looked just like him. Sometimes when Jonathan glanced at me with the same eyes as Jevn, I thought he somehow had the same legitimate complaints, too; the same well-founded suspicions, the same hurt, and the same unwillingness to let me get close. Sometimes I felt I was turning my back on both of them at once.

As I climbed the stairs to my apartment, I resolved never to reach out again. I'd take only what he would give me; I'd hold him only when he was handed to me.

◎ ◎ ◎

One night, Sleepy Amy invited me out to play pool. She was insistent that I should get out of my apartment occasionally and do things. And that night I saw a boy. I didn't know I could do that anymore—see boys as anything but long labors and distant mothers' sons.

He was wearing dirty white overalls and plucking an upright bass underneath a spotlight on a small stage. Curly red hair slicked back with pomade. I saw him that night, and then I found out where he would be playing another night, and another. I made myself available but I didn't make any first moves. Finally we got squished together in the threshold of a door when he was between sets, and we met. I said I liked his music; it reminded me of home. It turned out he was from Tennessee, too. At the end of the show, he came over and asked how I was doing.

"I'm just," I stammered. I already liked him. "I don't know, I'm just—" I didn't know where to start. My infinite guilt, my lost son. He didn't know anything about me.

He smiled. "Let's go outside, and you can tell me how *just* you are."

I found out he had hitchhiked, homeless, through the South and up through West Virginia to the Ohio River Valley, following spirits, avoiding full moons, collecting songs and stories of early radio history along the way. Oversized and ghostly on the tiny stage, he sang sad songs; his voice was deep and low, uncertain and crackling. When he wasn't playing in bars, he would busk on the sidewalk. I realized it was him I'd heard howling on the street corner from the window of my new apartment near the university. Songs from the South that treated grief and joy with the same unsmiling reserve.

I had always tried to distance myself from that music, playing Beethoven and Liszt to escape Tennessee. But lately I was drawn to it. And Graham was an archivist of this old music; he had a tune for every tragedy.

One day we went walking around the pond where I had labored. There were ducks perched, teetering, just on the edge.

"We should kick them in," I said, I'm not sure why. I wanted something simple like meanness to solve everything.

"But they just got dried off!" Graham laughed.

"But they're ducks; they don't mind the water." I didn't really want to kick them in. We kept walking, silent.

"Or you could kick them in the air, and I could shoot them," he said sweetly.

I decided to tell him about my summer. He already knew it somehow, but he wouldn't take his eyes away for a second. After a long pause, he smiled a little, nodded his head twice, and put his hand on mine, like he was my grandfather. The particular contours of my experience were new to him, but the weight and the complexity were familiar, and he bore it like he bore the full burden of his own sadness, without the faintest hope he could make it better.

"Trials and temptations . . . ," he said to himself, like he was adding my story to his collection of sad songs. The world was a solid stack of them, trials and temptations.

Now that it was months since the adoption, people I knew were mostly reminding me that it was my decision, and what they meant was that I was disqualified from being sad about it. Graham was the only person who seemed to understand that the hardest thing about it was that it had been my decision. He had so many songs about tragedy brought on by the one who suffers it. That's precisely what true tragedy was, I remembered from Shakespeare in sophomore English. Having to live with yourself, bound for eternity to the person who hurt you most.

Back at school, I was always getting the opposite of sympathy and understanding from Jevn. One night I left a note for him. He'd finished a stage of his thesis, and I wanted to acknowledge it. *Congratulations*, it said. I left it in his studio.

"You know it's a crime to steal," he informed me as we passed in the hallway the next morning. His Wilco CD had disappeared from his desk in the night, around the time I'd left my note, and though he didn't really think I was responsible, he was letting me know he had received my note, and that I hadn't made any kind of progress with it.

I told myself Graham was better for me. He trusted me and gave space to my sadness. He also made working so hard in studio all the time seem silly. He was part of a far more honest school. Sitting in the tiny booth where he worked as a parking attendant, he read what he was compelled to read, and he'd become impassioned about Greek coins, or Hindu gods, until he read about the Civil War and became impassioned about that. He'd leap up to chase cars that left without paying, his temper as hot as his fiery red hair, and then he'd sit back down and read science books from a hundred years ago and get evangelical about obsolete theories of medicine or physics. There was so much I didn't know about him, but I knew, lying on the grass observing the clouds, that I could count on him to be just as moved as I was. To not shut up about the glow of sunset around the rims.

My studio that quarter was about solid walls, made not of studs and surfaces but of weight, brick upon brick, that collects real warmth from the sun, holds it, and releases it slowly in the darkness. I was working one afternoon at my studio desk, designing a bathroom. I remembered a sink I'd seen in Sweden at a building I paid close attention to because Jevn had told me about it many months before, before I'd even planned my trip to Europe. The spout was just the end of a pipe that emerged directly from the masonry wall, and the basin was a trough that drained to an open hole in the floor. You could easily follow the movement of the water through the walls and cavities, like the masonry was just a screen that exposed and concealed the watery nature of the world.

I felt someone standing by my desk. I took off my headphones and said hello to Megan, a girl from my program who was a year ahead of me. I wasn't sure what had happened to her. She'd begun school as a curly-haired, fun-loving kind of Goth, but she had shaved her head and now she seemed genuinely dark and pensive.

"Heyyy!" she stumbled, ultracasual. She lengthened words and ran them together. "How's it going? I was wondering, would you want to go outside for a break in a little while?"

I was always finding reasons why I should take a break in a little while. Especially when it was nearing sunset, as our school had its beautiful northwest prospect, though no windows in that direction. We pushed through my favorite doors, which were weighted to resist us with three pounds of pressure, I'd recently learned. The same amount of pressure it would take to rip someone's ear off. Everything in architecture was scaled to some multiple of human proportions.

We walked around to the grass and sat against the building. It felt like summer. A year ago I had just met Paula and Erik.

"How's your baby? Have you seen him?" Megan asked me. This was why I liked her. She didn't just ask about studio. I don't even think she cared about studio.

"Yeah, actually, look—!" I pulled out of my bag a photo that I'd just gotten from Paula. He was standing up, wearing a blue checkered business suit with shorts.

"Paula said she's dressing him badly on purpose, to keep him from getting a big head." I held the photo so that we could both see, but then Megan stayed looking at it for a long time, smiling. Then she wiped her face hard with the edge of her hand.

"You know, I was pregnant, too." She breathed deeply to keep from crying. I was surprised. I was so preoccupied with my own aloneness, it hadn't occurred to me other people were alone, too.

"I couldn't do what you did. I kept watching you. When you got bigger, I thought, the same thing should be happening to me. And—when you talk about your son, I think about what my child would be like now."

I felt like I remembered now, how curious she had been about me, all the questions she had asked that other people didn't. "You're so lucky you have this." She took the photograph from my hands and studied it. "That you can know how big he is."

I didn't know what to say. I told her I didn't feel lucky.

I talked to Jevn a few times during his final quarter. We would e-mail each other to arrange our meetings because the chance encounters, though they happened all the time, were too startling. They put us immediately in our defensive positions, which by the end of the term had dulled and deepened. But we would always find ourselves there, anyway. Angry and hurt and determined not to talk again for a while.

Then one night Jevn came into my studio and asked me to come talk in the woodshop, where he was working that evening. I followed him there, his broad shoulders swinging, angling back occasionally, awkwardly, to make small talk as we walked down the stairs. We wove through the saws into the small booth with the special equipment that had to be signed out: the small tools, the drill bits, X-Acto knives, and goggles. He pulled a metal stool in my direction. Tiny gestures like that meant so much to me. A Plexiglas window shielded us from the table saws and drill presses and planers and intake fans, all operating at full volume.

I was not sure what prompted this talk, but I knew that Jevn had something to say. Every word would be carefully chosen. I was nervous and excited. Maybe that explains why I don't remember most of it.

I do remember we were interrupted. Jevn's job was to remind people to keep blade guards in place. Not to use that drill on metal. Wear protective goggles at all times. He sometimes had to tell people when to miter, when to saw, which saw, in what sequence. When he opened the door and stepped out of our little room, I breathed. I remember feeling it was one of those fragile, precious moments, when I would have a rare, real glimpse of him. Like the first time he told me about his father. I would not gawk, or push it, or respond. It was delicate, and I was bound to break it. He returned. His arm rested long on the tabletop beside him, and his hand reached for a drill key, spinning it forward and back.

He said he was adjusting to Jonathan's position in his life every day.

"There are moments when I wish I was his dad, but the situation didn't allow for that at all, and I'm very aware of that."

Maybe this was a kind of apology? A recognition of what I'd been through, too? Did wishing he was our son's dad mean he regretted it? Or was he advising me to push away regret, the way he was doing, by reminding myself the situation didn't allow for it. Was *I* the situation? Could I have changed the situation? These were questions not to ask. I didn't ask them. Each word, carefully chosen, was only itself.

"They were taking his vital signs and weighing him on that cart," he said as he leaned forward and looked down at the key, "and he grabbed my finger for the first time. It was such a delicate—intense thing." He leaned back and scanned the workshop. "All this energy gets converted into changing me, how I think and how I act. It affects how I am with everybody. I think I'm lucky in that respect. There isn't an end. That's a powerful myth. Beginnings are just as powerful." He paused and glanced at me. "So where to begin after tragedy, here and now?"

I was afraid to say anything. I was just grateful for the moment. I was bound to ruin it by making it about us, by telling him I loved him, or something else he wouldn't believe. I told him I thought I should go. He hugged me and gave me a kiss on the cheek.

I walked away feeling heartened and full, but I only felt sure about one thing. He was actually there, the whole time.

My Phenomenology of Film professor told us he'd misspent his youth as a pool shark in Knoxville, Tennessee, and one day I brought Graham to class to meet him, knowing they would click. Then Graham started coming all the time, though he'd never been enrolled in college, to watch beautiful films in the afternoons and to discuss their phenomenology.

One day after class, Graham and I ran into Jevn in the hallway. I froze for a moment. It was just a few days after we'd spoken in the wood-shop. I wanted to give that conversation space and air. But at that moment it must have looked like it had meant nothing to me; I'd listened to him quietly and let him speak, but I hadn't mentioned I was already over everything and busy with another relationship. Jevn passed, not looking at us, sliding along the wall.

After that, he buried himself in his thesis, and soon he had intricate models at three scales and a full set of drawings drafted by hand, at the time when everyone was just starting to forget how to do that. He was done ahead of time, and while everyone else scrambled to finish, his models were put on display in the school gallery.

We would pass each other in the halls, smiling awkwardly the way we always had. You might have thought we had a secret crush on each other, that we were just getting started, but you'd have never guessed we were inextricably bound, like love and fear, in a faraway son.

Jevn was the only person I'd ever met whose work was so good, you could call it a gift. Not a gift like a talent, but a gift to the world. You could be moved by it, even if you didn't know anything about architecture. At the end of the year, I passed by his final critique. Fifteen or twenty students were gathered, watching the professors review his work. From a distance, I saw him miming the slow swing of an imaginary golf club, or maybe a baseball bat, aimed for the outfield. Technically, he was having his final presentation to determine whether he would graduate, but everyone knew he had graduated a long, long time ago. As I came closer, I realized they were not critiquing. They were just taking it all in.

"How many teams of interns did you have helping you do all this? How many models do you have? Those two and then three, four . . ."

"And you did all of these drawings by hand?" One critic stood and put his face just inches from one of the drawings.

Finally, one of the professors said something about wanting to adopt Jevn as his own son. He was just trying to express how impressed he was, but I thought that was a very strange thing to say, given what had happened.

Paula and Erik brought the kids to Ohio for Jevn's graduation, and if I had any doubt about how things would be, Jevn clarified it by e-mail a week before they arrived. It would not be like the honeymoon of our long-ago Cincinnati double dates. Jevn had tickets for Jonathan's family, and he wanted a few of his favorite professors to meet them on Friday night. He wanted either dinner or brunch with them on Saturday, before or after the graduation. He said that I could spend time with them Sunday morning. He added that he was flexible on everything, but it was very clear that we would not spend any time with Jonathan together.

I chatted with Paula and Erik in the lobby of the auditorium while they waited for Jevn to emerge after the ceremony. Friends came over and said hello and met Jonathan and saw that all of it was really true. Paula and Erik stood, cheerfully disoriented by the throngs of people who passed, being introduced, trying to remember who was who, and in between gathering and releasing their children. Jonathan was now toddling.

I got a night at the pizza place with Nina, my parents, and Paula and Erik, and Jonathan and Sarah, and breakfast Sunday morning. The rest of the time they spent with Jevn, and new lines were drawn. Jevn and I had become independent satellites of our son, with our own independent risings and settings. And then, after graduation, he packed everything up into his car—his folding bed, his Aalto vases, his long row of books— and was gone.

TWENTY-THREE

Things normalize. Things as enormous and unthinkable as the Grand Canyon become background scenery. I am a mother, the worst kind of mother. I am bound forever to Jevn, but I may never see Jevn again. I have a one-and-a-half-year-old son.

When I was seventeen, I drove across Arizona with my boyfriend. "Look to your left, after the trees," he said, to prepare me. The trees fell away and the earth opened like a mouth. It opened and kept opening. I sank into my bucket seat, grasping at its base. We were driving a rental with the top down. I felt the mouth sucking me into it.

We parked, and I processed it in fragments, looking through my fingers. There was no middle distance. Near fell instantaneously into far. The canyon sides opposite us were crisp, brickish, and steamy. The distant rim seemed at once touchable and impossibly remote.

I wanted to kick it. Or kick something into it. I wanted to watch a branch or a rock catapult down the sides, banging and rolling, to show me how here became there. My boyfriend said there were hiking trails below and you couldn't do that or you might hurt someone. And it was too big, anyway. There was really nothing you could kick into it to get a sense of its scale.

Then I wanted to kick it to express my frustration.

We got out of the car and approached the edge. Trees hovered below in island landscapes, on the ledges and rock formations along the sides of the canyon. We walked down some stairs but then the magnitude of the canyon threw off my sense of up and down, and I fell to my knees and then clung to the ground like I was hanging off a cliff. My boyfriend picked me up and carried me back to the car, where we cut open the watermelon we'd had rolling around in the trunk since Tucson and sat at a safe distance, watching birds soar over the cavity. I put on my seat belt.

I decided then that there was definitely God. At least there definitely could be God. My inability to believe it was proof of nothing. I couldn't believe the Grand Canyon, either. I was sitting beside a thing whose cool breath could give me goose bumps in the desert heat, but if I was going to keep my balance, or swallow my watermelon without choking, I had to tell myself it was lavender paint spilled across sand.

Sometimes everything seemed so big it exhausted me to process it. Other times, everything was so big I pretended it wasn't true. It could still knock the breath out of me when I thought about it, and yet it all became background, the familiar setting for the rest of my life.

Paula wrote in January to say that Jonathan had started talking. *He says "cheese," "please," "Mama," "Da-da," a very plaintive "Uh-oh," and can tell you the sounds of the dog, cow, horse, truck, lion, bird, owl, and train. And he can not only point to his eyes, ears, hair, and fingers, but also to his chin and knees. When you come to visit, I'm sure he'll know more.*

I'd imagined once he learned to talk, right away he'd tell us everything: most of all, how he felt about his adoption. But Paula was always sending stories and photographs that reminded me he was still just a baby.

She also wrote to extend a generous offer. An invitation to spend a month in North Carolina that summer. She had arranged an opportunity for me to teach an art class as part of a program for incoming students in her department. She said I could live in the dorms or they could set up the playroom for me, and then I'd have a lot of leisurely time to spend with Jonathan, who she said was at a really charming age. It was a generous invitation, but I wasn't sure how to respond. The emotional toll of a weekend with my son wrecked me for days. I would return mute and numb, with nothing to say to anyone, and I'd be derailed from my most important project: creating a life that made giving up my son make sense. That project was becoming more urgent as I neared the end of school without having found anything in architecture that seemed worth it. I couldn't possibly afford a month away.

I didn't tell Paula how difficult her offer was for me. We used to talk about these kinds of complexities, but now adoption was their life; they'd built a real family on these foundations, and talking about the difficulties would only pose the question of an alternative. Talking about it would unbuild their home by unearthing the tangled structure that supported it. Instead, I said yes, I'd figure out my internship schedule for the summer, and I'd find a way to manage a month in North Carolina. There was just that one thing more important than my architecture project, and the nearest thing to undoing my first rejection was to never say no to him again. But I told Paula I thought I would stay in the dorms; I didn't want to impose on them for such a long time, and I couldn't survive a whole month without some kind of sanctuary, myself.

School had a firm grip on me as I approached my final year. My dad's brother died that year and so did my mother's mother, but I couldn't afford the time to visit them in their last moments or to attend their funerals. Cousins got married and had babies; I heard about it all from a distance. It was never a conscious thought, but I found I couldn't prioritize my family, even in those important moments, over architecture school, because I had prioritized architecture school over my son. It was a hierarchy that had to stand, if I was going to keep moving forward.

My final year would begin that summer with my final internship. I'd gotten used to the ten-week rhythm of internships; I was always getting ready to leave. It seemed like the thing we learned more than anything: how to pack our lives into our cars and drive away. To never have too many books or too many bonds to abandon a place. To be skillful in finding temporary housing, very cheap, no leases, preferably furnished, hopefully in a not-too-dangerous part of town. While other students were building college friendships to last a lifetime, we practiced transience and adaptability. We were never in one place long enough to make it home.

The rhythm suited me. I would learn the basic coordinates of any city: the good espresso, the train station and the drafting supply shop, a three-mile running loop, and then I'd close my eyes and open them in the middle of a fast-moving world of an entirely different nature. The miniature lives I built on internship were specially made to last ten weeks. By the ninth, they would begin to fall apart, in an arc I learned to choreograph. At the end of ten weeks, I'd break the news I was leaving, and when my new friends told me how much they would miss me, I would think, you have no idea what I can live without. I turned more resolutely to my next move; I wouldn't anchor anywhere. As long as I kept moving, I would never find myself in the living room at Christmas counting who was and wasn't there. Graham understood; he'd buy a Greyhound ticket to Asheville or Augusta and disappear, himself, for weeks.

I needed my final internship to remind me what was so great about architecture. An internship at another firm looking for red, or waiting for funding, or drafting vacation houses for New Yorkers, or calibrating parking spaces to building occupancies, would only prove I'd given up my son for nothing. I didn't want to *practice* architecture, I wanted to look at it, hard.

I sent another e-mail into the ether. I made a desperate last grasp at architecture to see if there was anything there at all. I targeted archaeology departments at Italian universities. I wrote asking whether there was anyone, anywhere, who might need an assistant of some kind. Surely a summer spent unearthing architecture would be as legitimate an examination of our subject matter as any internship in an office. I only got one response: *Meet me at the duomo in Orvieto at noon on June 8. Claudio.*

I flew to Rome and took a train to Orvieto. The city was built on the top of a giant volcanic rock that propped vertically out of a broad valley bowl. There were steep cliffs from the edges of the city to the expansive plains below, and clouds raced across the valley, like a giant mirror, in shadows. I waited on the steps of the duomo, high above the surrounding plains. Several people warned me the invitation was a scam. But it was an old habit. I was open to anything. It was what Jevn most mistrusted about me.

Noon arrived, and a little old lady approached.

"Amy?" She smiled and gestured for me to follow her.

We drove down the steep streets and hairpin turns of Orvieto, across the valley and back up into a wooded hillside to her cabin. The pillow I rested on at Claudio's mother's house that afternoon was at the same elevation as the city of Orvieto. I looked out the window straight across the valley to the steps of the duomo. On its side and at this distance, Orvieto looked like a toy city. Claudio arrived in the evening and we drove to the farm an hour away where his team of archaeologists was staying.

We woke early, boiled espresso, and packed our lunches. Just as the sun was rising, we would gather on the terrace of the farmhouse, over-looking the apricot and olive groves, and caravan fifteen minutes into the hillside, where an Etruscan settlement lay deep under the pasture. We dug all day, leaving our communal plastic bottle of espresso in the sun, where it stayed warm, and took swigs as needed. Experienced diggers wore long linen sleeves, hats and scarves, but I shed clothes with the heat, hunched atop an unearthed surface of *piedra madre*. Since I wasn't trained to care about tiny coins and shards of pottery, Claudio put me in charge of exposing the large stone wall that ran along one edge of my trench. In the evening we would cover our trenches with tarps, remove our tools, and pile into the vans to the little village, where I'd order a cappuccino at the café while Claudio deposited the day's finds in the laboratory there. When we arrived back at the farm, I'd put on my running shoes and take off into the winding hills above the house until dinner, where each place was set with two wineglasses, one for red, one for white, and both would be refilled like water throughout the meal. This, I told myself, was per-fect thesis preparation. I was studying beauty.

Beauty was rarely mentioned in school; it was an unspoken by-product of good design, not its driver. But the only class I took together with Jevn was a sort of show-and-tell in which we'd describe objects we found beautiful. The drinking glass I'd found on the street: *blue, transparent, bulbous*. Those qualities were certain, but why did beauty adhere to them? Jevn brought in a spoon and showed us how pleasant it was to hold, counterweighted at the handle to balance perfectly on your index finger. *Silver. Shiny.* But beauty wouldn't be so easily captured. Even as it sat solidly within those objects, it reached far beyond them.

Beauty was why I'd left the conservatory—there were many things the world needed more urgently than music—but beauty was the only thing that made architecture worth pursuing. Long rows of repeated forms to contain infinity; solid stone and shadows to record entire arcs of days and years. Buildings could teach us to hold what we couldn't touch. Reaching for beauty, I would grasp and keep every good thing. I wouldn't have lost my son at all.

Claudio could smell rain from two days away, and he could ward it off by furrowing his brow, silently, at the horizon. He would stand sternly above me, arms folded across his chest, to inspect my work. "That one," he would say, to indicate which stone I should remove next. Only he had the authority to determine whether it was part of a wall or meaningless rubble. One day, I asked Claudio if he thought the wall was beginning to curve. If the wall curved, I would remove a certain set of stones. Or I'd remove others and the wall would disappear straight into the untouched ground beyond the trench. I was getting close to a point of decision.

"You want it to curve?" he asked.

I shrugged. If it curved, it could mean it was a temple or a monument of some kind. Or a cistern. It would seem fitting, given my many nightmares about tanks and pipes and churning water, that I'd find myself unearthing ancient plumbing. But it didn't seem professional to want something. Claudio looked hard at the wall and exhaled. He pointed firmly at one stone, and another, and told me to remove them. Making way for my indefensible desire. The wall would curve.

"Art," he said, "not science," and walked away.

That July evening I went running as usual in the hills after work. I'd just received an e-mail from Jevn, who had entered a graduate program on the East Coast. He'd just been to visit Jonathan and said he was happy to see that Jonathan and Sarah and Paula and Erik were *a truly functioning family, a rare thing.*

I'm so glad about Jon's insatiable wish to be outside, he said. *I love his laugh.*

I smiled, thinking about Jonathan exploring the world as I was. I felt connected to him as I ran, burned by the same sun as I reached ahead to grasp the beauty of the olive groves.

Soon, the sky turned black and began pouring with hailstones as big as the apricots in the trees they pummeled. Big enough to knock you out. I hid under the branches of a giant oak and then ran into a chapel nearby. Hail beat the roof like someone's fist, determined to bring it down. But soon the sun was glinting across fields of silver leaves that shuddered in disbelief. I ran back to the house, avoiding hailstones rolled in dust.

Everyone greeted me excitedly when I got back to the terrace, handing me a glass of wine and a towel to dry off. "Are you okay?" they asked. Except that they sometimes made fun of me for putting on my running shoes after an exhausting day in the field, I didn't realize they noticed my absence at sunset.

"Did you come back with Claudio?" they asked. "He went out looking for you!" We turned to the road, and his truck was still gone. Just then, it skidded into the driveway. Claudio closed the door and walked across the gravel to the terrace, ignoring us. He turned a chair backward and sat down, lighting a cigar and gazing across the tops of the trees into the distance, as though he'd been sitting there for hours. He'd been worried about me, they all said so, but he didn't so much as glance my way. And I didn't thank him for trying to rescue me from the storm, but it fixed him forever in my affection.

◎ ◎ ◎

Days later, I woke when a screen door slammed somewhere above my head. I opened my eyes and tried to make sense of where I was and who had slammed the door. North and south were spinning as I realized I was no longer in the villa in Italy. But I could be anywhere. Cincinnati, Boston, Copenhagen. No, I was in North Carolina. Not a sunburned archaeologist but a mother. And still not a mother, exactly.

It was my son who slammed the door. I was staying with Paula and Erik for a few days before moving into the dorms to start the teaching job they'd arranged. Paula told me Jonathan sometimes got up, put his coat on, and went outside to play before anyone else woke up. His *insatiable wish to be outside.*

Still lying in bed, I returned to Italy. I'd been reluctant to leave. I felt I'd started something there. A life I could love, even without Jevn, without my son. Or—with all of it, with their absences and all the complications. But time alone with Jonathan was precious, so I rolled out of bed and walked to the window. In the gray, wet warmth of early morning, he was pushing a wagon up the little lane, and then back down again.

I joined him, walked beside him, asked him how he was doing and whether he'd enjoyed his summer as much as I had. He was silent. Busy. He trudged slowly against the friction of the rough pavement, and it occurred to me he might prefer to be pushed. I felt full and happy, and I wouldn't let his seriousness intimidate me. I scooped him up and put him in the wagon. I was going to run behind him. Like a mother bird, I'd returned to him with good things I'd found far away; I wanted him to feel the wind and the dry, bumpy road beneath him, like the roads I'd run in San Venanzo. He was supposed to laugh! We were having fun! But as soon as he found himself sitting, he clasped the sides of the wagon and began to pull himself out. I stopped pushing. Gravely, he stepped over the side and returned to the back of the wagon, glancing up at me with suspicion.

I crumbled, ashamed of my sunburned skin, the Etruscan dust beneath my nails that had reawakened and revived me. While I basked in the sunset in Italy, he was here, amid the broken beginnings I'd left him. And now I was back, thinking everything should be okay, standing on the porch with banana bread. He looked at me narrowly, just like Jevn.

For the rest of the month, I visited my son after class and on weekends. Most of the time he was happy. He pronounced the words he knew like percussion. *Big!* he would say, emphatically, always in reference to a feat he'd just done or was about to do. Or as though introducing himself by a name that more fully described him. He would puff out his chest as he said it. *BIG!* And jump off the side of the couch. He would say it to get the attention of men he didn't know. Or standing tall above their Yorkshire terrier, the only thing smaller than he was.

But then sadness came suddenly, fully, and unpredictably. I'd recognize in his wrinkled forehead my own ancient and irrational sorrows. This was exactly when I would have been sent to my room, and that was where I wanted to go when I'd see it come over him. Jevn had given him a beautiful smile and a tall stature, but I'd given him clouds to overtake him without warning. And then I'd given him up and given him something to really be sad about. I wanted to hide from all of it. But Paula would grab him and pull him close and whisper something I couldn't hear. The words didn't seem to matter. What mattered was the closeness of her lips as they tangled in his earlobe. What mattered was the funny tickling, the feeling that someone was not so far away and not afraid.

His eyes would explore the room as he listened, and the clouds, with the lightness and grace of water vapor, would dissipate.

I returned to Graham, to school, and to my final year. One afternoon, I got a call from a crisis pregnancy center where I'd left my name as a volunteer. Laura was four months pregnant and wanted to talk to a birth mother about adoption. When we met, I wanted to tell her, simply: *don't.* But then I also wanted to tell her, *do it, it will work out for the best, you have your whole future ahead of you. Everything is beautiful.* Then I would be able to watch, to see if I was right. She started taking steps. She found a few couples she liked and shared their profiles with me, but it seemed she wasn't looking very hard, if she really wanted to find someone. But then maybe she knew she didn't. I was there when her labor began, and for the delivery. And I was there when she wrapped her daughter in her arms in such a way as to make us all know what she would do. And made me wonder anew about my own strength.

I was denied internship credit for my summer abroad, and over the next few months I would find a hundred other ways to delay the delivery of my diploma. I couldn't think of a proper thesis topic, and when I was given one, I could not produce a proper building. One of my thesis advisers would pet herself nervously, from the side of her neck to her sternum, at my indecision, and another told me that my last name was a curse.

Graham began teaching me to play the mandolin, and for the last few weeks of school, we'd while away afternoons by the open windows, playing together. We practiced a fiddle tune for my sister's wedding; she'd returned from China, moved to Maryland, and found a husband, all within a year. It was a Bill Monroe tune, which, I later learned, had words, and those words warned women not to get married.

I spent the summer after my graduation at an internship practicing architecture to make up for my summer spent digging it up, and before I had my diploma in hand I was accepted to a graduate program in Philadelphia for the fall. As long as I never finished, as long as there was nothing with measurable dimensions, or clean rooflines made of materials as mundane as concrete and steel, then architecture could remain a beautiful mystery, and there was still a chance it was worth it.

TWENTY-FOUR

I packed a U-Haul and started driving. My cat rode atop boxes in the front seat beside me. I'd gotten her from some kids who'd found her, named her Scarlett Victoria, and were trying to get rid of her and her kittens on the corner in front of my apartment one morning. I told them I'd take whatever they couldn't get rid of by the afternoon, and she was all they had left. A mother cat without her kittens. Her long fur was gray and brown, more matted than plush, and she had one fang missing, so her jaw closed a little crooked, and her eyes were crooked to match. She was not a Scarlett Victoria. I renamed her Haystack. I petted her to comfort her, and Cincinnati disappeared in the distance.

As I drove, I undid all my doings there. Studying architecture, meeting Jevn. The amazing fortune of finding Paula and Erik, the only parents I could imagine for my son. Without them, my son might be surfing his hand out the window beside me. And Graham. Graham had found and chased me, scaled my apartment building wall, and ripped the groceries out of my hands and spilled them across the street and then chased me until my shoes fell off before I put it together that he was an alcoholic. But it was hard to let go, as the brokenness that drove him to drink was what drew me to him. Everything else was easy to leave, bittersweet; another landscape I'd loved and lost.

I bumped over the cattle guards, and the long, pocked farm road stood vertical before me. Sheep ignored me in the pastures along the sides, but the llama raised its long neck from within a dirty white cloud of them to watch me. I rose over the hump of a bridge my father had engineered to cross the creek for eternity. Beyond the crest of the hill was the house surrounded by tomato plants and bird feeders and grapevines and compost and tractors, assembled and not, and the cast iron dinner bell, mounted ten feet high on a metal post.

"Who's there?" my grandmother called from her recliner as I closed the door. I went over and bent down so she could lift an arm over me, a kind of hug.

"Good to see you, dear, come in. Sit down."

Wheelchairs, old office chairs, once-nice living room chairs, folding chairs, all floated in aimless masses like lily pads in the brick sunroom. Grandpa came in from his work with dirty hands and pants held up by suspenders, said, "Well, hello," and sat heavily on his chair, which was softened a little by a sheepskin rug. Sheepskin softened everything at the farm. Sheepskin on chairs, sheepskin for the dogs to lie on, sheepskins wrapped around the seat posts of the farm bikes instead of seats. Big, warm tomatoes were piled on the card tables beside giant cylinders of salt and knives of different shapes and sizes, rusty blades ground sharp enough for Grandpa to shave his arm hair off with them, as he would demonstrate with pride. Flies populated the walls and surfaces, and flyswatters, the old screen kind and new plastic ones, in different states of repair, were always within an arm's reach. Sheepdogs filled whatever space was left over.

Grandma was largely immobile, but she could put herself in her wheelchair to roll herself to the bathroom or to the computer, where she could forward good and bad and sometimes tasteless jokes to her family and friends, and she liked nothing more than a good story in return. From her recliner, she welcomed guests to sit and talk, and because her favorite topic was theology, often they were pastors or people from the church she could no longer get out of the house to attend. Whether theology or romantic dilemma, she would advise you to *broaden* your thinking. She'd grumble that phrase like faraway thunder, and she might roll into your shins in her wheelchair to show you how much she meant it. Sometimes she was blunt; she claimed she always said things with the best of intentions, but she couldn't be responsible for what happened after words left her mouth.

She was telling me about an e-mail she'd just read from one of her friends. "Some of my friends think that God has a body, but they also like George Bush!" She raised one eyebrow, glared at me, and relaxed it. "Love them anyway, even if they are totally mixed up."

Her wardrobe was limited to a few giant dresses with wide straps but no sleeves, all of them cotton faded to lavender-gray and worn to silky softness. She'd had a hernia for fifty years she didn't think worth the money to fix, and her right shoulder continually fell out of its socket, so she'd learned to use her left hand to maneuver the computer mouse. Dirt collected in all the edges of that mouse as it sat in the sun on the card table or nested between articles from *The Washington Post* she was saving for you to read when you got there.

She didn't think I should be moving to Philadelphia. She didn't see why I needed another degree, much less one in *landscaping*.

"Landscape architecture," I corrected her. My architecture history professor had told me that if I really wanted to understand architecture, I should start by studying the history of the garden. She told me not to worry about my accumulating student loans; they were a fact of modern life. I'd called Jevn, who was living in New York, to talk about the programs offered at different schools, and he'd helped me pick.

My grandmother speculated about how such a degree might help the homeless, which was what she had hoped my degree in architecture would do.

"I have a very unfavorable idea," she said. "I wonder how it could be implemented. A park for the homeless."

My grandpa breathed heavily, jaw half-open, eyes shut, head falling slightly back.

She continued, "A welcome atmosphere of benches which do not contain bars across the middle! Blankets to be borrowed and returned; comfortable seats to overlook the water. Maybe you wouldn't want to walk there after dark, but you ought to be home anyway."

My uncle Mick came in and said hello; then he continued back to the kitchen to make lunch. He and my aunt lived a tenth of a mile up the driveway and took care of Grandma and Grandpa. Grandma could no longer get to the kitchen, her movements restricted for the past five years to the sunroom, which had been added on to the house by my grandfather. She had determined the size and shape of the room based on where she thought she would like to sit and what she would like to look at while sitting, for the rest of her life. She could see cars coming up the driveway, tomatoes growing right along the windows in wire cages. She could see people coming in the door. And she could put her washcloth over her eyes and see nothing, while she listened to books on tape.

She was probably sitting there when my sister told her about the adoption, and when she forgave me and called me to tell me so. She would begin sending e-mails to Paula and Erik from that seat, and she'd be sitting there when she finally met my son.

"A warm building containing cheap, nourishing food, at every park," she continued. "Rice, noodles, beans sorts of things. But perhaps no fast food. Board games to be borrowed. A system of coupon payment in exchange for work done maintaining the park. Warm showers."

Grandpa opened his eyes and oriented himself.

"Was that Mick's truck?—*Dammit*, Helen!"

Grandpa always thought that Grandma had interrupted him. From the angle of their chairs, he couldn't see that her mouth had always already been moving. Grandma ignored him and lowered her voice and her chin to capture my undivided attention.

"Have you ever been told about how I got your grandfather to marry me?"

Grandpa leaned forward and put a folded fifty dollars in my hand. "Get yourself an apartment in Philadelphia," he said quietly, and leaned back. My grandmother's advice would be just as useful.

"I sat on him, when he was reclining on the settee, and pounded on him." She opened her eyes wide. "And now we've been married sixty-nine years and have had four children, one of whom died at age fifty-three, and fourteen grandchildren all told. And a bunch of great-grandchildren, but I'm too befogged to count. So you see it was effective for me to sit on him and pound. Is there a suggestion here for you?" She dropped her chin, her gray eyebrows growing wild, her jowls hanging low. "Forget about graduate school! I suggest you go after a man, and get him to the altar, and let him think about it later at his convenience."

"I'm going to landscape school, Grandma!" I said. Marriage and family were an infinity away. I couldn't possibly think about settling down and starting a family just three years after giving up Jonathan. Hadn't we all agreed I had a whole future in architecture ahead of me?

My uncle, slicing himself a tomato, weighed in. "Give me thirty thousand dollars; I can show you how to dig a hole and stick a tree in it." Uncle Mick was a blacksmith and a mason and a farmer and an inventor. He was best friends with my father when they were kids. They spent summers taking junked cars apart; they'd saw off the roofs and throw a cupful of gasoline and a match inside to remove the paint and upholstery. They'd race those cars through the woods, ragged metal edges right at eye level, and they spent many afternoons tormenting my father's sister, who later became Mick's wife. He was always skeptical about my big ideas. Vegetarianism, architecture, landscaping.

"It's not landscaping!" I insisted. "It's grad school. It's a really good program. I want to teach, or do research, or—"

"Tell me what you want, I'll tell you how you can live without it," my grandmother said. "Now, you may have already told me this, but I'm in the over-eighty group; when was the last time you saw Jonathan?"

I sighed, but I was grateful for this question. My grandmother was the only one who asked about Jonathan. Not Paula and Erik, not North Carolina. Jonathan.

"Just a few weeks ago," I told her. "He's walking and talking now. He turned three in July! Paula said they were making him a Spider-Man cake."

Paula had written to tell me she was thinking about me on Jonathan's birthday. They had hosted a combined birthday party for Erik and Jonathan. Paula said, "He'll now tell you very proudly that he is *free*."

"—but what a blessing they aren't possessive or feeling threatened," Grandma said as she moved some of the pile of newspapers on her side table.

"There it is, did you see that one?" She handed me a photo Paula had sent her. Jonathan wearing a green Windbreaker. "A beautiful child."

I handed it back to her. I knew that wasn't a compliment; she was saying it as a matriarch, her grandchildren her own accomplishment. Mick gave her a plate of food, and she positioned it atop her hernia like it was a table.

Her perspective about Paula and Erik had changed over time, as she'd gotten to know them through letters. They corresponded about theology and family, my grandmother's favorite things. After my uncle's death, she'd been looking for homes for his three youngest children because his ex-wife had been incarcerated. Grandma suggested that perhaps Paula and Erik might be interested in taking more Seek children, "seeing as they're doing such a good job with the one they have." I knew they were considering a third child, but I thought it would be strange for Seeks to outnumber them in their own home. Then it really would be like we adopted them, not vice versa. I mentioned it to Paula in passing, but I didn't want to be involved in the adopting side of anyone's adoption.

"They're unusual for adoptive parents," my grandmother said. "Most adoptive families are so on the edge of panic, they don't want contact. But so much can be added to the lives of those children if they don't build walls."

Grandma looked down the driveway to see another truck pulling up. It was Tunie, returning from her day job at the library. She passed without turning her head, on her way up the driveway to her own house. Mick wished me luck in Philadelphia, pulling the door closed behind him. Grandma lifted her plate for a moment and tugged the afghan up to her chin.

"We'll get him back, don't worry." She was not looking at me.

"What are you talking about?" I objected. "I'm not *trying* to get him back." Was I supposed to be trying to get him back?

"We'll get him back." She salted her sliced tomato. It was as certain as the sun would rise behind the dinner bell to her right and set somewhere over her left shoulder.

"He's legally theirs!" I was insistent. It had given me some comfort to know that my grandmother had come to terms with the adoption. If she, who had taken it so personally, could finally accept it, I could, too. My son one of the many things she could tell me how to live without. But if she'd only come to terms with it by telling herself it was somehow temporary or undoable, then there was no comfort at all. Getting him back could not be my only hope. I had to *not* get him back and keep going. *That* was the challenge. "I don't have any right to him. I signed away my rights! It's the *law*; it's not up to me!"

Grandma put her plate on the side table, where she kept a little bag of Dove chocolates, and settled herself to take a nap. I wondered about Uncle Johnny's birth mother, whether my grandmother knew anything about her, but I thought I knew the answer: he just showed up in the shed and stayed. Back then, there was no mother.

"Yes, but he is a Seek child," she said, "and he belongs with the Seeks."

"How would I even *do* that?" I scooted toward her in the squeaky metal office chair. She was folding her washcloth to put over her eyes. "Grandma! Do you understand that he's happy there? He has a sister; they're a family. I don't even want to take him back! It would be cruel."

"I don't know any of the legal aspects. I'm in the over-eighty group. It's not that I don't love you, dear, I do, but it's time for my nap."

She lay back in her recliner beside Grandpa, fast asleep in the places each of them would die. I was left alone in the silent, sun-drenched room, air conditioner feebly battling the heat stored deep in the red brick floor. A pack of my grandpa's yellow Carefree gum on his side table. Sheep baaaed in the pasture outside, and every now and then someone could be heard yelling over a tractor.

◎ ◎ ◎

I rented the cheapest apartment I could find within walking distance of the design school, sight unseen and in a bad neighborhood of a city I'd never set foot in until that day. My sister drove up from her new home in Maryland to help me settle in. We shopped together and then cooked together, and by the time she left, I felt like that tiny apartment, so small I'd have to roll a futon onto the floor every night to sleep, was home. For my first few weeks, I'd return to the places we'd gone together, buoys of familiarity within the sea of the new city. Like the checkout area of the Trader Joe's, where we had laughed so hard we crouched over and cried, and I felt as a consequence that that checkout area belonged to us.

School began the day after she left. Our studio desks were arranged in cubicles beneath sawtooth skylights that framed the shadowless blue sky. Sometimes a cloud might pass to suggest the world was turning. We designed vast cityscapes, rethought waterfronts of well-established cities, made attractions of militarized international border zones, and transformed industrial wastelands into bird sanctuaries and parks. We did not speak of flowers or trees; our profession was public space: the plazas and parks and open spaces you think of when you think of a city. It was not what I imagined, but it was interesting, and still, my curiosity veered toward the actual city surrounding us, which I would explore on foot as often as I could get out of studio.

I ran through my neighborhood, across the bridge and beside the river. Along the way, there were bronze plaques in out-of-the-way places, cast in nondescript sidewalks and affixed to bench backs, that said *This space not yet dedicated*, as if to offer those places up, to say the city was ripe for the picking; every corner waited to be claimed. I began to feel I was doing that; being part of the city, making it mine.

For one thing, I got a part-time job at a radio station. Listening to local musicians' demo tapes and pulling the best for airplay. One morning, as I removed some folders from the file cabinet, the receptionist pointed at my waistline in the back. "What *is* that?" she asked. I was still wearing the undies that had stretched with my stomach when I was pregnant, and it appeared some of the extra fabric was hanging out of my jeans. The next day, and many days after, there were little gift bags of underwear greeting me at my desk in the morning. Tiny lace thongs and zebra-striped pink-bowed short shorts like I'd never seen. Another day, she told me I should go out with Thomas, the guy who ran the other radio station in the building. "He's hot," she explained. I found out that on his off days, he was doing renovation work in a run-down neighborhood north of mine, and I offered to help him. We poured concrete and hammered shingles and lay wood floors and went swimming in the river farther north. After a few weeks of periodic manual labor, we were sitting side by side on his couch. I was wrapping my arms around my legs, folded into the hollow where Jonathan had been. Gingerly, he kissed my elbow and then apologized. He wanted to get close to me, but he sensed my reserve. I didn't have room for another person, another heartbreak.

I stayed afloat in school, but I fell in love with the city. As I ran, I stirred the big soup of me, all the things I loved and longed for, all the things I couldn't contain at once, embraced in the swinging of my arms. The city really began to feel like home when, like the Romans, I had augured a route around it, and for me that route became the city walls, as solid as stone, and everything within it I felt like I was somehow protecting.

Just as I was starting graduate school, Paula wrote to tell me that Jonathan had started preschool. She said he was reluctant to go, and so she read him a story about a raccoon mother who left a kiss on the baby raccoon's hand so that he could press it to his cheek if he felt lonely.

"I pulled out my lipstick," she said, "and left him with a big 'Sangria Sunset' kiss on his palm, and then he was happy."

These images I had of Jonathan bore ever less resemblance to the shadow he cast in me. There was him beaming brightly up at the camera in the black-and-white photos Paula sent, and there was the numbness I carried around the design school and said nothing about. There was him laughing with Sarah as I chased them around the house during a rainstorm last time I visited, them skidding in their socks and shrieking with delight. And there was my ambivalence when Thomas tried to get close to me. As my grief sank to inaccessible depths, my son grew more and more self-assured. I didn't feel any need to reconcile them. I simply felt I was looking at my son from a great distance. I let things divide and separate; the real boy Jonathan couldn't teach my sadness to go away, and I tried not to bring my sadness to bear on my relationship with him.

I thought by then they had probably begun to tell Jonathan the whole story. Adding detail as he grew and as his curiosity and understanding allowed, the way they did it with Sarah. Hearing she'd come out of her birth mother's belly, Sarah became fascinated with childbirth itself, and maybe because she saw me more often than her own birth mother, Paula told me she'd suggested Sarah save her childbirth questions for me. She would put a doll in my lap and ask me to give birth to it. She couldn't frame her question. It wasn't, Did it hurt? It wasn't, How long does it take? She just wanted to see it, as if watching it happen might help her understand what it all meant. I'd put the baby under my shirt and moan and groan like they do on television. Sometimes I'd be sitting on the sofa, deep in labor and about to deliver the baby, and Sarah would leave the room altogether, her question, somehow, or at least for the time being, answered.

But Jonathan wasn't interested in those things. He knew I was his birth mother, and that made me somehow special and specially his; I just couldn't tell how much he understood about what that meant. But I didn't want to interrupt a story in progress, one that was Paula and Erik's to tell. They knew his sensitivities and the best words to explain it. And they'd be there to answer his questions or comfort him, hours, or days, or weeks later.

That Christmas, in an effort to understand what I was going to graduate school for, my father took an interest in a diagram he found in one of the books I'd left by the fireplace. When he was not tending to the fire, he read that all soil could be divided into varying proportions of sand, silt, clay, and loam. Doubting this, he went outside and took a shovelful of frozen earth. He put it on a cookie sheet and into the oven to dry, and then he spread it across the table where my mother would have very much liked to set Christmas dinner. He pounded it lightly with a hammer to break it apart. He planned to put it into a jar and shake it until the component parts layered themselves, but he left it there for days, pounding it occasionally until after I'd returned to school, where in fact very little of my work had to do with soil.

I never thought about actually getting Jonathan back, but I often wished he could be there when my family was together. I wanted him to join us on our hikes in the woods. I wanted him caught between my brother and me, stringing the lights; I wanted him sprinkling Christmas cookies with my mother and sister, or stocking firewood with my dad. I wanted him captured in our web, held tight by everyone. But since he had his own family to get tangled up in, I just wanted my family in Tennessee to miss him. Or at least notice that he wasn't there. But then he had never been there, except the Christmas he was still within me.

I visited his family instead, before returning to school. After three and a half years, my relationship with Paula and Erik hadn't changed, though their circumstances were always changing. With Paula no longer bound to North Carolina for her doctoral work, they'd started applying for jobs in Chicago and other cities. I knew they were working toward a third adoption, maybe sending their Dear Birth Mother letters and corresponding with potential matches, but I didn't ask about it. They stayed in touch with my family, and I'd even heard that my aunt and uncle had visited them after the wool festival in North Carolina. As it was relayed to me, they just showed up on Paula and Erik's doorstep and were welcomed in. I could imagine the way Paula would laugh in surprise, delighting in exactly the strangeness that might make another family uncomfortable about the whole situation.

I visited every three or four months; usually I initiated it, but if too much time passed, they would. The days I spent with them seemed to unfold largely as they might have without me. Everyone dispersed casually throughout the house, unless there was a church service or an event to pile into the car for. If we were home, I'd often spend hours sitting in the living room or standing in the kitchen talking with Paula. Sometimes I felt like talking to her was the best way to catch up with Jonathan. She was always giving me funny stories and insights into his personality, a long-exposure image of him I wouldn't get myself on a quick weekend visit. But I'd always ask just as many questions about Sarah, or about Paula's sisters and a few of her friends I'd met. Visiting meant reuniting with everyone.

And I'd always spend a lot of time playing with the kids in the living room. Blocks or hide-and-seek, or anything we could come up with. I loved the moments Jonathan would inadvertently touch my skin, rolling a car over my arm or holding steady as he stepped over his toys. I'd keep still like he was a butterfly that didn't know it had landed on a person. I thought if I budged—it's *me* you're perched on—he might get scared and run away. His four fingertips on the top of my hand, the slight weight of his body against my upper arm. In those moments I'd remember there was a place only we had been and questions only we shared. But I was careful not to look at him in a way that bridged back to that place, and I was careful to make sure no one saw me thinking about those things. He'd go back to his blocks, always intent on his task, and I'd quietly catch my breath, there on the futon or cross-legged on the floor across from him. Then one of those times when we were playing in the living room, he crawled into my arms and said, "Amy, pretend I'm your baby." He put his thumb in his mouth and waited, looking right up at me.

I trembled—helpless and terrified, wondering whether he knew, or what he was saying, or what it all meant. But there was no time for questions. I held still and listened, making sure no one was nearby before I indulged his request, pulling him close and gazing down at him like he was my baby, my entire body shuddering at the chance to hold him like that for the first time since his adoption.

I was pretty sure Paula and Erik knew about those moments, because so often they would retreat to their offices, or they'd have somewhere they had to take Sarah, or they'd send me off for walks in the woods alone with Jonathan. When I got back to Philadelphia, Paula wrote to say that after I hugged them goodbye, Sarah and Jonathan climbed onto the couch and stood on their knees, looking out the window and watching me go. Sarah said, "I love Amy," and Jonathan responded, "No, *I* love Amy." My son had never said that to me, so it felt like a big deal to hear about it, even if they were just kids. I could picture them there, noses pressed against the window, trying to make sense of the world together. It was funny to think of love that way, as if one person's love could inch over and threaten someone else's. Yet it was the very conception of love we had to overcome to do what it was we were trying to do—and I was still surprised Paula had shared that story.

TWENTY-FIVE

Days before my sister's first baby was born, she was consumed with housework, finishing the tasks she knew she'd find difficult after the birth, but over the phone I asked her to pause for a minute to think: she was about to become a *mother*. Everything she cared about—her values and priorities, her relationships to her friends and family, her capacity for love and sacrifice—was about to change. And not because of the new responsibilities of parenthood, but because of a physiological event. If she was vigilant, she might catch a rare glimpse of primordial motherhood at the moment it implants itself, or rips open her heart, rending new cavities to make way for an unwieldy and excruciating and impossible new love. But she could easily miss it amid the flurry of contractions, and pushing, and midwives, and gifts, and then caring for the new baby. I'd missed it because I wasn't expecting it, and now it was among my most pressing questions: What is motherhood, exactly?

My sister sighed and said she had to paint the picnic tables. Cyan blue because that's the only paint they had at the store, and then she was going to put in the lettuce, which meant getting out the rototiller, and turn the compost. But she said she might think about it after that if she had time.

Within a few days, a few hours before my final landscape paper was due, she went into labor. I packed my research materials and my laptop and drove down to Maryland to be present for the birth. I timed contractions sitting at the edge of her bed, laptop teetering on my folded leg. But I found myself wondering what I was there for. She was going to get to keep her child. She would have a beautiful birth and then a beautiful life as a family to follow. There were no comforts I could give her that weren't already hers. And then Jacob was born, pale and blond and skinny like Jonathan, my parents' first legitimate grandchild.

That summer, Jonathan turned five, the perfect age to start to really enjoy doing dangerous things, and that was why my father suggested we all meet in Virginia to take a ride in the glider. It would also be a chance for a Seek Family Wave-Off before my move to San Francisco, where I'd accepted a design job. I invited Paula and Erik, but they had a full summer ahead of them. They were relocating to Boston for new teaching positions in the fall, but before the move they'd be traveling to Florida to visit Sarah's birth mother as well as Paula's parents and to Indiana for "Cousin Camp," where all ten or so grandkids canoed and swam and rode horses and otherwise hung out on Erik's parents' farm. And, the biggest event of all, they'd just finalized the adoption of their third child, Andrew, so they were busy getting him settled into the family. Between everything, they were packing and saying goodbye to their old home. It would be a lot to coordinate a trip to rural Virginia just to take a ride in a motorless plane. Nevertheless, they made it to the glider field.

My son was supposed to be the first passenger. He was beginning to look like a little boy in his red polo shirt. He was lanky and tall, white bangs trimmed straight across his forehead in a bowl cut Paula executed herself, using an actual bowl, but his head was always falling back in a wide, cheeky smile. In the shade of the open hangar, we unhooked the bungee cords that kept the cover tight over the curved glass of the canopy. The plane was seamless and smooth—bright white fiberglass, with long, narrow wings extending from the swell of the body at the middle. We rolled the glider by its wings onto the lawn, where my dad popped the latch, lifted the heavy glass lid by its frame, and began to show Jonathan the gears and sticks and knobs and pedals inside. My dad had learned to fly after returning from France in the sixties, and, fascinated with the pure physics of it, he joined a glider club in Virginia, where he and my mother first settled. The airfield was a three-hour drive from where they ended up in Tennessee, but flying was one of the few things my dad would take a whole Saturday off of work to do.

Under the bubble of the glass, the glider had a front seat and a back-seat, enough space for a pilot and a passenger, but when we were little my sister and I would ride strapped together in the back, with pillows to elevate us so we could see. When Dad would tilt the wing, my sister would tell me it was because I wasn't sitting up straight enough, and I might make us go completely over if I wasn't careful. My father tilted one way, then the other, steeper and steeper, and asked me over his shoulder and over the noise of the air rushing through the windows, to stop leaning. I bore flying like many things my father exposed me to, with no certainty I wasn't going to get killed.

Sometimes, he would pull the stick straight back and ascend until the plane stopped, vertical in midair. The nose would turn down and free-fall fast toward the ground, spinning like a top. He'd have to pull back on the stick fast enough that he wouldn't hit the ground (certain death), but not so fast that the force of the change in direction would rip the wings off (certain death). Pilots had to be able to do this trick to maintain their licenses, but I begged my dad not to do it with me in the plane.

We finished the tour of the plane, but Jonathan, seated and strapped into the backseat, decided that he was too scared to go up. And to my surprise, my dad didn't push it; he must have been uncertain about his privileges as birth grandfather. I wondered if he considered himself a grandfather to Jonathan at all. Instead of flying, Jonathan sat in the back of the plane while my dad told him about how they would fly someday, and how he would let Jonathan take the controls when they did. Which was true. You'd be soaring over mountaintops and he'd wiggle his hands in the air unsettlingly, to say, *I'm* not flying this plane—I hope you are!

While Paula and Erik each took flights, Jonathan and Sarah took turns driving me and my mother around in the golf cart that was normally used to tow planes to and from the grassy runway. Jonathan couldn't catch his breath from laughing as he floored it across the open field. When the afternoon ended, I tried to convince myself that it was enough. Enough time with my family, enough contact with the thing my father enjoyed most in the world. Enough contact with my father, just to be there in the place he loved so much.

The next day, we took a walk in the woods before going our separate ways. Dad helped Sarah spatula a wriggling snake onto a stick to examine it. While everyone else stood in a circle watching, Jonathan gently took my hand and led me away, into the woods. He explained that what my father was doing was very dangerous, and he kept looking back to gauge our distance from them until he was confident we'd reached safety. Paula told me he sometimes wore a toy football helmet around the house, just because it made him feel secure. I didn't want him to feel so fearful, but I was happy to be rescued from my father, and I was honored it was me Jonathan chose to save.

When the snake got away, we all wandered down to the creek where I'd been catching frogs and crawdads between glider flights since I was born. It was wide as a street and shallow as a bathtub, and the clear water made hunting easy. Tall trees shaded the water, but there were generous openings where the sun streamed in and deep pockets in the creek farther down where you could swim. We all rolled up our pants and stepped in, and my dad showed the kids how to skip rocks.

"Pick a really flat one," he told them, "like this one here."

The kids stood on their tippy-toes to see what my dad had in his hand. He cast it across the creek, and it popped up one, two, three, four times.

"Here's one!" Jonathan handed it to my brother. Because he was a white-water raft guide through high school, my brother read rivers like my dad read skies, but it was my father who'd taught him how to skip rocks. My brother threw it. One, two, three skips. Jonathan went looking for more. When he reached his hand to the shallow bottom, he was almost completely submerged.

Paula and Erik let the new baby wade in the creek with the others. Andrew was big and heavy with tan skin and curly hair. He cuddled into you and didn't cry easily, and he had a satisfying give when you squeezed him. He looked perpetually just-woken and wide-eyed, perfectly unbiased and open to anything. They had adopted him at nine months old. I didn't know the details about the adoption: his birth mother's situation, how they found her, or whether it had been as hard for her as it had been for me. Paula told me, but I guess I didn't want to think about it. I was just happy my son had a little brother.

Even though they had a long drive ahead of them, Paula and Erik let the kids get completely wet, let them run on the rocks, get muddy and destroy their day's clothes. This gave my father so much satisfaction. He said his parenting philosophy had been: when in doubt, increase freedom. He didn't have a single piece of advice for improving Paula and Erik as parents. He noted this quietly from his lawn chair, planted right in the middle of the stream beneath the trees, while they skipped rocks in the creek beyond us. I sat beside him, beside my mother. His pants were rolled up and his feet rested on a rock, half in and half out of the water. He smiled as he watched Andrew creek-walk up to his waist, his diaper floating loosely behind him. Then he got up and took Jonathan's hand and led him up the creek, balancing on slippery stones. It looked very much like my dad was the one who might fall.

◎ ◎ ◎

I flew to California in August, and for the rest of the summer I sat at the front of a vast open office with desks arranged like seats on a bus. Each landscape architect faced the back of the next one's head and only befriended them via e-mail. Taking lunch, social conversation, and hobbies were all frowned upon. Our work was so exactly not about horticulture, we weren't even allowed houseplants at our desks. There were no siestas or summer Fridays as you might have hoped, from the little you knew about California, and nobody left work early to go surfing. Happy hour was held in-house on Fridays and meant bottled beer in the windowless conference room, after which some people would go home, but many kept working. What was exciting was that I would be getting a paycheck on a regular basis, and I could start paying back several years of school debt.

I was introduced to the project I'd be working on by its project manager, who took over my very large desk with drawings and folders and trace paper. Over his shoulder the windows faced south and the hill rose along the side of the building. As people walked by, the long, horizontal window framed first their heads, and then their coffees, and then their knees. The project was a five-hundred-acre decommissioned military air base we would be converting into a park. We were competing against other design firms to win the project. I asked if we had any particular concept, some kind of an angle.

"Blue." Mark put a few sheets of trace paper down on my desk, diagrams drawn in marker. Red scribbles to indicate a circulation system, paths and trails and roadways and plazas, across the park. Blue scribbles for lakes and canals. Green scribbles for landscape typologies—woodlands, meadows, lawns. I was to make the scribbles into digital lines.

"Here, start with that." He began to walk away.

"Wait, but blue is the idea?"

"It's about water." He turned back around. "Recycled stormwater, recreational water, water for wayfinding. Yeah; blue. I think Hong Joo has space for an exploded axon, so build the diagrams as layers in one Illustrator file."

He disappeared up the stairs. Upstairs was where most of the senior people worked. Out their windows, you could see the round peak of Potrero Hill, and you could easily slip out the back door to get a coffee, and everyone would think you were just going to the bathroom. Unless you turned left, in which case the downstairs staff would see your knees, and your waist, and then your head, and know you'd probably be coming back with a coffee.

I'd brought one suitcase and a little duffel bag–like cat carrier containing Haystack, mutely acquiescent beneath the seat in front of me on the plane. I was accustomed to leaving. What was strange was that this was a permanent position, which meant I had no particular plans to leave again once I got there. I left thirty-three boxes in Tennessee. I left a piano there, too. Thomas had gotten it for me as a surprise, and it was so heavy, it took eleven water polo players from his team to get it into my tiny apartment. We put it where my kitchen table used to be. Hauling it back to Tennessee, I warned Dad that we'd need help getting it into the house, but he planned a system of tangled pulleys and ropes and, for show, had Mom tug it into place with her pinky.

I looked out the window at states I'd never thought about, and all those states were real: Missouri, Iowa, Nevada. They meant real distance from my life on the East Coast. I thought it might be better this way. The geographical distance would release me from any impulse to reconcile those two realities, my life with and without my son. Now far away, when I saw him, I'd be able to focus on him fully, and when I returned to California, I could be fully present there, doing the job I'd given him up to do.

At around seven one evening, Mark called my extension to take my dinner order; for the tenth night in a row, we were getting delivery. When we worked past eight, we got dinner paid for by the office; one of the perks that kept people working well past dinner every night. I asked for the pad thai, and then my cell phone rang. It was my father, calling from the East Coast.

"Th-this is Walter. Am I calling at a bad time?"

"I'm still at work!" The sun had set far beyond the rise of the hill to my right, and I'd missed it entirely. One thing I'd hoped: that once I got out of school, I'd leave work at a reasonable hour and have time for other things. I hoped that living on the West Coast, I'd see some sunsets.

"Oh! *Goodgoodgood!* I'll—I'll leave you alone. Do me a favor, call me when you get to a good stopping point. Bye now." It was exactly what my dad wanted to hear: I had a meaningful career that promised some level of financial security. I wasn't a single mother, and I wasn't eating dog food. All his fears about my future relieved. Unmitigated disaster, mitigated.

Several hours later I was still at work, revising diagrams, editing photomontages. At about five in the morning, I found myself on the concrete floor beside the printer, looking at the ceiling, wakened by the sound of the refrigerator door slamming shut.

"You're awake!" Brian said. He was carrying his coffee out of the long bar of a kitchen, its gray cupboards stocked with artificial sweeteners, coffee filters, and tiny packets of soy sauce. The printer was full of pages I was going to retrieve and collate for the proposal booklets. I'd fallen asleep waiting for them to print.

"We decided to leave you, thought you probably needed the sleep."

I told Paula about the beautiful landscape but all the late nights at work when she picked me up from the airport and asked, "How's California?" Jonathan had been smiling at me through the reflections in the back window as I approached the car carrying Jevn's old blue duffel bag.

"And how are you doing?" I turned back to look at him. He was wearing a bright blue Superman shirt. He asked if I wanted to see how high he could count. He made it slowly to twenty. Paula explained that by the time they got to Boston, it was too late to enter the kids into public schools, but since Erik had flexibility in his new teaching schedule and she could make time while she was finishing her dissertation, they decided to try homeschooling.

"Mom, after twenty, what is it?"

Paula was looking hard across me to see if she could make a left turn.

"One second, Jon, I'd rather not have an accident if possible!"

She pulled out, waving breezily at the two lanes of traffic that had made way for us. She did not forget his question.

"Twenty is a two with a zero beside it, right? Well, after twenty, you start over, with a two with a one beside it, and then a two with a two beside it. So twenty-one, twenty-two, twenty-three. Just like you did after the number ten."

There was a long pause in the backseat, and I could see my son in the rearview mirror, looking to the side, out the window. I was sure this lesson was too complicated to convey without props and paper and everyone's full concentration. He squinted, thinking hard. But then his head fell back and he smiled, "Ohhhhh! I get it!"

"That's what this homeschooling movement is—actually, we've learned Boston is a kind of mecca for it! It's funny, as if homeschooling isn't radical enough, they call it *un*schooling. There's no curriculum; you just take advantage of opportunities, according to the child's natural curiosity. And one of the great benefits, we've realized, is that without the time spent getting in line, and passing out work sheets, and disciplining troublemakers, there's so much more time in the day for the kids to just concentrate on playing and being kids."

They always approached new ideas with the exact right amounts of enthusiasm and thoughtfulness and skepticism and humor.

"I thought I was going to use homeschooling as an excuse to go see all the historic sites in Boston this year," she said. "I had no idea I was going to be thinking so much about what being educated means!"

We arrived at their new home, an upright two-story house with a big front porch. When we got out of the car, my son stood tall, higher than my waist and way too big to pick up. He hugged me, and I realized I hadn't anticipated the loss of the sustained contact we'd had when I could hold him. It was just lost, between one visit and another. He led me to the kitchen, where Erik gave me a hug and said hello, and where a chess-board was set out, ready to play. Jonathan challenged me to a game.

"I can't believe you know how to play chess!" Between one visit and the next, there were things lost and things gained.

Jonathan said that I could go first. "That gives you the advantage," he informed me. My father had taught me how to play, and just as he had, I made my moves with great deliberation. Part thinking hard, part pure intimidation. I cunningly calculated as many moves ahead as I could process. But just as I released my pawn, my index finger the last to lift off, Jonathan moved his like it was hot to the touch. "Your go." I glanced at him, skeptically, and then examined the board. With every move, I was setting a trap, like my dad had done mercilessly to me. My hand lingered over my knight as I surveyed the threats of the new terrain. As soon as I let go, Jonathan's bishop sped across the board.

"I know what you're trying to do," he said, narrowing his eyes at me.

I looked up at him and smiled. "I don't think you do."

But I was bluffing—he probably did know, exactly, what I was trying to do. That's why, when his brother and sister stuck out their tongues and made crazy faces for my camera, squeezing each other out of the frame, he was always shying away from the lens. He'd turn warily to me as I played with my phone, trying to take a photo when he wasn't looking— "Are you taking a picture?" he'd ask, and then I'd put it away. He seemed hurt, as if he knew I was going to parade photos of him to my friends; all the pride of a mother without the loyalty. His guarded looks weakened me; they filled me with fear. He'd been recording every wrong since his birth, and now that he was fully articulate, he could demand an explanation. He might tell me how angry he was that I left in the first place and that I was always leaving, back to school, or back to work, or now to California. And yet, as terrifying as it was, only in such a moment would I be free to tell him how much I wanted to have him with me.

Paula called us into the dining room to eat. We gathered around the table, and Sarah directed me to sit beside her.

"But she's *my* birth mother," Jonathan said.

"Amy's sitting next to Jonathan," Erik affirmed by setting a wineglass at my place.

We had pasta with vegetables for dinner. It wasn't a big bowl of food; they didn't seem to eat very much. I had begun to pack a few of my own things, a couple of apples, a bag of almonds, because over the course of a weekend there I often found myself hungry. I was used to eating much more. In California, I hosted extravagant breakfast parties—there were eggs and potatoes and crepes and a fancy rhubarb drink I got out of a magazine and big fruit salads and banana bread. Cooking was a way of caring about everything and everyone at once. It was how I cared about the groundwater and the topsoil and about my new friends in California. It was one of the ways I'd cared for Jonathan when I was pregnant—and it was hard to watch him pick listlessly at his food.

But it was not for me to say anything, there, at the dinner table. It was also not for me to say alone to Jonathan, either, that I thought he should eat more vegetables and complex carbohydrates and good fats. What did I know about getting a child to eat, anyway?

Over the weekend, I'd take opportunities to send texts to friends and orient myself to the horizon of my life on the other coast. And when nighttime fell, I savored a few moments brushing my teeth in the bathroom alone. It was then I'd notice that when it came to housekeeping, Jonathan's family was like my grandmother, who—aside from basic upkeep of the rooms neighbors might see—could think of many things more important to do than move dust around, endlessly. Or maybe this was just what having three young kids and two meaningful careers looked like. There were sticky places from spilled mouthwash and lotions and toothbrushes with bristles soaking in water left on the countertop after someone washed his hands. Bottles were toppled over. Washcloths belonging to no one, or, worse, to everyone.

I glanced at the mirror, surprised to see myself. I looked so out of place amid the squashed tubes of toothpaste in a house that wasn't mine, a world that only made sense without me. I didn't want to see myself, or try to comprehend what I was doing there. I looked into my own eyes just long enough to find the contact lenses and remove them, and then I appeared the way I felt: diffuse, dissolved, blurry and all but invisible.

Making my way down the hall, I sensed the intimate comfort of darkness weaving them together as a family. Bodies merged in sleep, trusting that togetherness wasn't the incidentalest of ties. They were rocked by the same small rhythms, rhythms that would drive them forever when they separated into the world. I heard someone say, *Goodnight, Mom!* and someone else, *Goodnight, Sarah!* The darkness erased our distance. I was close enough, in the next room, to say, *Goodnight, son,* but soon I was fast asleep.

In the dim light of morning, it was hard not to think about California, where the sunrise rips the sky wide open; where my affections were uncomplicated, and I could express my love freely. Any other Saturday, I'd be getting an espresso in the little alley, going for a run in the hills, riding my bike to the farmers' market, meeting friends in the park. I wondered if Jonathan could feel my thoughts escaping the room. Or the guilt I felt for letting them. It would never be as simple as telling him, someday, that I hated the life I'd lived without him, or that I longed for him every moment. I loved California, and I couldn't even picture my life with a five-year-old. And he was happy, too, with his sister and brother and friends and family. I was so glad. Otherwise I'd have given him up for nothing. But if we were happy, each in our separate lives, why continually reopen this wound? I sat among Legos scattered across the floor, trying hard to figure out what I was doing there.

"Do you have any four-ones?" Jonathan asked, and I brushed my hand across the Legos within range, looking for those that had four pegs in a single row. I handed him three of them.

"Here you go."

He looked down, his fingers working hard to make the joint secure.

He's mine, I thought—a thought I wouldn't have allowed myself a few years ago. It seemed harmless now because my feelings about it had grown so numb. *He's my* son, I said to myself; I had learned a certain way of being around him, flat and friendly, but I wanted it to *mean* something when I handed him my four-ones. I wasn't his babysitter or his aunt or his cousin. I wasn't a friend. I was here only because I was his mother, and yet that had no simple bearing on anything I was doing, and it was the one thing I would not speak about. I wanted to feel *something* so that I could at least hand him the Legos in a way that accomplished whatever it was we were here to accomplish.

"What about red one-ones?" He caught my eye, and I began to scan the floor. Did he know what I was doing now?

I found two red one-ones and handed them to him. We stayed silent after that, focused on our work. We piled Legos on top of Legos in a giant amorphous mass. We added room after room, expanding horizontally, low walls of wide, mismatched blocks, furnished sparsely, topped occasionally with antennae.

I had no idea what we were building and only the faintest feeling that it mattered to build it.

I was relieved to board the plane. A six-hour flight to cleanly separate me from the Northeast. I had no doubts when navigating my connecting airports. I could be myself as I ordered an espresso and then made my way through the narrow aisle to the back of the plane and sank into the seat to watch a dumb movie. We kept pace with the sun, as if time weren't passing and I'd never been there at all, and the Sierras soon softened into the Oakland Hills. We landed over marbled salt marshes, and I felt so lucky to call it home.

TWENTY-SIX

A single day in San Francisco; a million wonders. A million means of forgetting. Only the skinny arms of the Sutro Tower, holding steady through the fog, to prove the landscape isn't erased and reinvented fresh on a daily basis. It was a wild place, cold in August and blazing in February, and the only predictable thing was it would all be devoured by the four o'clock fog. There was no continuation of some old trajectory in such a place. There was not even any establishing new trajectories. It was just, keep your balance; continents are moving under your feet.

I put on my running shoes, and my friend Rachel picked me up in front of my apartment. We'd joined a marathon training group, and by the end of February our team was up to nine miles. We parked at the marina and gathered on the lawn while the fog was still perched on the bay. We took off along the sweep of the Embarcadero and then into Nob Hill, where the city grid confronts steep slopes head on. We'd talk about anything we could think of to distract us from the exertion. *Run with your ass, run with your ass*, we'd remind ourselves in chant to power our stride from the core.

Time really passed on runs that long; the slopes would start to shimmer with golden grasses and slip behind the clouds. The landscape seemed the stuff of dreams—the outpouring of a skillful hand experimenting fearlessly with beauty so richly strange it was hard to believe, even as it passed beneath your feet. Only seven miles square, but inside the city's folds were vast and varied landscapes, its seasons so slippery it gave no foothold to memory. I had the old familiar impulse: to write it in my diary, to inventory and preserve the fog and the prospects, and the prehistoric trees and the light, but it was too big. I had to run. Running was the only way to grasp it.

It was a city of self-determination, and, having finished school and found a home, I was finally in a position to make my life whatever I wanted it to be—but want had become so complicated. I wanted only everything or nothing. I was ambivalent about the finer details. The only thing that felt good was running. When I ran, I wasn't settling on anything at all. I leapt between unknowns, one foot in one territory, the other in the next, in between hovering nowhere.

Nine miles was longer than I'd ever run. It was late morning by the time we got back to the marina and spread out to stretch on the lawn. Rachel invited me to join her in the park after lunch, and we drove straight up the face of Filmore home—windows down and the air comprised of distinct gusts of cold and hot. As we neared Pacific Avenue, it felt as if we would fall backward. Out the sunroof you could see Angel Island.

"I'll try to stop by the park later," I said, as Rachel pulled over to the curb in front of my apartment. "I've just got a rehearsal at one. And there's this festival in Golden Gate Park, if you want to go. And I was going to meet up with Jen for dinner." When I wasn't working, my time was triple booked. I'd joined a mandolin orchestra in the winter, a gay clogging troupe and an art collective, started taking French lessons and volunteering on a farm south of the city. Besides that there were always bike rides, and sing-alongs, and scavenger hunts, and hikes in the Oakland hills—

"If it's too much, don't worry about it," she said. "It'll just be Jerry and me." Rachel diagnosed my condition: FOMO. Fear of Missing Out. The irrational compulsion to do everything, out of fear of missing anything. It was worse in a city as small and social as San Francisco, where you were not only bound to be invited to too many things but sure to hear all about everything you missed. Rachel didn't suffer from FOMO. She argued, "You'll always be missing something, no matter what you do. You just have to decide that you are *Where It's At*. Then you can never Miss Out." But her self-assurance was impossible for me.

"No, I'll be biking right past the park from Noe Valley after the rehearsal."

"Okay, does that mean you'll have your mandolin? Because Jerry was going to bring his guitar."

I slammed the door behind me and leapt up the stairs to my apartment.

My adoption counselors had long ago told me I would need hobbies to fill the void—why not learn to play an instrument? Or paint your toenails *fire engine* red? I didn't need this advice; I did these things reflexively. My grief was not simply a void but a vacuum. I said yes to everything and worked hard to fit it all in. It wasn't that I was thinking about my son all the time, and doing fun things rarely felt like a manifestation of grief. But they were tied to my son all the same. I knew from experience, it isn't a small matter, whether you decide to go hiking in Oakland or to a picnic in the park. A single no could throw your whole life off course.

My many yeses made for interesting reading for my grandmother, whom I regularly e-mailed scenes of the world of improbable things that happened in San Francisco. Like one night bumping into my high school prom date, who was wearing cowboy boots with spurs, reigniting our old affection and taking off to Reno by train. Or discovering that both my upstairs and downstairs neighbors played clarinet, unpacking my own, and starting a trio. There was always something colorful, something unlikely, and I was helplessly drawn to those things. The more unlikely, the more promising, because the weighty, obvious option was no longer accessible to me. My grandmother's only concern was that I not forget about Thomas, who was thinking about leaving the East Coast to join me. I took off my running shoes and jumped in the shower.

I missed him. Sometimes I'd listen to Philadelphia radio, and, hearing about a snowstorm there, I'd feel FOMO for that city, remembering the time we trudged through the abandoned streets during a blizzard on my birthday. Sometimes the missing would give me a kind of certainty and I'd feel ready to decide something big—that everything I'd been through added up to Thomas, and me, and a life in California. I put my mandolin in its case and woke my computer. That certainty didn't last. I opened my e-mail to get directions to the rehearsal, but Paula had sent a link to her blog—an intimate view of the life I was missing out on all the time.

For what seems like forever, I have been complaining about the kids leaving bowls of cereal uneaten. I decided I had to take matters into my own hands. When life gives you lemons, make lemonade. When life gives you uneaten bowls of cereal, redefine "frugal gourmet" by making Uneaten-Bowls-of-Cereal Cake!

I was lucky that what she wrote reassured me; there was no one else I could trust to raise my son. I felt pride in all directions, retelling her stories, and it meant a lot that so often they made me laugh. And yet, what was open adoption but a lifelong, epic-scale cultivation of FOMO? A perfect view of the world without you and proof that even in the role you were most meant to play, you were easily replaced. It left me detached from my own desires, devoted to happenstance, drawn to desire in other people, because there was no coming close to the thing I'd been most certain about. That night I told Thomas he shouldn't move to California for me.

I rode a bike I'd bought off Craigslist to work most mornings. My commute was a sigh down Sixteenth from the Lower Haight to the base of Potrero Hill, where to-the-trade interior design sales floors collected like fallen boulders. It was 8:30 a.m., March 24, 2006, the kind of clear blue morning that makes too many days feel like spring break in California. Shadows fell crisp and cool. I was approaching a vast intersection, where two roads sized for industrial traffic crossed, and one of them, Harrison, forked as it headed south.

The tow truck was headed west from Potrero. I was riding east. The driver might have seen forever in the distance, down the hill, across the city, and all the way to Sutro Tower—there wasn't another vehicle in sight. The light was green as we approached it. He turned left. I thought about my run and looked for his eyes, but *twelve miles* was all I could think to say to him as he hit me. The distance we were going to run in training that weekend. *Twelve miles* at the gray glass of the windshield. *Twelve miles* as the glitches of a universe self-adjusted, rendering me invisible even as my bike and I flew.

"That. Was not. Your fault." Immediately there was a woman grasping my shoulders and several strangers' faces hovering over me.

I felt myself detangling from my bike and rising to my feet. I saw the man step out, a young Mexican man, shorter than me, who began handing me things—identification, proof of insurance, saying he didn't see me, he didn't see me at all.

People gathered and collected the story, witnesses wrote their names and phone numbers on a piece of paper. They told me they were going to take me to the hospital. But I said I needed to go to work. Running over things is what you do to your neighbor's dog or a raccoon. I wanted to forget it. I walked a few blocks to the office, my hand pressing hard on the back of my pelvis. The man who had hit me followed me in slow chase, asking to take me to the hospital. I opened the heavy metal gate of my building and let it slam behind me. But soon my coworker had put me in her car, and we traced, by chance, my running route past the shy bald hill and Buena Vista to the hospital on Parnassus. The doctor asked me to walk to the water fountain, fifteen feet away, but by that time the injury had set in and I couldn't imagine lifting my legs from muscles in my pelvis. A nurse asked me if I was pregnant; I would need X-rays. They rolled me into a white room and began to assess the damage.

◎ ◎ ◎

I had herniated discs, a cracked pelvis, a hip labral tear, and some other, more complicated-sounding things. My doctor thought I might ultimately need back surgery, but she prescribed painkillers and bed rest. She would reassess when I'd had some time to heal. I told her I didn't want to take painkillers. I thought pain should be felt. It was a meaningful communication between me and my body and one of few things I could be sure about. Pain gave clear and decipherable boundaries, and if I didn't let myself feel it, I'd inadvertently hurt myself more.

"Pain is complicated," she argued. "Painkillers are not just about temporary relief—you need to take them to reteach your body how not to feel pain, so it will accept a pain-free condition when it has healed. If you let pain linger with an injury this significant, your body will remain in trauma, and it will invent pain to protect you, even after the injury is gone. Then you'll be dealing with pain the rest of your life."

She handed me a prescription but I never filled it.

"—you should also look into psychological treatment for PTSD. Do you have a therapist?"

"I don't think it was really traumatic—I could see that that guy really didn't mean to hit me." I saw his face and how sorry he was, and then I felt bad for him.

"It doesn't have to feel emotional to be traumatic. You've been injured, and you have a very active, physical life, which you aren't going to be able to return to anytime soon."

"Wait—what about the marathon? It's four months from now."

"No. No way. You need to be careful about this." She pressed her thumb into the inside edge of my kneecap and made me suddenly suck in air. "If we're lucky, we will have you running again. But for now let's focus on getting you out of bed and walking."

Days later, two oversized police officers surveyed my tiny apartment and loomed over my bedside taking an accident report, and friends and coworkers crowded in, bearing flowers and food. Among them were Paul, a boy I'd gone out with a few times, and Rachel. I couldn't sit up to greet them. When they left, I wrote to the marathon organizers to cancel my registration, but I started looking for races seven or eight months away. *I'll give it two weeks. Maybe three*, I thought. *And then I'll start running again.*

I'd always healed. I wasn't worried about long-term effects of the accident, and definitely not about PTSD. But I was shaken, and I couldn't yet see straight. A small part of me was grateful for the sudden interruption of everything, the imperative of pain to give me space to think. I had so much to think about, things that made the accident seem small. Most of all, that just a few days before the tow truck hit me, I'd found out that I was pregnant.

". . . I like you—I mean, I *love* you," Paul had said, stumbling, when I informed him, though our time together had done nothing so much as prove how incompatible we were. I was simply saying yes to everything. Yes to dancing till three in the morning, yes to missing the morning light, yes to Paul, whom I'd met through work and who was nice enough. But I didn't think I was saying yes to this, the one scenario a birth mother should know to avoid. And yet, my counselors had warned me it wasn't unusual at all—probably because, as she's casting hobbies into the chasm of her grief, a birth mother can be prone to thinking: What better thing with which to fill a child-shaped void?

But that wasn't what I was thinking. I knew well that another child could never compensate for the loss of my son. And yet of the very little I knew about PTSD, something I understood was that it makes you want to re-create the crisis scenario to give yourself a second chance to do what you wish you'd done. And maybe that was why in the midst of my frenzy of activity before the tow truck, drawn by someone else's desire, part of me really *was* saying yes to getting pregnant in circumstances no more stable than that winter when I was twenty-two.

Paul left with the others when they stood up from my bedside to go, and I wasn't surprised. We had nothing to talk about; I'd told him before the accident what I was going to do. I hadn't consulted anyone. I didn't want advice from anyone who wouldn't be with me bearing the cost afterward. I didn't want him to drive me there, or flip through magazines in the waiting room, or cook me soup after, or read to me beside my bed, or anything that might let him persuade himself he was doing fifty percent. And as it turned out, he didn't try to. Instead, I got hit by a tow truck, and when I got to the ER, they couldn't treat me until I made a decision. I had to sign a statement agreeing to treatment despite my pregnancy, and I had an abortion a week later. My neighbor drove me there, wheeled me inside, and brought me home. She comforted me with her own story and left me in bed with a stack of *Sex and the City* DVDs.

It was, in fact, what I wished I had done when I was pregnant the first time. Consulted no one; considered Jevn but listened to myself. I might have kept him, or I might have given him up a few weeks later when I was really ready. It didn't solve anything now, but lying in bed broken inside and out, I felt powerful, like I was beginning to make out a mysterious terrain, and I'd planted some kind of stake in it.

Beginning that March, I caught glimpses of San Francisco's teeth as they snapped at me, blindly, through the cold haze that hovered about

Sutro Tower, just visible through the high window above my bed where I lay, avoiding painkillers and swallowing turmeric on a jade pillow and an amber mat. The city and all its inhabitants were floating lightly on the back of an animal, living for the day. I turned thirty somewhere within the fog, celebrating with a twelve-piece mariachi, two old Iranians, and an Argentinean, each of whom took a bite out of a candle-punched Little Debbie they'd run out and bought at the gas station next door. It felt fitting that I didn't know anyone present, that I was in a Mexican bar with Middle Eastern men, and that the weather was nothing like January. The deeper my affection for this strange place, the nearer I came to its underside. Amid all the weightlessness, the teeth were real. You couldn't tie the city down and not feel it was looking for every opportunity to throw you, wild thing that it was, earthquake-prone and climatic lone wolf, lest you think you own it more than the next person basking in its wonder. Its special skill was to make you, and everyone else, feel like the only one.

◎◎◎

The accident forced me to delay plans to go to the East Coast, and so by the time I got there, it had been eight months since I last saw Jonathan. When I arrived, still learning my body's new limits, he was inhabiting his own body more fully. Cartwheels and forward rolls. And he'd grown closer to his siblings. They were always playing together in ways that made room for everyone's interests and inclinations.

"Pretend I'm Black Beauty!" Sarah was a racehorse, preparing for a derby.

"Pretend I'm Jetfire!" Jonathan was a Transformer—part robot jet, part farmer boy. Andrew was a silent but concentrated threshing machine, pulling up grass with both hands, sometimes fistfuls together, sometimes one at a time. Or, not a threshing machine, but a helicopter, he corrected me. One that operates upside down to chop the grass, to feed to Black Beauty.

"Sarah, pretend that Black Beauty tells Jetfire—"

"Jonathan, Black Beauty is a horse, and horses can't talk."

"Well, Black Beauty is also a Disney character," Jonathan reasoned, "and so is Garfield, and Garfield is an animal that can talk!" My son was always changing, and I was always learning him anew, but this was consistent: he was perpetually looking for loopholes. Sarah ignored him, preparing for her race. Tromping around on all fours in the grass, whinnying. Jonathan began to align himself with her.

"Transformers can't fly in horse races, Jonathan! It's not fair. It's only for horses!"

Jonathan shrugged. Unfair advantages were easy come, easy go. Then that game dissolved, or evolved into another.

"Pretend I'm having a baby," Sarah said.

"And pretend I'm flying a jet!" Jonathan elaborated.

And magically, they merged. Sarah was a woman giving birth to a baby. Jonathan was the pilot of the crashing plane on which she was delivering. Andrew was still, contentedly, a helicopter–threshing machine. The plane crashed and they rolled down the hill and piled on top of one another like real brothers and sisters. Elbows and ankles tangled and indistinguishable. Blissfully unaware that their bodies would not only isolate them from one another but would someday betray them altogether.

I helped weave the scenarios together, adding elements or story lines as needed. I was the race announcer, then a flight attendant. I had to think fast. They were no longer satisfied by simply being turned upside down or chased. There had to be a story to connect things, and it had to be compelling to all of them. At some point, I became the woman on the plane who was giving birth. Sarah was still interested in what it looked like, and Jonathan still had no such interest. Childbirth for him served only to heighten the drama of a crashing plane.

"Attention!" he said. "Attention, ladies and gentlemen, the engine is on fire, and we are turning around because someone is in labor. AAAAA AHHHHHHHHHHHHH crassshsshshshshshshshshshhhhhhh!!!!!"

When the story fell apart, we went inside and the kids scattered. Up the stairs or into the playroom, in all directions. Paula offered me a cup of coffee and I lingered in the kitchen with her.

"Isn't he looking so much more like a little *boy*?" she said giddily, like it was a good secret. He didn't like being talked about, so she told me quietly that the latest thing was, he'd just learned the concept of having something in common, and he was applying it all the time, like the whole world was a matching game—but we quit talking when we heard Jonathan leaping down the stairs. He stopped short at the kitchen door and looked at us silently for a moment, like he really didn't want to know what we were talking about. He asked if I wanted to go for a walk. I put down my coffee and followed him.

My hip was burning and I was trying hard not to limp, but Jonathan strode, loose and comfortable, and I felt proud—not because I was his mother but because I had the sense I was being seen in the neighborhood with one of the cool kids. He looked around, scanning the terrain, like he'd know an opportunity if he saw one.

"How's soccer going?" I asked him, nonchalant as he was, making conversation. But I was genuinely curious. Paula told me he didn't like it, and I wanted to know what he'd say about something he didn't like.

"It's okay," he said, pointing us across the street with an easy flick of his wrist.

"Yeah?" I was trying to be cool, but. "Does that mean you like it?"

"I like it," he said with a shrug, "but I don't really like going to practice. But I have to *pretend* I like it because there are adults there. And I have to pretend I like all the other kids." He was using his hands to explain it to me, his palms facing upward, then rolling his hands on his wrists to expose his palms anew, and then again, with every point of his explanation.

"Oh!" I said. I was charmed by his forthrightness. And I could relate. I remembered getting confused as a child, always doing things I didn't want to do because I couldn't know until I tried, and I was supposed to give everything a chance. I knew that for Paula and Erik it wasn't a big deal whether he played soccer or any sport at all. That they had probably encouraged him to have an open mind and a positive attitude and to try it out; that's what parents were supposed to do. But understanding your own desire could be so complicated, what a fine line it was, between healthy self-doubt and negating yourself entirely.

"Well, I don't like soccer at all," I said simply, so he would feel free to say it.

He smiled broadly. "Something in *common!*"

Then he turned to see if I'd registered it, too. I smiled back.

As we walked, going nowhere in particular, I would have liked to have talked about the deeper things we had in common, the inescapable things like our blood and our breath. But while he marveled at our similarity, I was forced to consider something else. That we now stood at such a distance that we could reflect on each other; something in common was an incidental bridge that gave a view of the vast space between us.

TWENTY-SEVEN

I woke up to another beautiful day in San Francisco. A beautiful day, tempered by a midstride shivering down my right leg, the weird warmth in my calf, a clicking weakness as my hip shifted loosely in its joint. The sound of the leaves when the wind blew was the first hint of fall, and I wanted more than any other time of the year to run. Fall was the year's sunset. And there *was* a fall in San Francisco, and that I could detect the subtlest signs of it made me feel at home. By now, more than a year since I arrived, I'd seen a full cycle, the city in her grandest and in her tenderest, early-morning moments.

For a moment I lay in the dark. I turned to orient myself and gasped: the full light of day was glowing around the edges of the blinds. Greg closed them at night, even though his bedroom cantilevered like a nest into the cool shade of a ficus tree. I had intense FOMO for morning light, but he was content to miss it entirely. We had been dating for a couple of months, but lately I was talking a lot about my plans to return to the East Coast.

"Do you know how hard it is to be in a relationship with someone who is always leaving?" he would ask me.

My experience of San Francisco had radically changed after the accident. For weeks, I could do little more than sit in my window, watching the day pass. Now I was biking occasionally, wearing cycling shoes that let me both pull and push using only my left leg. But what was drawing me back was recent news that my grandfather's health was declining. I felt like I should put myself back within range of my family.

We got up and got dressed, and as soon as we stepped outside, I said, "It's *so* beautiful today!"

He sighed and smiled, annoyed. "Can't you think of something more precise to say?"

He would kick me out on a Saturday morning so that he could work, when it seemed self-evident to me the only thing to do was to jump on his motorcycle and head north to the headlands. I wanted to work, wanted to practice mandolin, but the day came in my windows and pulled me out by my rib cage, despite my injury. Sometimes even the night did, like one night when the moon was almost full and the air was unusually mild, and I rode my bike to his house, pounded on his door, and, when he opened it, invited him for a ride to the ocean. We would pass through the world in its midweek slumber and see the buffalo in Golden Gate Park on the way. How magical to find them snoring in the moonlight! He had twisted his face incredulously and cited the time and the day of the week—*exactly* the reasons I wanted to go—as reasons we should not.

"I mean, your profession has to do with aesthetics," he reminded me, "and yet every day you say it's beautiful. It seems like you could be more articulate, and then maybe we could have some kind of conversation about it. As it is, you declare so emphatically that it's beautiful, I have no choice but to agree! Okay, it's *beautiful.* It's cloudy; it's beautiful! It's sunny; it's beautiful! How can you expect me to really engage with that?"

I sank into myself as we walked to the coffee shop. I remembered the time my sister took me to a formal dinner in China, where there were strict traditions we had to observe. She elbowed me away from the glass with the tallest napkin—it was for the guest of honor—and she whispered that I shouldn't eat the rice that would be served at the end of the meal; that would insult the host, who would think we were still hungry. I watched her quietly for other cues. The dinner began when the host placed a carrot, finely carved into the shape of a bird, on the turntable and sent it spinning. The bird made the rounds, greeting every guest, and when the device came to a stop, the host handed it to me—*me!* Not the guest of honor!

I took it in both hands and thanked the host, but everyone kept looking at me, like I hadn't yet done what I was expected to do. I couldn't see my sister clearly out of the corner of my eye. I cradled the bird in my hands and looked around, smiling graciously, but they were waiting for me to do something. And so I held the bird tightly in one hand and took a bite. What else do you do with a carrot bird? But I knew right away that wasn't what I was supposed to do because all the jaws dropped. I looked at the headless bird in my hand and had to get rid of it, so I chewed and swallowed the whole thing as fast as I could while everyone just watched.

My boyfriend reminded me I had the wrong responses. I'd forever be a foreign guest chomping heads off birds instead of admiring them beside my plate, or whatever it was I was supposed to have done. Everyone else was built for this world. Beautiful things made them do sensible things like plan picnics or get married. But beauty imprisoned me, demanded a response. All my settings were miscalibrated. I loved things so much I destroyed them; I gave up the things I wanted most. Running was the most acceptable way I'd come up with to handle the beauty, and now it hurt to even walk.

I told Greg I'd try to be more precise, but inside I took another step toward the East Coast.

That fall I boarded a plane for Thanksgiving. It was, to my surprise, already winter in Boston. It took a moment for me to accept I'd missed an entire East Coast fall, and I resolved I wouldn't miss another. Erik picked me up alone from the airport; the kids were watching the end of Jonathan's basketball game. When we found them in the gym, Jonathan ran up to me and hugged me like he really knew me. I picked up Andrew, gave Sarah a hug, and as soon as we got back to the house, the kids and I took off for a walk in the woods.

Andrew rode on my shoulders. He was quiet and thoughtful, but he had no hesitation about doing dangerous things. When he jumped off a rock, Jonathan, always more circumspect, would jump off the same rock. Few things about Andrew were very much like Jonathan, or Sarah like either of them, and every part of that seemed good for everyone.

I introduced a game.

"If I see something beautiful, I'm going to point to it, and if you see something beautiful, you point to it. Look! There!" I pointed to the bright blue doors of a building.

"Yeah!" Andrew said, satisfied.

As we walked through the woods, Andrew pointed at a church, a bridge, the mill. Sometimes the rhythm of the game got ahead of him and he was pointing without contemplating, it seemed, whether he really thought something was beautiful.

"That's beautiful!" Andrew pointed in the direction of some trees.

"What's beautiful about it?" I challenged him, invoking my boyfriend.

"I don't know; it's just beautiful!"

Jonathan and Sarah walked their bikes ahead of us. Jonathan was wearing a puffy red coat that went down to his knees. Sarah led the way, but as they approached the steps of the bridge, they stopped and waited, their bicycles too heavy to maneuver. They were whispering while they waited for us, and I heard Jonathan say something about Jevn. He and Sarah giggled. I leaned down to lift his bike up the steps, bracing my lower back as my physical therapist had taught me. Then Sarah's.

"What were you guys talking about?" I asked. "Did you see Jevn recently?"

They both burst into laughter.

"I saw them almost *kiss*!" Jonathan laughed as he ran over the bridge. I smiled and followed them, shaking my head. I didn't want to seem shocked at the mention of Jevn's name, but it had been a while. The last time I'd seen him was in a framed picture in the living room on one of my recent visits. I was unsettled and intrigued, but I tried not to seem surprised about that, either. There was Jonathan, squeezing Jevn around the neck from behind, both of them stretching their smiles and squinting their eyes to the limit. The way Jonathan wrapped his arms around Jevn, like seeing him was pure pleasure, I thought it must be simpler to be a father. Jevn never left my mind entirely, but I was still surprised to learn he had a girlfriend serious enough to be introduced to Jonathan.

Andrew and I lingered on the bridge, looking at the mill below and the tangle of forest that surrounded it. Jonathan sauntered back to join us. He asked if he could borrow my camera, in case he saw something beautiful. I pulled it out of my pocket, and he assembled his fingers so that the index, long and delicate, rested softly on the shutter release. He glanced up at me to confirm they were in the right places, and as he adjusted them, I recognized them as my own—and I had the strangest sensation that I was looking in a mirror. That those delicate movements were mine; it was like a flickering in my deep muscles as they engaged to support the gesture he was making. He was the image of Jevn in every other feature, but I clung to the sight of his hands, my heart pounding. Long skinny fingers extending from short narrow palms. And an infinite network of tiny lines. Hard and fast evidence of his birth and our connection. It felt like I should grab him by the shoulders and shake him and say, "Jonathan! It's *me*!" like I'd found a long-lost son.

But he was never lost. *He is mine*, I reminded myself, *and he is not mine*. Equally important, opposite realities. I'd practiced both thoughts so often my heart was a branch bent back and forth, weakened every time.

He clasped the camera and ran into the woods ahead of me. I walked slowly behind. We piled our coats on a log by the stream, and I sat down to rest. While the kids played hide-and-seek, I drew my finger across the crease of my hip; it felt like cutting off my leg was the only way the pain would ever go away.

"Look!" Jonathan handed me the camera. He'd spun it while he was photographing the stream. Leaves had been captured in the ice, and water flowed through cracks in the surface. The tiny middle of the image was in focus, and the outer peripheries were blurred.

"Beautiful!" I said.

He ran off to take more pictures. Sarah and Andrew were crawling on rocks nearby. I followed Jonathan. I held on to his hand, like ballast, so he could lean out farther over the water.

"Do you think we could walk on the ice?" he asked.

"No, see how close the water is underneath?"

We chased his brother and sister. His brother ran slowly, swinging his arms hard like he was trying to fly. His sister caught him easily, in full mastery of her body now, at nine. We played for a couple of hours, and by afternoon the forest had taken shape: the soft carpet of dead leaves in the clearing was our living room, there was our mound of coats, the hollow between the hill and the tree, and the big rock sitting in the sun, home base. Everything we could see belonged to us.

It was starting to get cold. I gathered the kids' things and called them. Jonathan gave me my camera and put his arms through his giant coat. The neighbors would see us walking home with red noses after our long day in the woods. They might think I am my son's mother, and I wished that simple mistake could somehow stay suspended in frost on the window glass. I was happy to think it might at least enjoy a tiny life in the passive imagination of neighbors.

When I got to the farm for Thanksgiving dinner, my grandmother had a surprise for me. She handed me a mandolin swaddled in an old potato sack. The body was round and it pressed into the hollow of my abdomen as I held it.

"That was your great-grandmother Louise's mandolin," she told me. "Grandpa's mother. She used to play every Saturday night. Your great-grandpa played fiddle." I didn't know anyone in our family played music! I thought my inclination toward music was proof I didn't belong in my family at all! I used to play piano like I was blindly patting a wall, searching for the hidden entry into a magical underwater cavern, the world where I was meant to be. But then my mother would call me in to dinner, and the tide would suck away from the shore. I held the mandolin on my lap and pressed into the indentations of Louise's fingerprints. I understood why, years ago, Grandpa yelled, "That ain't no mandolin!" when I'd played mine: for him the sound of a mandolin was the sound of *this* mandolin and the sound of his mother playing it.

But now my grandfather was silent. He couldn't hear anymore, and he didn't make eye contact so that he wouldn't have to tell you so. Still, Grandma told me to hand him the mandolin, and my cousin took a picture of him handing it back to me. He leaned forward uncomfortably as I knelt beside him, the mandolin between us, and smiled. I should have it, Grandma said, since it would mean more to me than anyone, and I felt myself bound in a special new way to Louise and to my grandfather. As long as I could sink my fingertips into the shallow cavities between the frets, I would hold on to the sound of his childhood, and I'd always have my grandfather. But as we left, I heard him ask, "Who was that lady with the mandolin?" and realized he hadn't known who I was.

Returning to my childhood bedroom in Tennessee, I felt lucky that it at least never changed. The quilt Grandma made me, my old drawings from art class, a giant chunk of wood from a tree Dad felled. My drawer that held my cat's tooth and the orange pill bottle with Jevn's last name. My son would never have this experience. He had already had so many homes. He adjusted well, but when I was in Boston, Paula said he'd realized recently that he'd lost one of his toys, and he wanted to go back to the house in North Carolina to find it. It had been two years since they'd emptied that house, but he said he thought he knew just where it was in his old bedroom, and he assured her it would be okay for them to go inside, because that house was kind of really *their* house.

Tucked into my childhood bed, I looked at the pictures my son had taken with my camera: fragments of arms and legs, blurry close-ups of leaves caught in ice, so many spinning forest skies. *He has my fingers*, I thought with that strange satisfaction, and my impulse to grasp and hold on to beautiful things. To find them, again, in their dusty, lost corners, and to hold on to them forever—things he couldn't possibly keep.

TWENTY-EIGHT

From China, my sister told me a story about a man who joined a group of her friends for dinner, which was served family style. He got radish and beef soup, and as he ladled my sister's bowl, he deliberately set pieces of meat aside. They had just met, but he hadn't forgotten that on their way to the restaurant she'd said she was a vegetarian. One of her other friends ordered tomatoes and eggs, remembering from dinners past that it was Julie's favorite dish. Later, she was tutoring a student in conversational English. They began talking about love. "Love means that you take care of the one you love," her student said. "If she is cold, you tell her she should wear more clothes."

My sister thought that was funny. She argued, "Love means you remember."

I could still picture vividly my sister's face the moment I signed the papers. I'd dressed for the occasion several times, but in the end we'd both worn delicate linen shirts she bought in China. Hers was mauve; mine was blue. They each had a single button made out of knotted linen at the top. I wore mine with a skirt she'd had made by a tailor in Nanchang. Her face matched her shirt as I wrote my name. Her sadness that day had given me some of my strength. And I counted on her to remember.

Her son was a year and a half old when I got a call from her. "Guess what little boy is going to have a little sister or brother!" I played along, but I was annoyed; she had no idea what some people have to go through to have children. But mostly I was busy. My office had just approved my transfer to New York, and I was saying goodbye to San Francisco every way imaginable: long last afternoons in the park, last rides out to Stinson Beach, last Monday nights with live music at the bar where I was always meeting people, last breakfast party on my roof, complete with clogging and a mandolin duo. And last espresso with my boyfriend, whom I finally broke up with.

I saw her just a few weeks later, when my family went skiing in West Virginia over the holidays. But she didn't ski because of her pregnancy, and I didn't ski because of my injury. Instead, we cooked and played games in the same cabin we'd stayed in seven years ago when I was pregnant. I'd hidden in my room and read *The God of Small Things* and was compelled to swallow a pickle every time I read the word *pickle* in that story about an Indian family that operated a pickle factory. We'd told none of my cousins or aunts or uncles who were staying in cabins next door. Seven years had changed so much; now, being pregnant and having children were things to proudly announce to everyone.

My sister had already ordered a birth pool in preparation for a home birth in the kitchen. After Jacob was born, she quit her job teaching English at a university to become a professional homemaker. She had additional freezers and refrigerators for her supply of grains, flours, beans, and nuts. She was part of a raw milk black market, and, concerned about the environmental impact of washing cloth diapers, she taught her son how to "eliminate" on command from birth by sitting him on a toilet at regular intervals and using a range of verbal cues. She and her husband occupied a parsonage in a D.C. suburb with strict neighborhood regulations. The neighbors minded her annual delivery of a pile of sheep manure from the farm, for use in her garden, and they minded that she sometimes "peed" her son out the front door of her house, saying *shhhhhhhhhh!*—a pre-lingual direction to urinate, and to be quiet about it.

For now, her motherhood was a frenzy of nursing and cooking and putting to bed, but eventually, I thought, she would have time to think about mine. I thought her own son growing up with white-blond hair just five years short of Jonathan would make her consider what I was missing at every step, and maybe she would feel for me what I couldn't even know to feel for myself. When we were little, we used to put all our coins in a pile and split it in half; it always felt better, whether I was gaining or losing, to have exactly the same as my sister. And when she cried so hard, more than I did, at the Surrender, it lightened the burden for me. I thought I could see she was taking on as much as any person could, her own share, of my grief.

But sometimes I wondered if her own son had made her forget. Jacob was the white-blond grandson of the family. We fed him and held him at Christmas, we played games with him on our backs, we helped him put on his shoes and walked with him in the snow, we got illegible notes from him in the mail. We knew his first words and his first steps, and all about his first successful poo in the toilet. We noticed my father in him, and when my father was filling out some medical forms at the doctor, Jacob would be the first grandchild he listed. Names would follow in order of age, but Jonathan wouldn't be among them. Maybe because, like me, my parents had no legal ties to my son, and tax forms and paperwork were not the time to go into it. Or maybe Jonathan registered more remotely in his mind, like a third cousin you rarely see but you love all the same. Jacob, on the other hand, couldn't be forgotten. Firstborn of the firstborn. Wanted of the wanted.

◎ ◎ ◎

I still hadn't left California when Abigail was born that August, the same month my grandmother had requested fulfillment of her long-standing wish to meet my son. She planned everything. She suggested everyone meet at the farm and then go enjoy local attractions without her. Then Paula and Erik could enjoy dinner in town at an "upscale" restaurant without the children, and finally, she asked that Erik sit down with her at some point to explain the book he'd written. It had to do with a theologian from the thirteenth century. She said she'd read the whole thing and couldn't understand a word of it.

As usual, Paula and Erik were busy that August. They were living in an apartment while Jevn oversaw the renovation of their new house in Boston. By September they would have lived in four homes in ten weeks. Paula tried to keep me in the loop. Her updates usually detailed the family's scattered coordinates, but sometimes they were just about my son. One of those nights, in one of their homes, she said, as Jonathan was getting into bed, he asked, "Mom, do you know what my mind is fixed on?" She thought it was funny he used phrases like *fixed on*, but she couldn't guess. He told her, "God and Jetfire." She said it was often late at night he'd say things like that, and she said he sounded just like me when he did. I liked to think about him contemplating God, the greatest and most untouchable thing, together with the smallest and most familiar, his favorite toy, a Transformer called Jetfire, making his mind bend around the mystery that somehow one becomes the other. Whatever he meant, it made me feel close to him, even if I wasn't there by his bedside for that conversation and didn't even know which house it happened in. I'd lost so many moments with my son, but Paula was always gathering them again to share with me.

Since they were already living out of suitcases, Paula and Erik accepted my grandmother's invitation and drove down to Maryland. When they arrived, the quiet brick sunroom grew noisy with kids and dogs, people greeting one another and the door swinging open and closed.

"Come over here and say hello!" my grandmother called to Jonathan from her recliner. Jonathan smiled and kept his distance, close to Erik. Erik pushed him forward, and he stood stock-straight beside her.

"Hel-lo!" my grandfather said to him, like he was speaking to a puppy, bowing his head and lifting his hand in a low wave that worked double-duty, as a greeting and to stop anyone from responding.

"Jonathan, tell Grandma about your birthday party!" I suggested. Paula said they'd watched a Star Wars DVD and eaten off of Star Wars paper plates. But Jonathan just swung his shoulders and looked at me.

My sister pushed the squeaky door open, carrying Abigail in her arms. Her white-blond boy, now more than two years old, slipped inside after her and stood in front of Jonathan. I thought maybe in this moment everyone would see: what we all understand instinctively about what Jacob means to the family is true of my son, too. Jonathan's towering height over Jacob might prove that all those meanings were actually five years more true of Jonathan. Jonathan was five years more of a grandson; he had five years more capacity to carry the family history. But mostly I hoped my sister would see our sons and remember.

Half an hour of hospitality was all my grandmother could substain before she encouraged us to go entertain ourselves. We caravanned to Harpers Ferry to take a walk and enjoy the sunset. We got big, expensive ice cream cones, and when Andrew dropped his on the brick sidewalk, Paula grabbed the empty cone out of his hand, scooped up the splattered ice cream, and handed it back to him before he had registered the loss. She looked away and swung her arms and continued walking. My mother laughed and laughed and retold the story many times to everyone who hadn't witnessed it.

When we drove to dinner, Jonathan rode in the car with my family. I sat in the middle in the back, between him and my mother, and I can't remember how it started, but Jonathan and I started tickling each other. We knew each other's ticklish spots and how to get at them, and he laughed so hard he couldn't make a sound. We forgot whose fingers were whose as we grabbed at them, twenty too-long fingers flailing for our lives. We thumb wrestled and arm wrestled, and when we got to the restaurant we tapped each other's toes under the table.

The next morning, we all met for a picnic before going our separate ways. A little place in the woods close to Harpers Ferry, where there was a pond, and a dock, and a place to sit and eat. The pond was full of algae, and my brother and the kids began fishing it out with long sticks. They lay down on the dock to reach farther out and collected gooey piles of it. Jacob watched Jonathan closely, like a container he would soon crawl into. Jonathan taught him how to say *ribbit!* They jumped down the length of the dock, leaping and squatting, leaping and squatting. *Ooh ooh ooh!* Jonathan said, hunching over like a chimpanzee, and Jacob tried to imitate him.

I was the photographer, documenting every combination of our ever-expanding family: Paula with Julie and her new baby. Andrew and Jacob, chasing my brother and Jonathan. My mother, eating her sandwich and chatting with Erik. My father, trying to show them all, again, how to skip rocks across the pond. When we said goodbye, Jonathan approached Jacob to give him some jelly beans we bought in Harpers Ferry. You could tell Jacob was flattered. He leaned in to give Jonathan a kiss, but Jonathan just watched with interest from above. It landed near his belly button.

That night, my sister and I stayed awake talking after her kids were asleep. I told her I wished that someone had taken a picture of me with my son when we were all at the pond. I had a lot of pictures of him from my trips to North Carolina, but since the day I signed the papers, when Paula snapped pictures of my sister and me, swollen-faced with Jonathan in my arms just outside of the conference room where I'd signed, I didn't have any of us together. I'd left the pond with a hundred photographs of an afternoon during which I didn't seem to be present at all.

I hadn't said anything at the time because I wanted someone else to think of it. At least as much as I wanted that picture, I wanted someone else to consider how much a picture like that would mean to me.

My sister's face turned red as she remembered.

And I remembered I was alone in all of this. It wasn't a burden I would ever share. My grandmother wasn't scheming to get him back, and my sister had all but forgotten that distant day. I'd always be the photographer in my family, and no paper world where my son was locked in my arms could give me what I really wanted. But after that, I found it hard to hear about my sister's children. I quit calling her on Mother's Day; I forgot her kids' birthdays. And I began to refer to Jonathan as *my son*. Not the name his parents had given him, but the nameless thing he had always been to me, the child who wasn't mine to name.

I returned to California for my last month there. It was fall; there were wrinkles in weather that made short-lived shadows where you could try to plant your memories. When the light fell long that October, and I began to see the subtle signs of fall in the sycamores, I felt the sweetness of familiarity, but I wouldn't presume to know what season it really was, or when it would pass. On one of those last afternoons, basking in the sunlight I was sad to be leaving, across a crowded field of hipsters, I spotted a boy. Tight red pants, tight red shirt, and a blue bandana, rolled around his neck. We didn't make eye contact, but I knew we would meet. I would sit in the park until we did. And soon he was there, squatting beside me and offering me a Popsicle he said his mate didn't want. Australian. No, Irish. He was done with San Francisco, too, heading to Berlin. Jevn was right, every ending is a beginning. Those last days in California would feel like the beginning of everything. Lying in a loft with him, watching *The Silence of the Lambs*, his dog, Reginauld, resting between us and him reveling in every moment I buried my head in his chest for protection. Waking with a distant window's light framing a pure blue Oakland sky. We said goodbye to California and then to each other, and I landed in New York in time for a real winter.

TWENTY-NINE

Breathe, Seekie," Caleb said as he threw my bag into the trunk. We were double-parked in front of our apartment in Brooklyn.

"I know, it's just Paula said he'd be finishing his Little League game at noon, and I want to get there. It takes longer than Google Maps says."

We were borrowing my sister's old Saturn for a few weeks as we got to know New York. We'd taken a couple of weekend trips along the East Coast, and that Saturday morning we were on our way to see Jonathan. We pulled the heavy doors closed and settled in with Reginauld in the backseat. Caleb started the car. *"Breathe,"* he said.

Jevn had told me the same thing. My piano professor had said it, too. Boys were always telling me to breathe. I knew there was something to it. In childbirth, breathing was a way of moving forward in the face of unbearable pain. In the conservatory, breathing let you bypass your brain, taking inexpressible complexities into your body, and letting them right back out into the world, through your hands. My professor would sit beside me, reading the music as I silently inhaled leather and worn felt in the soundproof chamber of his studio in the east wing of Memorial Hall. I would gaze across the couch, over the Buddha, and out the windows toward my high-rise dorm, which was always casting a shadow over the conservatory.

I thought music school would be a kind of arrival; I thought we would finally get to play the most sophisticated pieces of piano literature, like the *Gaspard de la Nuit*, or the *Arietta* of Beethoven's last piano sonata, which my teacher in Tennessee said I was too young to play. He said Beethoven was transcribing the sound of heaven as he approached it, and without some "life experience" you couldn't possibly make sense of it, no matter how easily you could read the notes. I took it as a challenge and practiced it secretly at home, feeling like I was stealing a surreptitious glimpse through the gates. But at conservatory we played only the most straightforward pieces, sometimes ones we'd mastered as children, and we had to play slowly, half tempo and less, accounting not just for the initiation of every note, but for the timing and nature of every release.

Some professors advocated long hours of practice, but mine didn't want me to touch the piano without care. He thought endless scales and arpeggios only taught your fingers not to feel. Every time you approach the piano, he said, you should be fully present and paying attention, even if that meant playing less and longing more. And I wasn't to touch the keys until I had *breathed* the music.

I would close my eyes uncomfortably and inhale; a pause midair before falling. I'd exhale the first phrase of the Brahms, imagining the restraint of pressing my fingers bluntly into soil. I would sink into the thick cushion of the bench, arching my spine intermittently in a slow rhythm, then lift my chest, rising again, taut, from my sacrum. The phrasing would come from my expanded lungs, not from my fingers, flailing to find the notes. Breathing was a way to embody movements and meanings too complex for thinking.

"He doesn't care about all your agonizing, complicated shit," Caleb said. "Just make sure when you're around, it's fun. That's what he'll remember." We found the highway and merged into traffic.

After we left California, Caleb spent a few months in Berlin before deciding to join me in New York, arriving sweetly on Valentine's Day but then playing it off as coincidence. His advice, simple as it was, was born of experience; I wanted to rub it like a rough sponge across all my jagged thinking and let its simplifying action simplify all the parts of everything. His life had been spread haphazardly across three continents, his passport taken by one parent, then he himself taken by the other; parents' lovers arrived and departed through his childhood, and he was the only one in his entire family who ended up with his last name—but despite the odds, he had come out *Solid. Gold.* That's at least what our relationship therapist said. We were seeing her because I wanted to be talking about marriage and Caleb thought we were already married, by virtue of living together and having his dog and my cat (whom he called "the kids") and being okay with having babies if that came to pass and being in all other ways happily committed.

Caleb would comment charmingly on our therapist's new hairstyle, ask her about her vacation and each of her sons, and she always came to his defense during our sessions. She challenged me about why I was in such a rush to settle down and why I doubted him. She questioned my desire for children, and I'd find myself unable to give a convincing explanation. I loved Caleb, I was finally ready, and I was thirty-two—soon it would be too late. Walking up the stairs out of her basement office onto the street, Caleb would draw a fist in to his chest. "*Yessss!* Won that round."

He was an accident, too, of his parents' brief romance in Miami. He grew up in Liverpool, and he occupied his space on earth without budging. When people bumped into him on the sidewalk or cut him off, he might grab them gently by their shoulders—"Pardon me, dear"—and smile, stabilizing them, as though it might have been his fault. "D'ya see that?" he'd say afterward, incredulous. "Ran right into me! Dozy cow." As a child of a very broken and reattached and broken again and stolen-away family, he said it had meant a lot to have good memories with someone, even if that someone didn't marry his mother or stay for long. He still remembered the little gifts his mother's lovers gave.

I had a knack for finding the boys whose lives made my decision seem weak. Boys raised by single mothers who'd made great sacrifices to raise them. Boys who had good manners pounded into them because their mothers couldn't afford for them to turn out bad. They grew up with a sense of reality, their own two feet, precarious, on the ground. And they found their own strength early, inside.

"You have to visit him more," Caleb said, definitively. "Once every two months."

"I know; we're going right now!"

"But you can't just jump in and have it all your way, Seekie."

I looked out the window; it didn't feel like it was all my way. Even if I saw him every day, he would not be my son, and it would not be my way. But I should try to see the good things about our distance, whether I was in California or New York: every time we met, we had the freshness and curiosity of new friends, and my feeling for him would never be tarnished by the dull daily habit of parenting. Caleb was right; I inhaled the complexity.

"He was excited to hear you're coming," I said, being positive. Paula had told me as much, when I asked her if it was all right to bring Caleb. "He got the idea that you'd have more to show him on the skateboard than I would!"

"Fancy that."

Caleb would be my first boyfriend to meet Jonathan. He was also the first one to really understand and accept that my son, even in his absence, was a part of me. On our first date after meeting in San Francisco, Caleb stopped along a sidewalk where someone had set out records to be taken. He began carefully perusing them and handed a few to me. "For your son," he said. And then I remembered our dinner conversation, and that I'd mentioned, in passing, the record player I'd bought for Jonathan.

I was excited for them to meet; I thought Caleb might make it easier, show me how to be, or start conversations with my son I wouldn't think of.

"You have to get him little things, doesn't matter what. Little presents, just so he knows you're thinking about him when you're apart. When he looks back, he just wants to remember the good things you did." He pushed Reg into the backseat—"*Oi!* In the back!—And you have to hug him lots, you're his mum, you've got to show him you love him."

I had told him how complicated touch was for me. It couldn't be the way it was for my sister and her children, who would pile into bed like a litter of puppies, the borders of bodies loose and unprotected. She would nurse one child as another lay across her calves or slept with its body pressed against her back. When they came to visit, we were a slumber party across every surface of my tiny apartment. I fell asleep beside Jacob and woke with his tiny arm, light as a feather, wrapped around my waist. He had reached out in the night and hadn't been surprised to find someone there.

I didn't think my sister's love was dulled by the daily habit of parenting, and, despite the advice of my professor, that kind of easy familiarity was what I looked for when I practiced piano, day after day. I would ride my bike in the winter without gloves and then sit down, fingers frozen, to play the *Molto animato* of a piece by Franz Liszt I had played for more than three hundred days in a row. I wanted to have the music in my body, cold. I wanted my fingers to produce those notes under any conditions with a gesture as natural as gathering and tying up my hair. I'd made my move to New York and already found my rituals: I passed the same Laundromat and drank the same double espresso standing at the same copper bar every day. I brought the things I loved into my body like its own blood. What about the intensity of a phrase you've breathed so often, you can feel it in the softness between your ribs?

That familiarity allows the deep feeling to pass through your fingers with facility. I remembered standing beside my father when he would be cracking peanuts out of the big red canister at the kitchen table, and many times he put his free arm around me as he read the paper and hugged me and asked, "Where did you get such soft skin?" Or I would lie cradled in my mother's arms watching television as she gently and involuntarily stroked my hand. Her touch was nothing more than the simple exploration of the provinces; flesh reuniting with flesh that was once and ever its own. Inexpressible feeling finding involuntary expression.

And cuddle, pet, hug, kiss—those casual touches must provide necessary relief. They must temper the wildness of a parent's instinctive hunger for a child. They must soften the question, What does it mean that I'm this child's mother? Questions peripheral to the daily habits of parenting—the waking, feeding, reading, disciplining, and tucking the child into bed—the child you still don't understand, the relationship whose mystery doesn't in fact diminish, that was initiated, surreally, the moment of birth.

I could snatch and squeeze Sarah and Andrew, and I didn't care if they squirmed. During the period when their favorite thing was to be chased and grabbed and thrown, I would clutch them by their ankles, I would tickle their guts out, I would hold them captive and turn them upside down and start again. That kind of play was just this side of pure, raw affection, and they squealed and screamed and ran away as they should, without a sideways glance.

I couldn't touch my son the simple way I did his siblings, and he wasn't mine to touch as a parent does, so the mystery of him consumed me. And though with my son I was always playing less and longing more, just as my professor advised, when I finally saw him, I tried to touch him without feeling. I wouldn't use touch to secretly share inexpressible things. I held my son less tight, for less long, and let him go before there was a chance he would resist. I let him determine the strength and the duration. I'd return to him every unit of affection he offered me, but not more. The older he got, the more he understood about his adoption, the more ambivalent he might feel about embracing me. It seemed like the very least I could do: to perceive and to honor his rejection.

But Caleb was telling me to *just breathe*. Quit thinking. Let myself feel, and don't worry about how complicated it all was.

"If they didn't want you there, they wouldn't have invited you," he said.

Yes, I would initiate the first touch. I'd move faster than my doubts, swoop him up, and hug him, whether he liked it or not. He would like it, that's what Caleb was saying. There was nothing to think about. Why couldn't I be *Solid Gold*? Our therapist said that I am *So. Intense.*

"What's your sister naming the new baby?" Caleb asked. My sister was pregnant with her third. Her second had been born in the kitchen, nine minutes after the midwife arrived. Her third would be born in the same kitchen, delivered by a substitute for the assistant to the midwife and by her husband, who was growing tolerant of her eccentricities.

"Did I tell you what Jacob wanted to name it? Starship Light Buoy! I think they decided on Nina." I always liked that name; it made me remember my Nina, who fed me grapes and delivered my son.

"I like the name Zsa Zsa. Or Mooba."

We parked on the side of the road in front of the house. Just hug him, I told myself; don't make it complicated. Be awake, and present, and show him affection. Jonathan met us at the door. He'd just finished his last Little League game of the season, and he stood there in his uniform. He was still only seven, but his shoulders were now broader than mine, and he was gaining on me in height. He was still growing into a different person each time I saw him. Every hug was a new invention, had a new diameter, a new elevation, a new strength. I tried not to think too much, but when I felt him loosen, I couldn't help but let go.

We'd told him we'd be bringing a skateboard (a little gift; Caleb's idea), and we went outside to teach him how to ride it. We let Reg out of the car, and he raced past us. As Jonathan turned around to watch him pass, Caleb pulled Jonathan's hat off and planted it back down, backward. I couldn't believe how casually he did it! Jonathan looked suspiciously back, hands on his head, preventing his hat from being removed again, still deciding whether to put it back on right. There was the penetrating gaze: he looked at Caleb, assessing him. Caleb didn't budge.

"That's how the cool kids do it," he said, dropping one end of the skateboard down and releasing it to the ground, his toes on the tail. Jonathan was still uncertain but used his hands to pat his cap down more securely, like the cool kids do, and turned his attention to the skateboard. Caleb showed him some basic ways of standing on the board and riding, but when it was his turn, Jonathan looked self-conscious, so I suggested an obstacle course. A game to give him something to aim for.

"What if you ride down there," I suggested, "then over that bump where the driveway starts, and turn again out of the driveway, and then go down the hill?"

"The bump where the driveway starts?" Jonathan said, very uncertain.

"Here." I walked it out. "Come down the road, then over this crack in the driveway, then up over the driveway bump again, and all the way down the hill." I pointed into the distance. "Does that make sense?"

As he started down the hill, long arms like delicate streamers floating at his sides, I braced myself. Gritted my teeth. Opened my eyes wide. Leaned, like you lean to guide the bowling ball after it's beyond your control. I yelled, "Yay!" involuntarily when he made it without falling. It felt strange. If I'd had a single wish in the world, I'd have wished for him to make it over the crack in the driveway, then over the bump, and then down the hill.

Andrew played alongside us. He'd found a half of a broken skateboard with no wheels. He sat on it, stationary and happy, calling it his "rhombas" board (his bottom, he explained, was his rhombas). I turned to him. "You want to try the obstacle course on your skateboard, Andrew?"

"Mine doesn't roll," he said contentedly, as though he were describing one of his board's enviable features.

Caleb scolded me that I wasn't paying attention to Jonathan. He told me quietly that Jonathan had looked up a couple of times to see whether I was watching, and I hadn't been.

"You improved so much, Jonathan!" I called to him, correcting myself. "Like, in just the last twenty minutes I can see you've gotten better!" I wanted to assure him I really was paying attention, I just didn't want to leave his brother out. And it was true, you could really see him starting to get it. This was the miracle of learning and what must make teaching so satisfying; someone could grow right before your eyes.

"Twenty minutes; that's ten minutes less than half an hour," he responded, robotically, dismissing my compliment. A small jab, I thought, to say he would not be so easily won.

We invented a few more obstacle courses, and then it was time for a break. Caleb and I followed the boys inside and took off our shoes in the foyer. Jonathan ran upstairs to put his skateboard away. We joined Paula in the kitchen.

"Jon came in very excited," Paula said. "He said you told him he'd improved a lot in just twenty minutes!"

She invited us to stay for dinner, but I had wanted to keep our visit brief so that I could be sure to sustain my energy for the duration. We'd have a great time, and as soon as I started thinking too much, fading out, it would be time to go. More frequent, shorter, higher-quality visits were possible now that I was in New York. I wanted my son to feel as though I was a short distance away, that I was always showing up, that it was easy to call on me, that it was always fun.

And sometimes I wondered whether long visits were hard for Paula, too. She was often relaxing on the couch or on her computer while I played with the kids, and sometimes I noticed slight tensions between her and Erik, and I wondered if I was seeing the complexity registering in her, whether she battled an exhaustion similar to mine.

I'd spare us both. Caleb and I had planned an evening in Boston so I'd have something light and fun to look forward to after seeing my son. We said goodbye and got in the car.

"Jonathan thought you were going to hug him again when we were leaving, did you notice that?" Caleb asked me after we pulled out.

"No!" I said, shocked.

"You hugged him, and then everyone else, but then you were reaching down to pick up your bag, and he put his arms out for a second, thinking you were reaching for him. But then you didn't."

"What? I didn't see that!" I looked at Caleb to reassure me it wasn't true. My son had reached out for me, and I hadn't responded? But thinking harder, I remembered. "I think I saw it, but I wasn't sure, and it was too late, and then it felt weird! I didn't mean to! I would have hugged him! I didn't realize! Do you think he felt bad?"

"You have to pay attention, Seekie. He looks at you a lot, and you aren't looking back."

I sighed, putting my face in my hands, staring at the floor. Shaking my head, wishing I could be back in the foyer and fearless, hug him again even if he wasn't reaching to hug me. So what if it was awkward? So what if he hadn't wanted to hug me twice, and he rolled his eyes at his silly mother who couldn't stop hugging him?

THIRTY

Our apartment was a tiny one-bedroom in a brownstone in Brooklyn. There was an eight-inch width of counter space in the kitchen and only one closet. In our first few weekends there, we built bike stands and bookshelves, a spice rack from scrap wood we found on the street and a desk that wrapped around the corner of the bedroom, a place for both of us to work. Every night Caleb would cook. He'd been a vegetarian since he learned how to spell and realized the chicken pecking around the barnyard in his storybook was the very same chicken in the meat case at the butcher shop. Often, he put a plate on the desk next to me where, after work, I'd focus on side projects. I was developing a program to help low-income Brooklynites buy produce from local farms. I'd also signed up for an online degree in food policy. Caleb would look over my shoulder as I took notes on my readings and marvel that, after ten years of school, I still hadn't had enough of my nerdy stuff.

In the mornings before work, I'd do my physical therapy. I'd lie on the floor with my knees bent. Reginauld would walk over, giddy to have me on his level, to lick my face, and Haystack would stand on my belly, staking her turf. With a washcloth under one foot, I'd concentrate on engaging certain vertebral muscles as I slid one leg slowly into straight.

Then, without letting those vertebral muscles go, I would slide my leg, ever so slowly, back into bent.

"You awake?" Caleb would ask, stepping over me.

Two and a half years after my accident, I thought I would have healed, but instead, I was beginning to think I might not ever run again. I couldn't do the simplest things without feeling I wasn't built to do them, and I found myself talking about my accident all the time. It explained why I couldn't meet up for a day in the city, why I couldn't stand for long at the bar, why I'd never go dancing. The pain had taken over, starting with my hip, slowly draining me of my most basic appetites.

My doctors were always speculating about why I was still having so much pain. One of them said that chronic pain often has an unrelated emotional cause. She said some griefs are too big to be borne by the conscious mind, so they find physical manifestations, which, troubling as they are, are often easier than emotions to manage. She said perhaps my grief about the adoption was homeless until the tow truck hit me, and then it took up residence in my hip, where there was an actual injury and a valid excuse for pain to reside.

That made sense, but it also made it harder to heal. The only thing that had ever helped me tolerate the grief was running itself, but I wouldn't be able to run until I got rid of it.

That spring, my grandfather died in his recliner, beside my grandmother in hers. I got the news at work and left immediately. I cried all afternoon, and then Caleb and I planted tomato seeds out beside the garbage cans in front of our apartment. I decided I would save the seeds from those tomatoes and replant them every year, and every spring I would think of my grandfather.

At the funeral, Grandma rolled to the front of the tiny church and insisted we stop crying. She couldn't find it in herself to want anything for Grandpa that he didn't want himself. Once he could no longer build things or plant things or fix things, it was no longer a life. She tried to make us laugh by reminding us about the time she fell in the driveway and couldn't get up. Grandpa ran to the barn to get the backhoe and carefully bounded toward her—careful because the brakes were shot, the edge of the steel bucket was sharp, the ground was bumpy, and he didn't have such a good view of everything from his seat. But he rolled to a stop just behind her, lowered the bucket, scooped her up, and returned her to her feet like a gentleman.

After the funeral I sat in the sunroom with her. His chair had been moved out and there was a giant emptiness there. I talked about my love life, asking her advice as a way of inviting her to talk about Grandpa if she wanted to. Caleb and I had been fighting about the marriage-and-kids question, and because I worked all the time and Caleb wanted me to relax. Grandma said that I was like my grandpa, who thought having fun was a waste of time. "But I don't think Walter and I fought much," she said. "The way I remember it was: He bossed if he was right, and I bossed if I was. And if he wanted to boss the times when I was right, he just yelled louder." She seemed hollow and drained. "Just remember, all the time you spend fighting takes time away from doing things you'd really rather be doing."

Things like playing Wiffle ball in the park, Caleb pitching and Reginauld covering outfield. Or walking down to the lake, where Reg's full-bodied abandon as he leapt into the water gave me a vicarious feeling of physical strength and freedom that made me sure I would run again. These were the things I should think about.

I used all eight inches of our countertop to chop onions to make vegetarian chili according to Paula's recipe, in preparation for my son's visit that fall. All five of them stayed with me while Caleb was overseas visiting his mother. We took the Staten Island Ferry tour of the Statue of Liberty and wandered through Central Park in the rain. And before I knew it, they were gone, just a pile of towels and sheets and sofa cushions in their place.

And within a week, Jevn came to New York on his own business. He was moderating a panel discussion related to his recent book. I hadn't seen him in four years, but from the back of the room in Midtown he looked the same, except for the bright lights and his suit jacket, and except for the way he adjusted the microphone, as if adjusting microphones was now something he did all the time. He was half-hidden by the lectern, and I was a safe distance away, concealed in shadow in the back. It seemed right, to be standing in the audience. I was always, in a way, merely a fan. Jevn spoke in the understated way he always had, about the same things he used to, but now it was his professional persona. I studied his face and realized that now Jonathan's was more familiar to me, and I could see how different they actually were. Jevn was sharp and stern, but Jonathan was soft and smiley.

I couldn't listen. I was too busy watching him stand, and move his jaw, and shift his weight, and pause with care, and hold his thumb and index finger half an inch apart. I took breaks in the lobby, browsing the architecture books for sale as the caterers set wineglasses in neat rows.

When the lecture ended, people stood and got their coats and made their way to the wine and cheese and unwashed grapes, and Jevn and I made eye contact over their heads, across the room. He came over.

"Amyseek," he said in the way he always had, as if my name was a single word with no accented syllables.

"Hi! How are you?—great job!" I said, heart thumping but telling myself to breathe.

"Thanks!" His same open-mouthed smile.

"Shouldn't you be schmoozing?" I asked. I felt self-conscious about monopolizing his time.

"Yeah," he said, and continued to look at me, waiting for the next thing I might say.

I wondered if he had forgiven me, or if I still owed him, somehow. I wondered if I would still be under his spell. He left me for a few minutes to schmooze, and then he asked if I'd like to go get a drink. Everything felt strange: his height, trying to keep up with him as I walked beside him on the sidewalk, entering through the door, sitting so close, side by side, together at the bar, angling myself to talk to him. All things that had once been old habits. Jevn ordered a beer, as he always used to, and I ordered a whiskey, which I'd only started to do after Jonathan was born.

"May I have a Jameson, neat, please?" I said, because Caleb had kicked me at a hundred countertops in coffee shops and bars before I got used to saying, *May I*. People behind bars are people, he said, and proper English and the opportunity to say no are the least you can offer. He would also stick his finger in my mouth if I yawned without covering it; I imagined these were his mother's techniques.

Over the course of several hours Jevn and I talked about our professional lives and our romantic lives. I insisted on addressing his love life because I didn't want to get any more information inadvertently from Jonathan. I asked him about the girl Jonathan had seen him almost *kiss*! When he confirmed she existed and they were serious, I could see her immediately. Someone mature and sophisticated and confident and sensitive and beautiful and careful with words. Dark, voluminous hair. Tall. A hearty, full-throated laugh. Wide-legged slacks. Big sunglasses. A watch and a proper purse. Someone who buys flowers at the farmers' market and fish at the fishmonger. And puts them all bountifully in the basket of the bike she rides glamorously in heels.

And I was surprised by how it sank me. Not just imagining her; I was sad that we could talk casually, as if the past had no presence and our son was just an accident. I wanted us to brush away the weightless things— just years, just geography and experiences, just other boyfriends and girlfriends. Some part of me still felt a claim on him, because we were once together and we might have stayed together, or because we were together, and always would be, in Jonathan.

Jevn still spoke of Jonathan with the deepest reserve and care. It seemed to be difficult for him, but I could not make out precisely why. He said Jonathan was one of the most intense people he knew and that they were already "good friends." He said that finding Paula and Erik remained one of his proudest achievements.

I agreed, but then I mentioned a frustration I'd had when they visited, that Paula wanted to find a McDonald's or Starbucks to duck into, out of the rain, but Jonathan wanted to find a hot dog stand, and I wanted to help him have a real New York City experience. Fortunately, I didn't know where any McDonald's or Starbucks were; the closest place I knew of was the café by the model boat pond in Central Park, so we went there.

Telling the story to Jevn, I just wanted a moment with the only person who lost the same son I did to take stock of the particular things we lost. But Jevn wouldn't indulge me. He said he imagined my relationship with Paula wasn't simple, but that he didn't make any assumptions about anyone. He said he was just grateful to know Jonathan. And grateful for Paula and Erik.

Looking at him, I remembered a river. The Ohio River, as it flooded the valley the year I met him. Highway ramps looked like boat ramps; overpasses interlaced underwater. Collapsed buildings were saggy skins, mouths ripped open, gaping with driftwood. I'd ridden my bike beside it, still heaving heavily like the fat barrel of a horse, its obedience generous. The river, that stream of gut certainty Jevn had always told me to tap into—but rivers could overflow their banks and destroy the city, and still my son was the only river I'd ever had.

For a second I felt my old anger. People were always impressed with Paula and Erik's generosity, and it was as if I should just pull a blanket of gratitude over all the loss. But recognizing their generosity undermined my own. I was still, every moment, every day, giving them my son. Surely Jevn could see that; surely he felt it, himself! It trivialized the care we took to find them and create this arrangement, which we'd all done together, and the pain and guilt and exhaustion I experienced all the time— didn't Jevn feel those things, too? Letting us see our child was part of the deal; it was the least they could do, and it didn't compare to what we'd sacrificed. Grateful as I was, I wouldn't tell myself it solved anything.

But I didn't say any of that. I just agreed that we were very lucky. Jevn was a blank, blunt wall that wouldn't be penetrated. His friendliness and warmth, the particular give I could see he had for me, did not lead to an opening. I hugged him goodbye, but I couldn't find his edges. He was a smooth, warm white wall, going to infinity in all directions, and my eyes still could not make out whether he was near or far.

THIRTY-ONE

H i." My son's name appeared in the lower right-hand corner of my screen at work, overlapping my drawing. My heart raced, surprised at his sudden appearance, completely unencumbered by planning, or packing, or traveling to see him.

"Hi!" I responded. I smiled and then glanced around the room and then waited anxiously.

"What are you doing?" he asked.

"Working," I told him. "I work every day, from morning to night!" When I'd arrived in New York, there were twenty-five staff; now we were down to five. Those of us who had survived the economic collapse were just trying to keep our jobs, despite increased workloads, pay cuts, and mandatory unpaid days off.

"Man! You have a lot of work."

I told Jonathan he should be outside instead of on the computer, and he told me I should be, too. He said he had to go.

I closed my chat and returned to work. I was trying to finish a layout for a park in London that was already under construction; landforms were being built at the speed we could design them. The project was enormous, fast-tracked, and understaffed, but I was accustomed to working under pressure. I knew how to time production for color calibration, for file size handling, for last-minute concept overhauls. I had work-arounds for every issue, and I'd seen enough sunrises over Tribeca to be confident I could produce efficiently around the clock.

I tore off a piece of trace to go over the contours again and paused for a moment to think. I gazed down at my tabletop; I adjusted my lamp and paused in its warmth. And then I said it to myself: *I love him.* I looked all around me, trying to orient myself. The windows still facing south, the last moments of sunset passing between the buildings, car horns sounding the early end of Friday. What I felt was beautifully automatic; it leapt ahead of me, holding and claiming him. I *love* him, I said to myself again and smiled, surprised that my feeling was persisting, that I hadn't found a way to shut it down.

Those words felt new; I hadn't said them to Jonathan since before his adoption, and I didn't think them to myself when I pictured him. I might tell friends I loved him as a shorthand for the many feelings I felt for him that were too complicated to name, but I always knew it wasn't love, exactly. Love was something different from desire, or pain, or guilt, things that rose easily to the surface when I thought of my son. Love was light and free; it was among my many feelings, but it was held down by heavier things. Love felt good, and I wouldn't normally allow myself that indulgence.

I thought I remembered saying I love you in my mind as I held him when he was still a baby. But my love had no arms to wrap and keep him. I'd pushed that feeling forward like a birthday wish, or like a boat I was shoving off a sandy shore that scrubbed the surface of the ground, lightened, and was gone. I trusted it would go somewhere, but I had no control, and I didn't watch to see it disappear. If I'd tried to say it out loud then, only Paula and Erik would have understood, Jonathan still so little, and I thought it might undo Entitlement. I thought if they heard me tell him *I love you,* they might think I was claiming my motherhood, or experiencing regret, or flaunting a feeling they were working hard to achieve. *I love you* did damage. I stayed silent and smiled at him, weighting my love till it floated forward and away.

When he got older, I could have said it, but how? After he took my pawn and I took his bishop? When we were playing basketball? Or riding bikes? No, those were words you whisper to your child as he's falling asleep. Or when you're sending him off to school, to remind him you'll be there when it's time to come home. Love was a comforting already-known, a balloon you tap easily, to keep it in the air. The right time would have been as I was leaving, when everyone was gathered in the foyer, saying things like "so good to see you," "good luck next semester." But then, that was not the right time to say it. "I love you," directed at my son, was completely unlike "Goodbye, thanks for having me." Instead of giving gracious closure to my visit, *I love you* would rip this structure wide open and point directly to my unique relationship with Jonathan. It would beg the question, If I loved him so much, why was I saying good-bye at all?

And since his adoption I hadn't felt a thing that was light and free, or that compelled me to say it. I had sedated my instincts, and there were no secondary instincts for a surrendered son that would bubble spontaneously to the surface with an appropriately timed and tempered statement of affection. My son was always examining me with narrowed eyes, and I thought he knew that the feeling I felt for him wasn't simply love. Saying I loved him would make him doubt my love; he would think I just threw words around carelessly. It was enough for him to see that I was there, committed and available.

But now, I did feel it. I was saying it in my head; I was saying it to all the fibers of the gray carpet. I couldn't work because I was busy saying it. It felt brand-new and incredible, a whole new identity, a whole different terrain. What wall had been moved? What had changed in that moment sitting at my desk that freed this involuntary feeling, that brought my son so close to me, for the first time since his adoption?

I thought back to a moment on the Staten Island Ferry. The ferry was pushing through wet fog as the kids and I played a chaotic game of tag that had us running back and forth through the interior to the outer walkways on opposite sides. The ferry was almost empty that afternoon. On one of my sprints through the cabin, I found Paula and Erik and sat down with them to catch my breath. Soon, I heard the kids screaming. I got back up and peeked my head out the door and looked down the long walkway. I saw Jonathan, standing still but laughing and breathless, his back toward me. He yelled, "Where's Amy?"

"Over here!" I called back, darting away from him down the walkway, and our game resumed.

It was such a small thing that I hadn't told anyone about it. It was nothing—but it was everything—to see him looking for me. It seemed, in that moment on the ferry, he freed something that only he could. And now it was rising up in me, like butterflies.

And yet, when we signed off of our chat, I hadn't said it. *I love you* claimed to know and understand him. But I didn't know anything. I didn't know how he entertained himself on a lazy Saturday or what he thought was funny or his teacher's name or his favorite subject in school. And he didn't know me, because I hadn't let him.

I also didn't want him to feel like he had to say anything back. So instead, I just said: <3. Building a heart out of pieces felt true.

His response had been unrestrained: <3 <3 <3 <3 <3 <3 <3.

Then Caleb appeared on my screen.

"Pow," he said. "How you getting on?"

"Good; my son just chatted me!"

"Coolio. What'd he say?"

"Nothing much—it was just amazing to have him contact me."

"Good they gave him your e-mail."

"Yeah." I hadn't really thought about that.

"What's the difference between *than* and *then*?"

"*Then* is time-oriented. *Than* is a comparison. I am taller than her. I was younger then."

"Right. I knew that. Just confirming. What you want for din? I'll have it on ice for you if you're working late."

☺ ☺ ☺

My grandmother asked me to keep writing her e-mails and telling her stories, and when I had a free weekend in April, I went to visit her. She lay back in her recliner, and I sat close by in the green barrel chair with the wicker back and tried to entertain her with stories about my friends' love lives. I told her she couldn't possibly understand how complicated relationships were these days, because she'd married a really good man. Now there were not only no good men but hardly any men left at all. I told her about the bar I'd gone to in Brooklyn where my friend and I counted twenty-two women but only one man. And of course the one man was on a date with one of the women. I told her about all my friends trying to get pregnant through IUI and IVF and donor eggs; I told her about a friend who just found out her husband had been cheating on her for almost ten years and all of my friends who had boyfriends who wouldn't commit.

In light of all that, I said I was grateful for Caleb, who was at least loyal, even if he didn't want to get married or plan for kids. He just wanted things to happen, naturally, and there was something beautiful about that. If I could get myself comfortable with the idea of building a family without the security of marriage, which he insisted was illusive, I had no doubt he'd be a devoted partner.

My grandma just lay there with a washcloth over her eyes, but at some point she began to rouse herself. Slowly, she got up and into her wheelchair and rolled her wheelchair into my shins.

"The best man." She looked at me hard. "I married the *best* man."

Caleb hadn't come with me to visit her. My family didn't find him *Solid Gold*, and he felt it. They thought he dressed funny; his jeans were too tight, you could see his bright teal underwear when he bent over, and Julie didn't like his dog. My mother thought he should marry me if he loved me so much. He won my parents over when he cooked dinner for them one night and they finally saw how generous and charming he was, but it was already too late. My grandmother was getting sicker, and I felt like I was in a race to start my life before my family slipped out from under me.

I couldn't do it the way Caleb wanted to—get pregnant by accident, and then try to explain to Jonathan why, still unmarried, still financially unstable, this time I kept my child. And I couldn't just wait indefinitely for Caleb to change his mind, only to become one of those infertile people I'd met ten years ago. I couldn't bear to think that the only child I'd ever have would be the one I gave up, and I absolutely could not adopt. Caleb was standing by the bikes in the far corner of our apartment when I got home one afternoon and told him I wanted to break up. He helped me carry boxes and dismantle our bookshelves; he gave me all our joint stuff and made me a bike rack he painted hot pink to hang the bike he'd built for me. We put the pots for the tomato plants on my new fire escape. And he gave me a digital camera, a little present, he said, "for your son."

My new apartment had counter space enough to roll out Christmas cookies and a view of the sunset over Brooklyn. Haystack liked to stand at the windowsill overlooking the city, and she didn't miss Reginauld at all. Sometimes she would walk out onto the metal grate to assert her long-lost independence, and one night she caught a mouse out there in the tomatoes; she brought it inside and ate it like a burrito and then reclined across the countertop as if she'd paid her half of the rent for a lifetime. I tried to make it a little home. It had everything I needed, all of it within a little more than an arm's reach.

But I realized that when I fell in love with Caleb, it was the first time I'd dared to think, *Maybe* this *was why it all had to happen*. Before that I'd rejected reasons—they trivialized the loss. But meeting him was a consequence of a whole life's worth of accidents that included my son's adoption, and wanting Caleb meant wanting to keep them all in place. It meant loving my son, who he was now, eight years old, three hours away, and adopted, instead of holding on to him through grief.

Breaking up with Caleb undid all that. Or maybe it was nothing more than habit. I loved with abandon; my love always let go, as if the fullest consummation of love was to destroy it. To love from afar and watch love float away.

Fresh, piercing pain to distract me from older, duller pains.

◎ ◎ ◎

Paula wrote to tell me she'd been thinking about me and thinking about my grandmother. She said Jonathan had just been through his First Confession, and she herself helped him to write down his "very short, very earnest" list of sins. She said the confession was in preparation for his First Communion, and she invited me to come share it with them.

"I wanted to make sure you know that we would be happy to have you with us."

Their conversion to Catholicism had happened after much "talking, praying, and thinking," and though it meant my son would be raised in the same mysterious faith I'd been raised in, a distinct connection to me, I was mostly happy to be reminded that as solid and stable as they were, they never stopped moving and thinking and responding and growing.

"Jonathan will be resplendent in his all-white," Paula said in her e-mail, "which, as you can imagine, makes him look like a very beautiful, small, slim, virginal used-car salesman. At the very least, we will send you photos!"

But my grandmother had been admitted to the hospital the same weekend, and I went to see her instead. She lay, shadowy and half-alert, in a room lit by a dim bulb hidden in a long, horizontal sconce above the window. Sometimes my cousins would come in and rub her head or her cracked heels, as they had been doing since they were little. What more important reason to have a child, than to have someone to rub your feet as you die?

"Precious one," my grandmother said when I got close.

Her face was gray, her eyes vacant. It was not the time to remind her about what she'd said about getting my son back. I wanted to know what she meant, and if she still thought it, and how I was supposed to do it, now that she'd be gone. She only said something about how life never gets less painful, and she said it like she was disclosing what now, on her deathbed, she knew for sure; the world's worst-kept secret.

She died in her recliner at home two weeks later by her window that looked down the road and out to the bird feeder. The day she died was the same day the program I'd worked to develop began distributing fresh vegetables from a New York farmer to a low-income neighborhood in Brooklyn. After the distribution, I went home and stood in my kitchen. I wanted to call Caleb, but instead I placed an order for a thousand worms and built a worm compost out of two nesting plastic containers to sit in my kitchen, oozing and squirming, producing rich soil out of cantaloupe rinds and tomato stems, in honor of my grandmother. There was something about putting my hands into the earth that connected me to my family. Something about tomatoes, which my grandpa would slice with his razor-sharp knives, and worm castings to fertilize my fire escape garden, like it was in my blood to do. Taking the earth in my hands, I was embracing all of them, all of it.

THIRTY-TWO

I felt myself falling forward, rolling head over knees in darkness. I heard someone saying the word *breathe*. That word that had guided me so many times now seemed to be a quality of the black landscape, *breathe, breathe*. I heard the word repeated, but it appeared as a row of trees, chopping the sunset into a million pieces as I drove fast through the forest.

"Breathe, Amy, breathe!"—louder and clearer. I could no longer sense the pins tapped deep in my neck and my lower back, and my ankle, and the meat of my thumb. I'd taken flight, off the edge of the road, and I'd lost sense of up or down. There was just that word, a rhythm that could swallow all the world's complexities. Of the many possibilities, most of them were invisible; none of them had meaning. One of them was *breathe*; it was the string of a balloon rising faster than I was in the darkness, and as it nearly touched the edge of my hand, I opened my fingers to take hold of it.

After I opened my eyes, I sucked in the air. I was shaking and wet. The acupuncturist treating my injury said that I'd had a seizure. She was shaking herself. There was no real explanation. Just another confusing manifestation of my injury, or my grief, or just bad acupuncture. But it scared me. It made my injury, which had become an old friend, dull and familiar, seem newly potent and dangerous.

I had embraced the pain, thinking it was honest and simple. It communicated danger and had no motive for trickery. But pain was just a communication between the body and the brain. And like any relationship, it could turn dysfunctional. The physical injury and my son were all tangled up in my mind and in my blood and in my neurons and cells. I'd always known the knot wouldn't be undone by pulling hard on its ends, but now I knew time alone wouldn't loosen it, either. More than that, I understood that grief wasn't a friend, and that the tangled knot did not somehow contain my son.

When I recovered, I walked home strangely vigilant. I watched cars carefully, feeling vulnerable, under threat. I knew that I'd been at a fork in the road and that I could have decided anything; it hadn't even felt like a decision. But we are always making that decision, pushing through impossible pain, a thousand futures crumbling with every step. *Breathe*, I told myself, as I crossed Fourth Avenue.

THIRTY-THREE

N o physical contact," Jonathan said, lifting a bucket of water in the driveway.

"No spitting," Andrew added.

"No spitting," Jonathan confirmed. "Um, pretty much anything besides throwing water on people is not allowed—"

"And walking around and breathing and living," their neighbor Madeleine interjected, holding an empty cup and pouring it over Jonathan's head in mime.

"Anything besides throwing water on people is basically illegal." Jonathan put the bucket down between his feet. "Besides, like, walking and living and that stuff." His hands rotated slowly in a juggling motion, to capture in a cloud the world of processes and activities he couldn't enumerate comprehensively, but which you couldn't have a water fight without.

"Breathing," Madeleine added again.

"Can you jump?" I asked. I was supposed to be the referee.

"Yeah, you can jump if you want. You can, um . . ." He held his hands, one nested loosely in the other. "You can't really pick up any items. Throw them, use them." Each arm, alternately, moved out and around in a tiny backstroke to indicate everything in the yard around us that you could not pick up, throw, or use. Jonathan tried to lasso the unwieldy world of things that could not be done, and then he would try to encircle the universe of things that had to be. What water fights were, exactly, would not be pinned down.

"Rock throwing?" I asked.

"No, definitely not," he said seriously.

"Okay, are we ready to start?" I tried to gather the participants. Sam and David called to Jonathan from across the street. Kids were always emerging from every corner, passing through the yard, coming home from church. None of them informed, this particular morning, that a water fight was about to commence.

"We are preparing for battle," Andrew warned no one in particular, placing his own bucket into position, "and don't get in the battle-rabble!"

"Okay." Jonathan took a timid step back and spoke to himself. "Madeleine is coming with two weapons, and I guess that's okay because I didn't say anything about that." I turned to see Madeleine, the least threatening little girl in the world, teetering toward us with a cup of water in each hand.

"Do you wish you had said something about that?" I asked Jonathan.

"Yeah." He laughed, as if that were an extreme understatement.

A plastic tub was stationed below the basketball hoop, rolled there atop Jonathan's skateboard after being filled at the faucet on the side of the house. It would serve as the refilling station for the various weaponry: buckets and cups and squirt guns. But it became an excellent defensive fighting position for anyone who remained there, waiting for empty-weaponed aggressors to approach, seeking a refill. This Jonathan discovered, and the fight escalated in increasingly egregious challenges to the spirit of his carefully laid-out rules, until everyone but Jonathan was soaking wet.

He was nine. I'd attended his birthday pizza party; it was the first birthday I'd spent with him since he was born. Normally I celebrated alone, invisibly, a glance at the sky as I went about my normal routines, and I celebrated early—on the day before his birthday, the day I'd spent the full twenty-four hours in labor—so that his birthday itself could be his. I'd send him an e-mail, and I'd often hear from Paula. But on his ninth birthday, together with him in person, I told him nine was special.

"It's the last year you will be a single digit!" I told him. "For the rest of your life, you're going to be double digits." I remembered the rough texture of my blue bulletin board as I gazed into it, trying to grasp the profundity, when my father told me that. Jonathan smiled up at me. His baby teeth were gone. Replaced by front teeth with a space between them, just like mine.

That early image Paula and Erik had described in their Dear Birth Mother letter and over e-mail before my son was born, a life centered around books and friends, had begun to flesh itself out. They'd moved to New Haven and bought a large, old house, where each of the kids could have a bedroom; there was a formal living and dining room as well as a sunken family room and, upstairs, a proper guest room, where they often had friends or colleagues staying. They'd always hoped to end up in Chicago, but New Haven had many of the things they wanted in a city: it was walkable (Paula could see her front porch from her office window), had a functional public transit system, and gave both Paula and Erik good career prospects—they had both acquired teaching positions. And since they planned to stay for a while, they quit homeschooling and enrolled the kids in an elementary school two blocks away.

This was the place the kids would remember as home. Paula and Erik had purchased the empty lot beside their house, splitting the cost with the neighbor on the other side, creating a very large combined yard, which functioned like a neighborhood park. Kids were always congregating there; you could generate a bike posse of probably fifteen kids without trying, and there were spontaneous dinners among neighbors. Doors everywhere opened and closed without knocking. And because I was to my son's friends not quite a kid but definitely not an adult, I was dragged through kitchens and bedrooms and basements of neighbors' homes, unannounced and uninvited, and sometimes I'd be standing face-to-face with a father or a mother, sometimes not properly dressed and certainly not expecting company, when I'd remember I was not a kid at all.

Paula had picked me up from the station alone because Jonathan was still at basketball practice. She told me all the news: Andrew was taking piano; Jonathan, guitar; and Sarah, violin. They were all involved in sports, and Sarah was getting some extra tutoring in math. Oh, and Jonathan was training to be an altar server at church. Everyone was busy.

My news was that my dad had been diagnosed with esophageal cancer over the winter, and his prognosis was not good. Mom had called to tell me when I was at work. I'd hung up and gone home. In those moments, how easy, how necessary and natural it felt to abandon my work. I understood its limits as I hadn't when I chose it instead of my son.

When we arrived back at the house, kids were gathered in the yard, and I approached them, looking for Andrew or Sarah. Someone emerged from the group to greet me, and I vaguely remembered him.

"We've met before," I said. "Do you remember who I am?" After all this time, I still wasn't comfortable saying.

"Yeah, you're Jonathan's mom," he answered. "Lone Wolf," he referred to himself, with a closed fist beating softly for each syllable in front of his heart. He added over his shoulder that I seemed too cool to be a mom. Then Andrew spotted me and leapt into my arms. We found Sarah, who was now a teenager, and she gave me a teenagery hug.

◎ ◎ ◎

It was early May, the sky full of glorious, high clouds, and just warm enough for a water fight. When everyone left to put on dry clothes, Jonathan invited me upstairs to see his room. I sat on his bed and looked out the window, trying to assess the tiny rectangular space as one measure of his childhood. The exact proportions of this room were determined long ago, when I was looking through profiles, trying to anticipate what couples' promises and photographs might mean for the eventual shape of my child's life. And this was it. This was where he woke, his head pointing toward the window. This was the ceiling he gazed into, and these walls were the color blue of his childhood. Then I noticed there were two framed photos, of me and of Jevn, sitting on top of the hutch above his desk.

He was looking for something within the messy pile of toys beside his bookshelf. Finally, he pulled out the Swiss Army knife I'd given him, engraved with his name. He handed it to me, and I admired it, having forgotten all its features. It still had the toothpick and the plastic protector for the corkscrew, which I thought he would have lost by now.

"Does the pen still work?" I asked. He said it didn't, and I told him I thought we could order a refill. But by then he was handing me the remote control helicopter I'd given him that never got off the ground. Now it was broken, and I felt bad. It wasn't the best gift, but it was hard to buy him gifts. Caleb said to send him little things all the time, but I'd go into museum shops and the things just looked like things. An eraser shaped like the Guggenheim for my abandoned son? Finger puppets to say I wish I had him with me?

He'd sometimes send thank-yous for the things I did send: *I got that Mars Mission ship, and I love love love love love love love love love love love love love it. You picked out one of the most famous ships in my Lego-land. I can't wait to see you again because then you can give me challenges on my skateboard.*

But I wanted him to get rid of the broken helicopter; I would get him the amazing toy helicopter I'd seen in Berlin that was so easy to fly. I told him as much, but he pointed to some of the propeller mechanics and said he had an idea for how to fix it, an idea that involved paper clips and pennies and tape.

"I still have this," he said, showing me the camera that Caleb had given me to give to him.

"Oh, yeah!" I took it from him and examined it. I realized he wasn't looking for anything, he was just showing me things I'd given him. "Does it still work?"

"Yeah, it does video, too." He showed me how to turn the knob to the movie camera and then put it down on the bed beside me.

Then he held out a photo album I didn't recognize at first. I'd put it together in a kind of daze, right after his adoption. It contained family photos, childhood photos, my whole family history in twenty images. As I turned the pages, I remembered I was going to give him a letter to go with it, the story of his adoption, but I'd left several such notes unfinished when I was pregnant, unable to picture my child or to make sense of my feelings. And after he was born there was never the right moment;

the story didn't feel finished. We were always somewhere in the middle of it. It even seemed a little strange for him to have these photographs. They weren't the ones I'd choose to represent myself anymore.

He threw something onto the bed and I reached for it, another photo album. I was surprised to see childhood photos of Jevn and his brother; Jevn had made an album, too. We'd talked about compiling our photos together after the birth, but by then we were trying to heal apart, and I never knew whether he'd sent his own. During that time when there was such deep silence between us, Jevn was sharing his most precious things generously with Jonathan, photos I'd never seen, even one of his beloved uncle.

Finally, Jonathan stood up, finished, and glanced at the pile. It was surprising, the number of moves those things had made it through. I liked knowing he had some special category in his mind for the gifts I'd given him, but I was glad he didn't have a special box for them. That his toys were broken and played with, and the albums containing our precious family histories were worn and sticky like children's books are, telling their ever-changing facts of the real world—not unlike the books on insects or sharks that sat sticky beside them on the shelf.

Over the course of that year, my father's cancer was treated with aggressive chemotherapy and surgery, during which his vocal cords were mistakenly cut, leaving him unable to speak above a whisper just when I wanted to talk with him most. I'd quit my job in the city and started working for a small garden design company in Brooklyn. I was following in my father's footsteps, building a business. He struggled to hear, though he wanted to know every detail, and he struggled to speak, and I hated to make him repeat himself. But one day, walking home from work, I called to tell him about some business strategies we were developing at work, and he said very clearly that he had only one business strategy.

"Don't overcharge people."

"That's not exactly a business strategy, Dad!"

"All I ever needed," he whispered with conviction.

In the periods between treatments, he continued working in his office and on his side projects. When I went to visit in the early summer, he was busy building a twelve-foot-tall cannon-like device with a long, open channel made of two-by-fours, string, and PVC. The barrel of the cannon had various strings and springs and pulleys along it, and it leaned on a wood frame. From a distance, it looked like a tall, narrow, almost completely unthreatening easel.

"We're calling it a gasoprong," he said, smiling at me, though no one, not even he, knew where he got that name. "We have to get on the Internet and find out what it's really called."

"And what's it for?" I asked him. His tools were scattered across the floor in the garage. And plastic chairs from the deck were positioned at his different workstations. Every word, every movement made him pause to catch his breath.

"Shoots a lead weight. There'll be a string attached; it'll go up over a limb." He gestured with one index finger looping around an imaginary high limb and smiled, as though the delightfulness of this should be self-evident.

"But why?" I asked.

"It's for making swings. Really high swings." He smiled and wiggled his eyebrows once. Like an engineer of old, he had to invent a machine to create the thing he really wanted to make. The actual thing was a swing that would float on multiple hinge points through the forest, like a Jacob's ladder, like Tarzan. He wanted swinging to be as much like flying as possible, and he planned to make this new swing in Baltimore at my sister's house. He had surveyed her yard in the freezing cold of that previous winter, my sister manning the ranging pole, to determine possible trajectories.

Her backyard was a playground of custom-designed and hand-built hazardous things. There was a zip line that launched off a high platform and ran a hundred feet through the trees. It had two settings: dangerous and, with an ingenious mechanical adjustment even a small child could manage, very dangerous. He hand-knotted the safety net, a complex matrix of big bowline knots of heavy rope and little bowline knots of a lower-grade rope. My mother said he sat working on it for hours. There were swings of all kinds, tire swings, infant swings; the backyard was a field of magical seats that swung from branches so high you couldn't easily see where they attached.

My dad couldn't say I love you, but he built things. The rare times I'd dated boys who couldn't build things, I would wonder if they cared about me at all. But as long as shelves were built and knots were tied and gardens were planted and swings were hung, then I knew.

"Let me show you the power of this thing," my dad whispered as he invited me to pull back on the mechanism, an eight-foot-long trigger that stretched a massive spring at the top to cock the device. I pulled down with both hands on opposite ends of the screwdriver that was serving as the handle for the cocking mechanism. Tugging with all my body weight, I could only get it halfway cocked.

"Don't let it go," my dad said, smiling.

My brother and I carried the gasoprong to the backyard and stationed Dad's plastic chair at its base. We acted as if nothing was abnormal, though he was skeletal underneath his clothes. He had hammered new holes in his belt, and his pants were cinched around his tiny waist. We just enjoyed the evidence he was still the same person inside, even as we had to help him in ways we'd never had to before. We took his direction and moved the gasoprong into place. And soon, the tall inscrutable device was set up and ready to test.

"I'd like to be a little farther away from it when it fires, since it's marginally dangerous," he said. It was an inventor's conundrum; how to be close enough to pull the trigger, but far enough away not to get hit with a lead weight. "And since I'm not sure how marginally."

He moved his chair six inches back and sat down. He tilted his head and scanned the length.

"Looking at it," he whispered, "where does it look like there's potential for failures?"

"What do you mean?" I asked him.

"It's going to be easy to figure it out after it doesn't work. What's hard is to figure it out before it doesn't work." He began to position himself to fire it. My brother and I were pensive, but we didn't know what success would look like any more than failure.

"Where's the safest place to be?" I asked.

"I think probably behind it," he said with a scientist's reserve.

"Am I behind it?" my mom asked, suddenly scrambling with no direction. "We ought to warn our neighbors."

"Less exciting if we warned them," Dad said. "Is everybody ready?" He tugged the string that pulled the trigger. The whole device hopped and nothing happened. Except that it became a little more clear what he meant it to do.

"Okay. Back to Plan A. I've got to adjust my trigger mechanism."

"The neighbors just pulled up," Mom said, as if putting a hole in their roof would be more conscionable if they weren't home. And without warning my dad shot the device at low tension from half-cocked. The lead weight flew up in the air and swung back, almost knocking him in the head; he was slow on his feet from the chemo. But he declared that test a success, inasmuch as it was a definite failure.

When I woke up in the morning, I reveled in the sound of my mother clinking dishes in the kitchen and my father's thought-laden steps, now slower and lighter as he made his way to the bathroom and then down the stairs. The exact dimension of the space, the particular echo of the hallway, everything was perfectly positioned to deliver those sounds to my bedroom to comfort me with the world's unchangingness. I used to lose myself in the textured ceiling, trying to comprehend eternity, and sometimes I would try to comprehend my parents' deaths. It was like touching my finger to the sharp edge of a blade to feel the sticky scrape of the narrow edge. It was a kind of thrill to imagine the horrifying un-imaginable only to remember that it wasn't real. But it was also import-ant to chip away at it, because someday it would be.

I lay in my bed and thought, *There will really not be many more mornings like this.* But this news was not news. I'd always known my dad would die. I cried, but wildly. I cried for common knowledge. I cried for reality. I cried at confirmation that everything is invisibly slipping out of your grasp; the world had elbows that were sharp inside you and growing, without cushions, as you prepared for the inescapable moment when you would have to let it go.

THIRTY-FOUR

My heart leapt, seeing Jevn's name on my screen, that singular sequence of letters, the special shape of the spaces between them. No part of me could dismiss it or put things in some removed perspective, or stop thinking so highly of him. An e-mail from Jevn meant something, it always had. And the whole world disappeared.

He reminded me of our entire story. His momentary happiness when he found out I was pregnant and then my certain and shattering rejection.

I'd forgotten how articulate he was and how generously he loved me. Everything I hadn't forgotten, I didn't know in the first place. I didn't know when I met him how hard it was to find someone good, and honest, and true. I didn't know how few men I'd want to make a father, how very few men I'd want to love in a son.

He said that he couldn't imagine me without my dreams, and for that reason he was glad I'd corrected his delusions and broken up with him. But, he said, *I have never felt so much for anybody, learned so much, misunderstood so much, or apologized so much.* Despite everything, he wanted to do it, wait at the bus stop every day, read every bedtime story—my heart was racing and my hand was shaking, scribbling the word in the beating of my blood before I could find a way to communicate a trembling but certain *Yes*. It was simple! There would be nothing to mourn for!

I looked around to the seats ahead of me, behind, to remember where I was. On the train, almost halfway to New Haven. I flinched as I returned to the present. And back to my computer screen, Jevn's e-mail dated December a decade ago. I'd found it looking for something else. I couldn't remember having ever read it. The trees catapulting across my field of view made me forget for a second that I couldn't fly. But I was ten years down the road I'd dared to close my eyes and fall asleep imagining. Pressing reply wouldn't change anything.

Regret was always doing that. Turning things inside out, making it feel as though time were just a rubbery toy, and I could bend this part to touch that part, and reconnect the pieces in an entirely nonsensical sequence. Regret was always giving the most inaccessible possibilities life and bringing them so near I did not have to reach, or roll, to find the warmth of his tiny breath. I felt I could press reply, and these ten years without my son would be a loop I closed again.

My father's declining condition made it worse. It made impossible things urgent and imperative. Most of all, I had to have children to remember him. But I had done the math a million times. Two years to find a husband, a year to get married, another year to have a baby, eight years until my child would really have memories of my father, two more until he really got how funny my father was, maybe two more till he saw the sweetness. That was sixteen years. How had we not anticipated this? My parents married late and encouraged me to marry late. We had built a super-efficient structure entirely lacking in redundancy. Generation lapped generation by the smallest possible measures of time. And now there was no time left.

I twisted time frantically in my too-long fingers. I would undo his cancer. I would take away his mouthwash, or his cigars, or his antacids or whatever made him have that cancer. I would make him go to the doctor sooner. I would undo his surgery so he could still speak. I would undo my age. We would have a hundred turnip parties, a million peanuts, all the togetherness he wanted. I would find a husband tomorrow. I would have three kids fifteen years ago. They would rub his feet as he died. But that wouldn't happen for thirty more years. I would do everything I had to. I had to do something. And then I realized the impossible thing I really had to do, though I didn't know what it meant, and I didn't know how to do it, and it was scarier than all the other impossible things, but scary as it was, it seemed somehow less impossible: I had to get my son back.

I arrived in New Haven late at night. I had arranged to stay with Charles, a man I'd been dating for a few months who happened to live there, too, and who could not, if his life depended on it, build anything. He'd told me he could see how much I wanted my son, desired him in an unreasonable and impractical way. A way that could never be satisfied, but had a life of its own. And he said that, on that same primal, fundamental, never-to-be-concretized level, he very much did *not* want him. Seeing a photograph of Jonathan, he remembered meeting Jevn by chance in Rome. He told me that no man can fully embrace the child of another man; the child is an intrusion on his territory.

I appreciated his forthrightness. His ability to speak rationally about irrational impulses meant he had sympathy for my own. And it had no bearing on his support for my relationship with my son. He said he did want my son for my sake; he wanted me to have what I wanted. He wanted me to get him back, whatever that meant. He sent me off in the morning with an espresso and an egg.

On the commuter train, I wrote an e-mail to Jevn, asking how he was doing, and he wrote a short reply, saying nice to hear from me and that he was doing fine. He had no idea what I'd been about to write him yesterday. I arrived early. I had time for two minutes in the bathroom at the station. A minute to buy another espresso, just for comfort, at the café. I tried to take my time, take control, like I'd been taught at the piano bench. When you step out onstage, don't rush to start playing. Walk slowly to the bench. Sit, test the height. Roll the seat down, sit and test. This time is yours. Adjust yourself. *Breathe.*

My son was in the backseat next to Andrew, beaming. I waved hello. I wanted to hug him, but it didn't seem natural to open his door and lean in. I just smiled into the back windows as I lifted the handle in the front. I was already not being brave enough.

"Hello!" I said to Paula as I jumped in.

She reached over to hug me. I had the impulse to say, "Happy Mother's Day!" but my imagination cycled through potential worst-case scenarios. Our motherhoods were like one of those optical illusions where you are going up stairs and down stairs—but it's impossible for your brain to comprehend both at once. Would this day be hers or mine? It wasn't for me to decide.

"It is so beautiful today!" I said, instead.

"It is!"

I should have brought flowers. But flowers would seem too much a gesture of gratitude, when I thought we both had reason to be grateful on this day. If either of us had money to spend on flowers, we would have put it into the kids' college savings.

When we arrived at the house, Jonathan, Andrew, and I went straight to the backyard so they could show me their parkour. They'd started learning it the previous fall when Jonathan was getting too big for the swing set and had started climbing on it in a way it wasn't built for, and so I'd said it reminded me of parkour, and then I'd shown him some videos on YouTube. "Amy, is this parkour?" he'd ask, leaping off the monkey bars. "Is this parkour? Is this parkour?" Andrew would run and jump over the end of the slide and then fall and roll across the yard. It was all parkour, as far as I could tell. Parkour is urban gymnastics; it is running the skyline of the city, it's enjoying full ownership of your lungs and limbs, it's jumping off roofs, balancing on handrails, leaping down stairways, making stunt props of every obstacle. Paula signed Jonathan up for gymnastics so that he could enjoy all those dangerous things more effectively. And now, seeing him walk on his hands or attempt a forward flip, knowing he'd been practicing since I last said goodbye, I felt proud. I was seeing the imprint of something I'd said on a whole chapter of his life. Then I quit thinking that. It would probably make him look at me with suspicion.

I went inside to say hello to Sarah and Erik. Sarah was cradling a rabbit, one of the many small creatures she kept in her attic bedroom, its sloped ceilings painted like the sky. I gave her a hug and spotted Jonathan slipping in through the sliding glass door. As soon as I unwrapped Sarah, he grabbed hold of me.

"I didn't hug you yet," he explained.

I squeezed him hard, as if I was compensating for my negligence, but really it was less hard than I wanted to squeeze him, all the time. I was glad he made it happen; I'd been trying to figure out how to negotiate a hug after the car ride home, without it being awkward, without everyone wondering why I was suddenly laying a hug on him, and—there it was. I got it.

I hugged Andrew happily after that, picking him up.

"How much do you weigh?" I asked him. I'd started to love him somewhere along the way. He was easy to love. It made me think about how difficult it must have been to give him up.

"Fifty pounds," Andrew answered earnestly, as if it was a natural question for one person to ask another.

"Only fifty pounds?! You feel much heavier." How much, how much weight was hidden in those fifty pounds.

Erik got breakfast ready while Paula set the table and put the bagels on a plate. I gravitated toward my son, waiting for me in the dining room. He sat down and told me which seat was mine: the head of the table. He said it with such confidence, I thought maybe it had been decided by everyone earlier, and I sat. Maybe the mothers were taking each of the heads of the table. But no, Erik took his seat at the other head. Paula sat down along the side. I, the fertile concubine. Her in the trenches, with the actual children, with the dirty job of being a mother. Or maybe all of that was the opposite. I was the dirty producer, and she was the acting mother, the one with dignity. She should be here in my place, for sure. Aiy. I hoped everyone understood Jon told me to sit here, and I was only sitting here because he had.

Erik had made a massive breakfast. Usually meals were very small when I visited, and since Paula was usually in charge of cooking, I wondered if she simply lost her appetite when I was around. But not today; Erik made me a mimosa to start, and the table was laid out with eggs and spinach, fruit salad with strawberries and cantaloupe, croissants, fried potatoes, and bagels.

"Wow, Erik! This is extravagant," Paula said as she sat down. "I guess I'll be going grocery shopping again this week."

These were the kinds of paradoxes of being a mother-mother on Mother's Day—even with breakfast made for you, you still don't get a break. Erik poured my coffee. I decided not to eat too much and not to ask for a refill on my mimosa. Jonathan wasn't eating the very small scoop of scrambled eggs I'd given him.

"Jonathan had doughnuts at church. He doesn't have room for eggs!" Erik winked at Jon. Erik was always eating leftover food off the kids' plates, like father-fathers were supposed to do.

Usually I wouldn't say anything, no matter how hard it was to see my son not eat. But my father was sick, and Jonathan was my only son, and I had to somehow get him back.

"Even if you get full eating bad-for-you stuff, you still have to eat good-for-you stuff so you can get enough nutrients," I said, boldly.

Jonathan thought about it and picked at his eggs.

"If you're going to get any good at parkour, you need protein, and iron, and B-twelve, and all kinds of nutrients you can't get from dough-nuts and Lemonheads and those kinds of things." I was parenting from the head of the table, right in front of everyone!

He took maybe one more bite.

"That's really good reasoning from Amy, Jon," Paula said. I wondered if she thought I was trying to do her job, or trying to suggest she was negligent in the role I gave her, and whether she wished I wouldn't or whether she welcomed it as someone who welcomes any person taking an interest in the good of her children, or welcomed it exactly because I am her son's birth mother, having a relationship she has always wanted me to have with my son. I was probably not paying enough attention to the other kids and whether they were eating their eggs.

"Jon, have you told Amy about your interest in philosophy?" Paula asked. "I'm going to a conference next month and the kids will be going with me. Maybe Jonathan will present a paper at the conference?" she suggested coyly. Jonathan smiled broadly and began to think.

"You'll have to get started on your research!" I tried to participate. It was fun to imagine my son as someone who would one day do research.

"I think I'll gather some props," he said, eyes darting around the room, planning the talk he might give. "Like Black Forest Gummy Worms! And what's a big word I should use? *Controversy!*"

He distinguished philosophy as a world wide open; he made a broad, sweeping gesture like a swan dive into the everything. He said he knew that the questions of philosophy were ultimately unanswerable. But, ask them or not, they'll haunt you the rest of your life. I savored for a second his inclination toward uncertainty. Yes, he was very much theirs, the child of academics, but he was also very much mine.

Theology, on the other hand, was built from argument upon argument. He crouched and squinted his eyes at the tiny bricks he was laying in the air, argument upon argument, building a wall with surgical precision, using index finger and thumb of each hand. He used the word *argument* derogatorily: he meant those boring conversations that took place between his theologian parents and their theologian friends in the living room, in the side yard; his world was full of theologians having arguments.

"You're very good at arguing, though, Jonathan," Paula challenged him. "Remember a few nights ago, when I said it was time to go to bed, and you said, 'Can I have just five more minutes?' Wasn't that an argument?"

"I was asking a *ques*-tion." Jonathan slowly enunciated the word. Questions were the hallmark of philosophy.

"Questions are a basic component of arguments—"

"*See?*" Jonathan exhaled, exasperated. "You're arguing with me *right now!*"

Paula asked how my father was doing, and I told her all I knew. He had not been totally debilitated by chemotherapy, and the cancer hadn't metastasized, despite its advanced state when the doctors had discovered it. His years of eating well and staying active had paid off, but I had no sense of his prognosis. I told her I'd really like it if they could visit him that summer. I said it casually, as if my father wasn't dying, my son not my only hope. Surely they would understand the importance.

"Well, the one big thing we have planned is Andrew's birth mother's wedding. Andrew is going to be the ring bearer!"

"Oh, wow!" I wasn't about to try to take something away from my son's brother's birth mother.

"The wedding is in July. We were only planning for me and Andrew to go, but let me think about how we might all do both."

Then Erik asked about my injury, and I told him I still wasn't running. It was a constant preoccupation, but I didn't linger on the details, maybe because they didn't elaborate the details of their own lives, either; we caught up in broad strokes. Or maybe because my life was just the story of a prolonged adolescence, an endless series of phases, lacking any of the milestones that warrant conversation: getting married, buying property, having children. My son's adoption had established their family, hearty and real, but it made me altogether weightless.

They never passed me the potatoes. They sat eternally to the left of Erik's plate. I wondered if that was to deprive me of them so that I would starve to death and then Jonathan would become more fully theirs. Or maybe they thought I'd ask for them if I wanted them. But I took only what I was offered. I'd already expressed my desire for Jonathan to see my father and to eat his eggs, and those efforts had exhausted me. It was enough of what I wanted for a day.

The kids brought out a cake with two candles on it. They set it directly in front of Paula. All this thinking about my role, but there was really no doubt about it.

"Should I blow them out?" she asked. But before anyone answered, she did so quickly, as if to eradicate the implications of that question. Why two candles? I wondered. If there were two mothers, there were four mothers to remember at this table. I wondered if Sarah and Andrew were thinking about their own. Paula announced that we were all too full to eat cake, but I thought I would have liked a piece of cake, having not had much breakfast.

I was now older than Paula was when she'd already adopted one baby and was e-mailing me in the evenings to talk about adopting mine. Ten years ago, they were the adults, and I was as much in need of parenting as my son. Our distance had given me a certain security in the decision, but now I'd caught up. I was old enough to parent my son. I'd traveled and finished school and explored enough to know there wasn't really anything out there better than loving a child. And so even as I was accustomed to adoption, it seemed my regret grew more, not less. And every day they knew more than I did what I lost and how deep that regret should be.

"Screen time is up, Jon. No more videos on the computer." Jonathan and Andrew had slipped away to the laptop that sat on the kitchen island. Paula parented casually, as if to remind me that the decision was already made.

Erik began to clear dishes, and I could tell Jonathan was bored waiting for our eternal breakfast conversation to end. I asked him if he wanted to go for a walk. He nodded and sat down in the foyer to put his shoes on.

"You can't come, Andrew," he said, seeing his brother getting ready, too. "You're too young. You'll get in the way." Andrew began to cry, and Erik took him upstairs to talk. I imagined he said something about letting Jonathan spend time alone with me. We knew early on that Jevn and I would likely visit more than the other birth parents, but Paula had assured me they would never deprive Jonathan of time with me just to preserve an illusion of fairness for the other kids. Still, I felt guilty for the pain my visits may have caused the other two. I thought I should pay more attention to them, but I knew that wouldn't solve the problem. And I'd recently decided to stop pretending my son wasn't special to me.

I slipped out, myself, wanting to escape the whole exchange. As I did, I passed Sarah, who was speaking to Jonathan.

"Jonathan, you saw Jevn last month," Sarah scolded him. "Andrew hasn't seen his birth mother in a long time. You're being selfish."

Jonathan ignored her, and when we got out the door, I asked him about how often Sarah and Andrew got to see their birth parents.

"Not very much," he said, and he didn't seem interested in the question. David, who lived next door, joined us, and we walked across the street to the campus. They leapt over rails, walked along the tops of walls, jumped onto picnic tables. I watched every move. I responded to every trick. And I could see that Jonathan was watching to see that I was watching. I made sure not to disappoint him.

"You sure take a lot of video!" David stopped and looked at me suspiciously. I was taking videos so they could see their stunts, but I was also secretly hoping stills would give me pictures my son would never pose for.

"You guys aren't all that good at parkour, so it takes a lot of footage to get any decent content." I held my ground.

They both laughed and we moved on.

We continued, finding challenges and surmounting them, all across the campus. When we encountered a wall they couldn't climb up, I suggested they visualize the feat first. Think hard about it, see it in your mind, and then—do it!

"I think I should think *easy*," Jonathan contended. He stared the wall down and then ran up it, leaping to the lawn above.

David asked if I thought he could jump down a long set of stairs. I could see he wanted to, and I wanted him to. I said I thought he probably could. He backed up to get a running start and I prayed, *Pleasedon'tkillyourself, pleasedon'tkillyourself.* It was only when we passed other people that I thought perhaps I should tell them not to climb on this or that, or maybe say something like, "Be careful." But it wasn't in my heart. I wasn't afraid for them; I was happy to see them taking over the world. I wasn't sure if that made me more of a mother or less.

"Do you think we look like we could be brothers?" Jonathan put his arm around David and looked up at me as we walked. I thought about the Norwegian ancestry that distinguished Jonathan from his olive friend.

"No . . . not really."

"Well, we're making our *own* family, a parkour family!" Jonathan said, and they both laughed. He must have naturally felt empowered to do such things, having learned family to be an inclusive and self-determined thing. Compelled to self-create, to take back his choice.

I asked David if he had any thoughts about philosophy. He was also the son of theologians, surrounded by arguments. "I have thoughts about philosophy," he said. "My first thought is, Why's that a job?"

Jonathan was the ancient voice that values the pursuit of the unanswerable question, but he listened without concern as David maintained his position, that there was no use in asking. "My cousin is a philosopher and once he asked me, 'What does it mean to be?' I said, 'What does it mean to be what?'"

"HEY! What does it mean to be?" Jon yelled to someone passing by. "No answer?—Let's go!" He leapt off the wall and David followed him.

We passed a group of college students going through Dumpsters to salvage things thrown out at the end of the semester, and Jonathan and David joined them. I stood by and tried to balance chaperone and kindred spirit. They found a perfectly good wire mesh garbage can, a swim pillow that went between your legs to help you focus energy on your arms, a baseball cap, two highlighters, an unopened Valentine's box of Snickers, which they sampled, packs of Pez, a desk lamp, a leather purse Jon would give Sarah, and a table fan. The college boys occasionally smiled at me. I wondered who they thought I was.

We went home to drop off our first round of things and to equip ourselves for deeper digging. Jon was telling Erik about all our finds just as Paula walked in.

"Jonathan was just telling me how much fun he's having Dumpster diving!" Erik said it to Paula, in part, it seemed, to ask Paula whether Dumpster diving was a thing to let the boys do.

"Good!" she said, unsurprised. "It's not like it's the first time they've done it. What did you find?"

I was so glad she didn't mind. That she approved of my lax parenting. I was glad that she didn't rain on the parade of his childhood with worries about germs or rules. And I couldn't help but think she didn't want me to feel I had increased any dimension of his life, today. That I would have to search harder to find something she had not already provided for him. Even among criminal pleasures.

Jonathan had outfitted himself in a winter coat and gloves, and we returned to the campus. On our way, he gave one of the college students a double take, and the student noticed and glanced back at him.

"Nice sunglasses," Jonathan said, oh, so coolly.

The student smiled in thanks. I could tell he was genuinely flattered, but he didn't break his stride. I wondered how my son came to be so comfortable in the world.

Before we made it back to the Dumpster, we happened upon a group of boys and their parents wheeling an enormous television out of the dorm. Jonathan approached them boldly.

"Are you getting rid of that?"

"Yeah, and you're welcome to it!" They looked at me to find out if that was okay, and I'd forgotten I was there.

"You're not—his mom?" the mother stammered. I didn't know what to say. I wanted to say yes. *It's complicated, but yes.* I wondered what he would think if I said yes? Or if I said no? If I waited long enough, I thought, maybe he would respond and I would find out who he thinks I am.

"Um, his mother lives there." I pointed to their house across the street. Then I asserted a little parental authority, telling him I wasn't sure about the TV, as if to say, *Never mind what I just said about his mother, watch this and see if it's not obvious to you who I am.*

"It works," they assured Jonathan. "We were watching a hockey game up until a few minutes ago. There's just always two pucks."

It was a horrendously large and heavy object. It looked like a giant Atari. I called Paula on my phone. She astounded me by saying she would come over to see it. From a long distance we saw her see the TV, and she bent over in laughter. Jonathan smiled and laughed, thinking it was a good sign. But as she got closer, Paula was circumspect. She turned soberly to Jonathan.

"If we take the television now, do you understand it's not a decision to keep the television? It's only a decision to start a *conversation* about keeping the television?"

"I'll only use it for video games, and I'll spend more time outside! I promise! I need a television because—"

"Jonathan, it seems like you're trying to talk about keeping the television now. I don't want to have that conversation now. We can take the television, but we'll have a conversation later about whether we're going to keep it."

"Okay!"

Paula asked me to call Erik to bring the car over, and he pulled up a few minutes later.

"What do you think?" he asked me as he stood and assessed Jon's find.

"I don't really like TV, but I think for the sake of how happy it would make Jonathan . . ."

"I'm just concerned about how disappointed he'll be if it doesn't work. Or if we decide not to keep it." This was how parents were supposed to think. He out-parented me.

They loaded the television into the trunk and secured it, hanging halfway out the back, with bungee cords. One of the neighbors walked across the yard to join us and asked, "Did you buy a television?"

"We don't even know if it will work, but we've bought an adventure." Paula laughed. I laughed, too. That was how they thought about everything, and that was exactly what made it work.

Jonathan leaned out the car window, like a proud hunter coming home with his kill. Erik walked behind the car to secure the television in the trunk, and Paula was at the wheel, taking direction from him.

"Slow down!" Erik called to Paula. "Actually, go as fast as you can, I don't want the neighbors to witness this!"

But soon there was a crowd of neighbors and kids, guiding and advising and laughing and loading the enormous television into the basement, where it was never so much as plugged in.

Charles arrived to pick me up. Jonathan greeted him, eager to show him where I was, and Charles joined us in the living room. He greeted everyone and wished Paula a happy Mother's Day. Paula said her evening plans were to go out to eat with her three girlfriends; it had become a Mother's Day tradition to be left alone to do something extravagant without the kids. She made a gesture of shoving them away and laughed. Entitlement achieved; her motherhood was now a thing she could take for granted. In fact, she had to fend them off.

I hugged Andrew, who was always so sweetly sad to see me go.

"Amy, what should I call you?" he asked, pensively. "My birth aunt? Or . . . my stepmom?"

"I'm sort of like those things, I guess, but I don't really know, Andrew!"

Jonathan and Charles talked a little, and I wished they could talk more. But we were leaving, and Jonathan was going over to David's. It had been such a short day, but I felt the exhaustion coming. Then Paula said it had occurred to her that if the whole family went to Andrew's birth mother's wedding, they wouldn't be more than eight hours' drive from Tennessee. And maybe they could visit my father then, if that timing worked. I said that sounded good to me. *Please let it work.*

We hugged goodbye, and I embraced Jonathan, letting go too soon, and he ran out the door. I was still feeling the urgency of that thing I'd come so determined to do; I just didn't have any energy left. I wasn't sure how I was supposed to get him back. But I knew they'd keep giving him—in weekend visits, in long walks alone, in time with my family—until I figured it out. I made Charles drive by David's, to see if we could see Jonathan again before we left. I wanted to say goodbye again. I wanted to be brave and hug him twice. Charles pulled over and asked if I wanted to jump out, but it was too strange. No, I just wanted to see him. Maybe they're playing basketball. Can you back up a little?

"Go see him if you want to see him," Charles told me.

"No, no, no. It would be weird."

We returned to his house, and exhaustion overtook me.

THIRTY-FIVE

When the earthquake happened in Haiti, Paula posted a warning on her blog against adopting hastily from there. She wrote that really helping a child orphaned by the storm means not just loving it and lifting it out of disaster, but being willing to embrace its original family and community and to "shake your fists at the heaving ground and crashing buildings that took those people away." In precious moments alone with the child, when it's most possible to forget everything that came before, she said, it's an adoptive parent's obligation not just to love the child but to "love it *more* for all the people who couldn't be there."

My dad's weight was down to 147. Mom said he was as thin as he'd been when he was all legs in his ski pants in the Alps, fifty years ago. He had shingles on his back, and his whisper was getting weaker. His hands were bruised, and he patched his skin together with painter's tape; it was so thin and delicate it would rip under the slightest stretch. But he always remembered his Mardi Gras beads when he returned for chemo. And as weak as he was, he couldn't stop building things. That spring, lightning had struck one of the trees that supported the zip line in my sister's yard, and a giant branch had fallen, crushing the railing of the launch deck and detaching the cable. He had to fix it. Building things was a kind of compulsion for him, as it had been for his father, as it was for Jevn. Building was like a first language for these silent men, comprised of saws and hammers and drills and rope, communicating the fundamentalest things.

When I found out he was heading to Baltimore, I told Paula and Erik that this would be the best opportunity to spend time with him. I didn't want to wait until he was dying. I wanted Jonathan to witness him alive and in his element, and perhaps to feel in his own blood the early resonance of something that had always meant so much to my father. I had asked Jonathan once if he was interested in learning how to build things. Jevn had built a playhouse in Paula and Erik's backyard in North Carolina and designed the renovation for their house in Boston. I wondered if it had sparked his curiosity about construction.

"Yeah, but nobody really has to teach me," he responded. "I've known how to build things since before I was born."

I laughed at his so casually taking ownership of a period of time when he was very much within me. He was all mine then! Mine to feed, mine to float in the water, mine to bake in the sun. It must be how mothers feel, I thought; as soon as you teach a child to speak, it will tell you it never needed you.

"Well, that's probably because you went to architecture school with me every day for nine months!" I fought back, playfully, happy to have him push me away and give me an excuse to pull him back.

I knew it would be difficult to coordinate, and I knew what I wanted was excessive and impractical: for my son to have a memory of my father with a hammer in his hand. But I told Paula what my mother had told me, that my father had been refusing to eat. She said she'd make seeing him a priority. Everyone except Sarah would be able to come.

When Jonathan got out of the car, he walked right up to my sister's son, standing by the tire swing. Both still blond and skinny, they stood for a moment before the mirror of each other. Jacob was nervous and shy; he battled a stutter, and he looked up at Jonathan warily, but Jon wrapped his arm around his shoulder like they were old friends, and they walked into the yard together. Paula and I said hello and stood side by side as we watched them.

"A little too sweet, isn't it?" She laughed. "Jon is drawn to kids younger than he is; he's really protective of them. It's so funny to me!" But she was positioned to be surprised by her children. She had no particular expectations, she said, because as an adoptive mother she never saw her children as miniature versions of herself. She said she was always aware that her kids were on a "completely new adventure called themselves." We were both, all the time, between hugging and holding on to him—perpetually, reluctantly, letting him go.

"Jonathan," my dad whispered, emerging from the house. He'd been taking a nap, trying to build up energy for the work ahead: rebuilding the zip line launch deck and its railing.

Jonathan walked, stiff-shouldered, up to my dad, who appeared pained as he stood in the driveway, one hand clasping the threshold of the garage. There were two-by-fours propped up on plastic kids' stools on top of the asphalt, prepared to be cut at an angle drawn in Sharpie. My father handed Jonathan the Skilsaw. He knelt down and showed him how to align the blade with the mark, instructing him to err to the left if at all. Then he stood and caught his breath, and Jonathan looked up at him. My father pointed to the mark and smiled wearily.

"Yeah. G-go ahead. Cut there," he whispered, resting immediately after the exertion. My son seemed to understand that there was good reason he wouldn't get more instruction than this. Erik passed by carrying suitcases into the house and took a casual interest in Jonathan's work.

"Danger-parents, I think that's what we should be called, right, Jonathan? I think I'm supposed to be discouraging this kind of behavior!" He laughed.

My dad smiled, though I'm not sure he really heard Erik. But Jonathan heard him and looked up, unamused. He was by nature extremely careful, unlike Andrew, who returned repeatedly to the emergency room without acquiring any sense of his own fragility. Put together, Jonathan became a bit more daring, and Andrew might sometimes think twice.

We worked all afternoon. Jonathan was the primary laborer, given minimal direction just before having to execute, having no real sense of the overall scope of the work or when it might be complete. After the wood was sawed, the project moved to the yard, just beneath the launch deck, and my dad sat in a plastic chair while Erik and Jon assisted him. My dad showed Jon how to take slack out of the steel cable with the come-along, notch out joists, lay floorboards. Slowly, he showed him how to tie a bowline knot.

"It's a very useful knot," he said. "Doesn't slip much. Doesn't slip any. All these knots here are bowline." He pointed at the safety net. "Now, slip that around the two-by-four." He handed Jonathan the looped end of the rope.

Every time I looked, my father was standing, seeming light-headed, taking a deep breath with his mouth open and squinting his eyes, or he was sitting, his head in his hands, occasionally handing a drill or an extension cord or a wrench to Jonathan. Jonathan worked while the other kids, too young to help, played on swings nearby.

My sister, now pregnant with her fourth child, came outside carrying a bucket of vegetable peels and cores and seeds. Jacob followed her, eyeing the construction site.

"Mom, what happens if the zip line falls on us?" he asked my sister, looking up at the thick, twisted cable above him as she dumped the compost into the garden.

"Then I consider how lucky I am that I have other children, man," she said. Jacob's eyebrows furrowed. This was the kind of thing my family was always saying to me when I was little, reminding me at every opportunity that I was an accident. I hoped Jacob knew she was kidding. I followed them back into the house, where Paula and my mother were sitting at the table, talking about all the perfectly good things that get thrown away at the end of a college term. My mother described the way my brother, now a university professor, would drive around picking up furniture and lumber to salvage.

"That's a great idea!" Paula put a hand closer to my mother on the table, leaning toward her in her warm, engaging, friendly, easygoing way. "That's what we're always saying; there is so much stuff thrown away! Someone should organize a Goodwill or something to sell this stuff back to other students. I mean, lamps, and beds, things that parents spend a lot of money on. It's not like those things have had ten years of use."

Julie put a plate of buckwheat burgers between them. She didn't coordinate proper meals the way my mother had; she just continuously cooked and continually put food on the table.

"I'll have to think about that," Paula continued. "Some kind of exchange center for college stuff. I'm sure it wouldn't be that hard to organize." Paula was often, breezily, coordinating bake sales and hosting refugees and renovating their downstairs apartment to provide cheap housing for students.

My sister had made a giant spelt pizza, and she called the kids over to the cyan picnic table outside to eat. Jonathan looked over at them.

"Let's just get three more floorboards tied in, okay?" I said. "Then we can go eat pizza." It felt like a betrayal of the purity of our relationship, untainted by parenting, telling him what to do, as if I had any authority at all. But my dad was losing stamina, and every time he handed Jonathan a hammer, or helped him tighten the screws, or showed him how to avoid stripping the screw heads, Jonathan was seeing him, and there was a chance he would remember him. Jonathan glanced at me, then down at the drill, like I was laying claim to something he was unsure about giving me.

But I didn't have time to worry about it. My sister needed help carrying more things out to the table. Cauliflower-quinoa cakes, nettle soup, pumpkin custard, buttermilk smoothies, sautéed greens from the garden, rhubarb chutney, chard frittata, peanut butter balls, cucumber salad, corn on the cob. My mother was nagging her to clean up the kitchen while she cooked instead of leaving a disaster to clean up in the morning. Paula was telling Erik that she was exhausted from the trip. Jacob was screaming at Abigail, two years younger but meaner. There was too much going on for me to think about who my son was to me; if anything, at that moment it felt like our loss was an incidental fray in a larger fabric. My son was part of the swirl of family, and when I looked over at him taking direction from my father, I felt, I *love* him, and I didn't think our bond at that moment needed tending. I could take it for granted so that I could pay attention to other things. To Paula and Erik, who I wanted to make sure felt comfortable and had what they needed. To my father, who often needed help silencing the commotion around him so he could be heard. To my brother, who I hadn't seen for a while, to Andrew, and to my sister's kids. I saw my son more often than any of them.

And I actually felt that. I could take him for granted.

After the pizza, the kids dispersed in the yard and the loose forest became a sunset paradise of children swinging and chasing lightning bugs as the adults sat at the picnic table and talked. In the hazy distance, Jonathan and Jacob shared a tire swing. They faced each other and swung lazily in a long arc between the trees. What could they be talking about as they floated, so ponderous and slow?

Dusk fell and my sister had another idea: fire. Jacob gathered sticks and helped her start it as my father had taught us to do, and all the kids gathered around. Jacob placed firewood as Julie directed him. She went inside and came back out with marshmallows and graham crackers and chocolate. The kids looked for long, straight sticks and taught one another to make s'mores.

Fire was among his favorite things, but my father had gone to bed, and I went inside to check on him. He was lying on the sofa bed, unfolded in the playroom. The lights were still on.

"Are you okay, Dad?"

Without opening his eyes, he pointed me to the spot, and I reached out to massage his neck. His body felt hard and stiff as it never had years ago, when he'd beg for a back rub and I'd sink my fingers into his meaty shoulders. I didn't know how to press this new hardness to give him relief.

He was worried about getting finished in the little time we had left. He was still working full-time and had to get back home for a job. Usually, he would hide these kinds of concerns, but I could see the worry in him.

"I'll finish laying the floorboards first thing in the morning, before anyone gets up, so that part will be done by the time we get started," I offered, desperately, to ease his mind.

"Oh, oh!" He stopped me, lifting his head. "L-let the kids do that!"

He smiled and nodded. He was worried, but finishing the project wasn't more important than everything we'd come here to do.

He lowered his head, and I stood above him, stroking his neck so he'd have strength for the morning, pressing carefully at his left shoulder, praying my son would really see him, rubbing his back like I was rubbing raw wool, that cloud of complicated bonds that secured us, a tight and tangled felt.

We had frittata and pancakes for breakfast. Everyone took a plate and a seat as they became available. My sister made the performance of motherhood she was so good at.

"Julie, what *is* this beautiful table?" Paula asked her, sliding her hand across its marbled and many-colored surface. Julie was cutting an apple into skinless, bite-sized pieces and dropping them into Nina's bowl. "It's oak underneath, but I knew the kids would destroy it, so I got a piece of acetate cut for it, and then we finger painted the acetate."

"That's brilliant!" Paula said. "The colors are so beautiful."

Motherhood didn't have time for uncertainty. The hot frittata in the oven, the pancakes sizzling, the applesauce simmering on the stove, the leftovers in the fridge, the lists of chores pasted to the refrigerator, the basket of chocolate hidden on the highest shelf in the cupboard, the cabinet stocked full of dry goods, and the facility with which my sister managed conversation with Paula while she peeled apples and cut servings for people gathered at the table—these were the unromantic realities of parenthood, and they always felt like blows meant to crush any illusion I might have had that I was somehow, also, a mother.

Paula leaned in the threshold of the door, empty plate in hand, articulate and charming, representing and fleshing out and legitimizing our motherhood as she shared tricks of the trade with my sister. I felt as if we were partners, sharing different burdens in the same project. One that happened to look nothing like my sister's. Her plate full, she made her way around the corner of the table and sat next to Erik. My dad sat at one end of the table, eating slowly and carefully. He looked up at Erik.

"I was thinking"—he was asking for silence—"I-I'd guess birth fathers typically aren't nearly as involved as Jevn is, would you say that's about right?"

"Do birth fathers typically design additions for the adoptive family's house? If that's what you're asking, Walter, I'd say probably not!" Erik agreed. He glanced at me and smiled.

My father turned to Jonathan, who had just sat down at the table. "How would you like to take the controls in the glider next spring? Would you like to try that?"

Jonathan smiled, but my heart sank. Next spring. Could we really count on next spring? Could we count on ever flying again?

We gathered outside in the church parking lot, adjacent to the parsonage, an expanse of asphalt that sat empty most of the week and which provided an ideal surface for teaching kids to ride bikes, and roller-skate, and dribble a basketball.

Suddenly realizing he was being watched, Erik stepped back self-consciously and explained—there'd been a fender bender, the damage was superficial, a ding in the bumper, and it had never gotten fixed.

"But the lingering problem, which we discovered on the way down, is that the hood flies up just when it's least convenient for it to do that."

My dad inspected Erik's work. It was just like every single vacation I could remember from childhood. Cars breaking down, new cars being bought or assembled in some backwoods junkyard in the mountains. Crossing our fingers we would make it to our destination, or at least somewhere close.

The kids were scattered around the parking lot, some of them playing with long balloons, twisting and tying them into shapes, popping them, letting them go, accidentally sending them squiggling across the pavement. Paula held Nina's hands as she took some steps. My mother tugged on the bottom edges of Jonathan's T-shirt to flatten the image on the front: *How to Avoid Chores*, it said, and she asked him to explain it. I wondered if it would be the last time my son would see my father, and I wondered what that meant. Then, everyone was strapped into the car, and they backed out. Jon stuck his head out the window; there was something else he needed to tell Jacob. I picked him up and held him at the window.

"You know the action-adventure game?" Jonathan asked.

Jacob nodded.

"Space bar—that's *fire*."

Jacob smiled, they pulled out, and we gave them a Seek Family Wave-Off.

THIRTY-SIX

When I was in architecture school, I asked several of my professors to admit that architecture was not the most important thing in the world. Only one of them would. *Of course it's not!* He laughed at my constant struggling. He was the theory professor who had visited me in the hospital after Jonathan was born. Then he looked down and started thinking. "But what *is* the most important thing? Maybe memories? What are we, human beings, but what we remember? What else do we keep?" I agreed. Memory could definitely be among the most important things.

"And can you think of a single thing that has happened in your life," he continued, "without some kind of picture of the place where it happened?"

Roller-skating in the basement. The cabin by the Arkansas River. The moon through the bamboo in my apartment the night I labored. He was right. Every memory had a place attached to it.

An exercise we'd done in one of our classes had demonstrated the same thing. We had to ask family members to draw their hometowns and describe them as they drew. My mother drew her old village in a map only she could decipher, and the memories flooded back, as if the lines themselves somehow released them. Considering the exact adjacency between the barn and the summer kitchen, she remembered that all her neighbors spoke French and everyone's last name, including her own, was Vallimont. *That's funny, I'd forgotten that!* she kept saying. Locating the chestnut tree by the chicken house, she remembered her many hiding places and the junkyard in the woods where she collected glass bottles. She drew the front porch of her house, remembering the adult bike her dad bought her and how he laughed sitting on the steps of that porch as she tried to teach herself how to ride it. Sometimes she'd ask to go to the candy store, and he'd throw his hat up in the air and say, "If it stays up, we'll go!" but it always came down, and they'd always go anyway. Sometimes to the store, or sometimes he'd take her and her brothers and sisters to the entrance of the coal mine where he worked.

Seeing her see all of it, I could envision her as a child, someone dreaming of leaving her little town and riding a motorbike and never guessing a man might one day drink champagne out of her shoe.

My professor continued. "So if what makes us human, in a way, is our memories, then architecture, when you think about it, is nothing more than a frame for them, a way we try to keep them"—he shrugged—"and maybe I was wrong. Maybe architecture *is* the most important thing."

That kept me going for another couple of semesters.

THIRTY-SEVEN

That winter I started walking. After three years of physical therapy, I had learned to flex muscles most people don't know about and to silence muscles they don't need to. For whatever emotional complexity was involved, my physical therapist explained what was happening on a physiological level like this: my tiny, deep muscles, traumatized by the accident, had receded entirely, forcing the more major muscle groups to cover for them, which is common after big accidents. Those major muscle groups rise to the surface during trauma, to enable you to lift a car off of a person or walk away after a crash, but you have to coax the small, deep muscles to return to work because they are responsible for the microscopic stabilizations of your whole body when you so much as contemplate movement. The big muscles alone do a clumsy job of the deep stabilizations, resulting in chronic pain. I had refused painkillers, and letting the pain linger made those deep muscles settle into their hiding places, as if there was still a threat. But for all these years, my therapist had been instructing me in various ways to call on my cowering deep muscles and assure them there was nothing to be afraid of anymore.

Pulling my laces that first morning made tiny clouds of dust; puff miniatures of the bulbous San Francisco hills where I'd last run. I zipped my jacket, pressed into the cold, and remembered my old friendship with the world in all its seasons. My leg burned and my hip clicked. *Dynamic stabilization*—I reminded myself of what my physical therapist called it—the healing that would come about as my body relearned a hundred microscopic adjustments. Stepping over puddles of icy water and blackened piles of snow, I concentrated on the tiny but essential gap between my sacrum and my pelvis. I watched the world getting ready for work in the early-morning silence as if I were an icicle, observing its passage in my own long, passing lens.

Walking every morning before work, I carved out a space for someday running. And when I wasn't walking, I practiced. Standing at the subway platform, I engaged my multifidi, those deep inner-vertebral muscles that were at war with my meathead hip flexor. No one knew how much concentration it took for me just to take a step.

One morning waiting for the train with Charles, engaging my multifidi, I told him I was impressed with something Paula said when Jonathan asked her how we know there's a God. Paula told me she'd talked about the hunger we're all born with for truth and justice and love, and Jonathan said he knew that hunger. She explained that perhaps the best evidence for the existence of those things is simply our desire for them. That, having small tastes, we only want more, and so we believe it must be out there, in some perfect form, somewhere: perfect love, and perfect justice, and perfect truth. And maybe those things are God.

Her answer was just enough solid stake in the ground and just enough give.

"What? What's so great about that response?" Charles demanded.

"I think it's thoughtful, not too complicated for a kid but open-ended and powerful. It makes you keep thinking about it, testing it."

"I think you have an unfair perception of Paula as a good mother and you, for some reason, as not as good. You would have been able to handle that question, and I'd be much more interested in your answer."

"But I have no idea what I'd have said to that! I'm just really happy they have those kinds of conversations. Why can't you just listen to what I'm saying?" Sometimes I wanted to say I regretted the adoption and have Charles comfort me, and sometimes I wanted to talk about how happy it made me that Jonathan had his family, his brother and sister, his neighbor friends—and I wanted Charles to celebrate with me. I wanted to cry about it and be silent and numb for days; I wanted to be grateful for it! Laugh about it! What was so difficult about that?

"I'm not charmed like you are." He was frustrated with me. "You're determined to minimize your own capacities; I don't get it."

"I chose them over myself to be my son's parents, so of course I'm charmed! And maybe I see them as great because if they aren't somehow great, then that makes this whole thing tragic. But even if my feelings are complicated, and I'm biased, that still doesn't mean they aren't great."

"Amy, they're like master hunters, taking three different mothers' children. And then raising them as their own—it's a very hateable and unnatural thing to have done. To not accept what nature told you, that children are not for you."

The train came, and we got in. By then I'd forgotten about my multifidi, and the pain in my hip returned. It was too crowded to keep talking, and I didn't want to have a fight. He was good at defending me in our conversations about my son's adoption. He was always on my side, against me.

That winter, I had a dream about my son. It was like the blizzard from Kurosawa's *Dreams*, but instead of a group of men trudging steadily in the infinite white snow, it was me and my son, walking slowly toward each other. The distance seemed endless; we were on opposite sides of a great expanse. I couldn't make out his face, only the swing of his shoulders over a shimmering horizon. It was a white space, white sky, clean white ground, the arc of the earth visible in the distance between us. The whiteness was warm and yellow, and waiting was easy.

As he got nearer, I felt a flush of satisfaction that must be the particular sustenance of parents, who feast on the sight of their children healthy and grown. I was content that I could see him there on the horizon and that his movements were filled with confidence. But it was undercut by terror, the greatest fear I know, that he was old enough to frame his question, and, slow as he was coming, he was approaching faster than I could concoct an answer.

I had braced myself for his questions a few times like that in real life. When he was eight, living in Hyde Park, in Boston, we were taking a walk, and I told him that when I had an internship in Chicago, the neighborhood I lived in was also called Hyde Park. Then I remembered that London had a Hyde Park, where I stayed when I was twenty-two on my way home from visiting my sister in China.

"Oh! And Cincinnati has a Hyde Park, too! I almost completely forgot about that."

"Cincinnati!" He brightened. "That's my password for my computer game."

"Really? How did you come up with that? It's kind of hard to spell!"

"Because Mom told me I was born in Cincinnati," he explained. I inhaled, filling my chest, calming my heart. I didn't know whether that word, *born*, and the idea of his birth were for him connected to me. I wouldn't remind him that I was there, with him, in Cincinnati. I wondered if this would be the moment he would finally ask.

But I wouldn't initiate. Beginnings are delicate, and whatever Paula and Erik had told him, he had grown into a secure and happy boy, which was all that I could want. I might have liked telling him about how much I loved him, but maybe his parents' story was focused on my inability to care for him and how much they loved and wanted him. Maybe it would confuse him to know how much I enjoyed him in those two weeks I kept him and that after all this time, I felt certain there never would be a thing I want more than him. No; I wouldn't draw his attention to what we didn't have.

I thought about the conversation they must have had when Paula suggested *Cincinnati* for his password. She might have suggested her own hometown, or Erik's. She might have suggested the town where Jonathan grew up. Why would she want him to be reminded, every time he played his game, of a place where, for a brief moment, he was mine? What efforts was she making, all the time, to bring our history into his life as an everyday reality, fearless of the complexity, fearless of the pain? How often must she talk to him about me, that he should greet me so readily, and want to spend time with me, and keep all the things I gave him?

How had she made sense of that place he was born—the place I let him go? To begin with, it seemed, she taught him how to spell it.

I remained silent as we walked, side by side as we had so many times before, steeling myself for the possibility he might finally ask, certain someday he was bound to, and I would have to find an answer. Steeling myself, too, that he might not ask today, and that I would have to continue to wait.

"When did Mom and Dad come after I was born?" He did draw a connection, his birth and his adoption, and me. He understood a certain sequence. He understood: first he was mine.

"They came right away. They'd been waiting for you."

He was quiet. I was never sure if he was really interested when he was quiet, but I wanted to be very careful not to give him more information than he was asking for.

"How did you find them?"

"I interviewed a lot of people. Most people weren't quite right. Jevn and I spent so much time searching. We wanted to find a really good family." Was that okay? Had I said enough? Too much?

But after that he seemed satisfied, or bored, and changed the subject. Were those really his only questions? And had I really answered them, just like that?

I had my own questions, if he would let me ask. I wanted to know whether he had survived the experiment I'd entered him into. Was he okay? Had I done damage he couldn't repair? Had my visits only aggravated the pain? Was he happy? Did he wish I'd kept him? And I'm not sure what answers would hurt more.

In my dream, when he finally got close enough to speak, he was towering over me, as tall as Jevn, maybe taller. The light behind him blinded me, and I couldn't see his face, I could only feel the shadow of his broad shoulders shaped so much like Jevn's. What would he ask, finally? Would I ever be ready? As he moved even closer, I caught a glimpse of that old suspicion in his face, his clouds, my old sadness, the sadness of all accidents, the sadness I gave him by giving him up. What could I say to comfort him? I felt myself shrinking under the weight, a burden I'd been bearing for years, and then I felt a new heaviness—the weight of his gaze, and then the weight of his arms, wrapping solidly around me. Space collapsed as he enfolded me. He bent his head to bury it with mine and answered questions he didn't want me to ask. He hugged me so hard he stopped me from speaking.

A few days later, the whole Northeast was as white as my dream. I trudged through the snow in silence with Jonathan and a whole pack of his friends. They ran ahead, throwing snowballs, trying to surf down tiny descents. The temperature was reported to be negative thirty degrees Fahrenheit with the windchill, and I was dressed only to sit inside the whole day drinking tea and playing Legos.

But I'd arrived to some confusion. No one was home. I waited in the car until one of the neighbors noticed me, and then recognized me, and then invited me inside. Paula was at a pro-life march, they said, and Erik was playing basketball at the school. They called Jonathan, who was at another neighbor's house. They told him he had a guest waiting for him and asked if he'd like them to come get him. He said, "If it's Amy, then, yeah." When he came through the door, he hugged me, and he seemed really happy. I asked him what he'd been doing.

"Trying to make something extremely dangerous," he said, cryptically. "And failing."

Erik returned and apologized; he'd thought I was arriving later. I settled into the warmth of the living room, catching up with Erik, but when the whole neighborhood of kids wanted to go sledding, and they needed a chaperone, and they begged me, I couldn't refuse. I enjoy this special advantage over Paula and Erik: I have no parental rights, therefore I am fun.

On our way, irresponsibly and unparent-like, I told Jonathan about a horror movie I'd seen in which some kids get stuck for days on a ski lift. It was relevant, a gripping story about cold. I told him about their attempts to jump, getting eaten by wolves, trying to walk with their hands along the cables.

"Amy! Can we go through here?" one of his friends yelled, pointing out a shortcut through deep, fresh snow. I felt so funny to be the one to make this decision for them. I was such a bad parent I couldn't figure out why it was even a question.

"Sure!" I said, and turned to Jonathan for reassurance. "I'm not sure I make a very good chaperone. What do you think my responsibilities as chaperone should be?"

"Make sure nobody's leg bones come out of their knees," he said, recounting the horrors of the story I'd just told him. "Make sure nobody gets eaten by wolves or frozen to death, and nobody puts their hand on metal so they have to rip it off . . ."

Perfect, I thought. I liked having my role so clearly defined, and by my son himself. I could measure my success or failure easily. Our conversation meandered as we walked, wolves compared with dogs, the food choices he was making because of his recent conclusions about climate change.

We found the little hill, which was nothing compared with what I sledded on when I was little. And their flimsy plastic sleds didn't compare to our long, waxed, wooden toboggan with the leather pillow seat and ropes down the length. We had to hold on tight because with all those kids piled on, and sometimes my dad, too, we'd get going fast, and whoever rode in front, the only person who could see to steer, always got a blinding faceful of snow. I couldn't believe it was just a memory now. Something my son would see in seventies color if I told him.

This hill was just a five-second drop, but the kids were making the most of it. Face-first on their bellies, or rotating wildly, or standing as if their sleds were snowboards. They were screaming, nearly missing each other. The colder I got, my thin oxfords planted in snow twelve inches deep, the more fun they seemed to be having.

I started running in place, gently, cheering them on. The cold made my back tight, and I lost control of my deep muscles. My hip burned, even as I shivered. But I wasn't worried about my injury; I began to worry that I might lose my toes if I stayed much longer. Except that you couldn't lose your feet to frostbite when you were in the suburbs of New Haven, less than a mile away from home—or could you, if the temperature was low enough? Maybe it doesn't matter how close you are to all the comforts of civilization, if you choose to forgo them? But the alternative was telling everyone the fun was over. Parents are supposed to sacrifice everything for their kids, I thought, and I wasn't going to miss a chance.

I jumped up and down to stay alive, and I played it off by cheering at the kids. Some had set to work building a ramp that created messy pile-ups as one of them would come barreling down the hill before the last accident was cleared. Most of them weren't dressed much more warmly than I was, but they had that endless resistance to cold that kids having fun in the snow enjoy. Jonathan came down the hill, dodging the mound of kids in his way. I hooted and hopped. When he picked himself up, he watched the action from the bottom of the hill. Then he turned to look at me. He studied me, as I more self-consciously jogged in place. He was so deliberate, so sober, he might have been positioning himself to confront me.

I stopped running and braced myself as solidly as I had in my dream. I had to be here for anything he might say. It was all I could do. I had to endure whatever might come. I didn't have answers, but I was the only one who might, and it was the least I could do to be there for the questions. To have enough proximity and history that he could get everything I had to give. His eyes narrowed. I stepped a few times because my feet were going to fall off, but I held his gaze.

Then he finally spoke.

"I can see you're cold," he said. It was not a question.

"No, I'm fine!" I insisted. "How about three more runs?" But he was looking at me with the old suspicion. He could see right through me.

"How about *one* more run?"

In my dream, I experienced the relief of ages; peace I didn't know I was waiting for. It was like stepping into the water when I was pregnant and feeling floating where I'd grown accustomed to weight. I had been waiting for it for eternity. How could I have guessed they would find a way to make it simple for him to love me? That I'd get him back, but only when he reached for me? I had a taste of a feeling I didn't know I could feel. It was like the feeling of running, all my cells part of the earth in exactly the right places. All the complexities accommodated. But with this feeling I didn't have to keep running to sustain it. With this, I could just rest.

There was another moment I didn't know I was waiting for until it happened, a year later. The day I reached down to the floor to pick up the lead for my father's mechanical pencil. Lead he had carefully placed in a ziplock bag, which went inside his briefcase, on his bedside table, along with his scientific calculator and the big green book of engineering standards he had helped develop in graduate school. He waved his hand, *No, no, don't get up*. But he was paralyzed from the chest down, and I had been sitting there, pretending to work, waiting without realizing it for just that moment.

He had always asked so many questions about the world, but he didn't ask any questions at all when he could no longer move his lower body, his spine finally devoured by the cancer. He just smiled sheepishly at the nurse who lifted and rotated his ankles, saying "You can't feel this? Nothing?" He shrugged his shoulders, the lowest part of him that was not paralyzed, like he was embarrassed, or sorry to disappoint her, but he couldn't lie. He had come home from work and couldn't make it out of the car except with a cane, and then he couldn't get up the stairs. He was paralyzed in a matter of hours, but he took that information in like it was simple arithmetic. Nothing there to study. It added up the same way every time. But who knows what pain he was hiding from us, to spare us.

With his unparalyzed but shaky hand, one afternoon, he indicated the number three. There were three things he wanted to talk to me about. He smiled his upside-down smile. I could tell it tired him more than usual to do it. I could tell that this upside-down smile, unlike all the others, was part frown.

Immediately, I started talking. About my brother's ex, about my trip to L.A. with Charles, about his new job and the apartment we found him there, about the lemon trees in his new yard, about the reservoir full of black balls in Elysian Park, about my job in Brooklyn, about our crazy clients at work, about my flight down, about Charles's separate flight down. About how we met by chance in the airport because my flight was rerouted. About meeting my brother's new girlfriend, who was waiting with him to pick me up.

"Th-three things." He smiled gently, stopping me. "One." His lips were wobbly. I got wobbly. "Why do you think it bothered you so much to know you were an accident?"

It was worse than I could have imagined. He cut to the heart of everything, my very beginning, everything I was made of. Suddenly all the curtains were drawn and everything behind it exposed. It was because of him, because of my sister always reminding me, that I thought what I thought, I wasn't wanted, I was in everyone's way, but now he was questioning me. I stammered, saying nothing.

"Well," he continued, "you *were* an accident." He was stretching his face longways to give more space to his eyes to catch the water that was welling up in them. Distending his jaw a bit, opening his throat, lifting his eyebrows. It made his eyes wider; there were no eyelashes, or shadows, or blinking, to buffer his question.

"Your mother had had a couple of miscarriages before Julie, and we weren't sure she could have a baby. We had your sister and brother, and we thought we had lucked out. When you came along, your mother was older, and we were scared you might be disabled somehow. And then there was the money. I was starting a new business in a new city, and I wasn't sure I could support three children. My business partner had left and taken all our money." I had only seen him cry at his own father's funeral. "But once you got here and we saw you were okay—"

He paused, shaking his head, trying again. "When I try to think of the world without you . . ." He gestured with his hands, fingers spread, slowly erasing the horizon, shakily, back and forth, pushing back that wall of water and unbuilding my foundations. Addressing the imperfect circumstances of my birth and my imperfect understanding of them. Our whole lives can be built on the slightest misunderstanding about our origins. But with that tiny gesture, as effortless as a signature, as insignificant as a hundred visits that amount to nothing, until they add up to something, his shaking and imprecise hands made space for me.

"The second thing—" He dried his eyes with the edge of his bedsheet and smiled apologetically because it was no doubt not a time for emotions, but all the things were fallen. All the constructs of our relationship we'd relied on for no reason at all, since I was born.

"Do you know how old you can be and still have children?"

"Dad!" It felt so good to be exasperated with him; I wasn't sure I'd ever get to feel that again. "Charles is moving to California! It's not going to happen with him, and it's not a thing I can really control."

"Well." It was so against his nature to give advice. "The way I see it, I think you have lots of good things in your life. But I don't see why you can't have everything you want. A-at least, I think you want kids." He smiled. "I'd think it would be awfully nice if you were pregnant by, l-let's see, August of next year."

August 2013, I registered to myself. It had a magical property. It was the most concrete advice he'd ever given me. Don't kill spiders. Get pregnant by August. And dads understood things daughters couldn't. August 2013 was the right time. And maybe it was less a project he was assigning me and more a prediction he was making, from the wise perspective of his paralysis. I felt my anxiety about the whole issue release, enclosed by the safety of his generous, yearlong boundary. Surely I could do it in a year. Find a man; have a kid. I wanted more advice, more challenges on my skateboard, each one specially designed and incrementally harder. I wanted all the advice he had never given me.

"I—I don't mean that you don't already have a child. I know that Jonathan is your child."

"I know, Dad, yeah, it's okay—" I stammered. I didn't want him to feel guilty for anything.

"I just think you'd like to have a child you get to raise." The upside-down smile. "Okay, okay, three."

I could barely take another thing.

"The blue van. It needs oil, needs a new spare. There's some rust that should be patched. Look in the back, there's a rust kit. I'm going to sell you the van, a thousand dollars."

That time I smiled. He was still afraid of spoiling me. But even as he lay there, legs like solid rocks, I couldn't imagine he wouldn't need that van anymore, that he wouldn't be pulling up in the driveway again with a box turtle in the back.

It was only after speaking to the ICU nurses, later, that I found out the real nature of August 2013's particular significance for my father; they'd given him that long to live, and he wanted to see me on my way to having everything I wanted before he went away.

He was eventually moved out of the ICU into a rehabilitation facility. With his unparalyzed parts, he continued to study and work and learn. He occupied himself with engineering jobs and with questions that filled his clipboards. One afternoon, an architect called demanding drawings, and I impatiently informed him of my dad's condition. I found out later that Dad had called back, apologized for me, and resumed work. He drew on a large clipboard and had his loyal draftsman, Wayne, come by the rehab facility in the afternoons to pick up redlines.

Another day I saw his clipboard, full of calculations of a different nature. They weren't associated with a drawing, just endless math and a couple of angles. I asked him what he'd been working on. He said he was trying to figure out the exact degree of daily change in the sun's location.

"I'd tried to figure it out about fifty years ago," he whispered. "I spent twenty, thirty hours on it. I figured it out last year, but last night I realized I forgot it again. So I redid the calculations. It's a sine curve, roughly."

In the afternoon, when he had put in a full day's work, the nurses would sling him up in the Hoyer lift and lower him into a wheelchair, and I'd roll him, cringing at every bump in the floor surface, outside to the front porch. Mom would bring dinner she'd made, and we'd all look out over the valley at the sunset, and then the moonrise. One of those sunsets, he said to her, "Days like this, you just don't want to end—d-do you?"

He would tell me that he loved me, and, forcing one word to follow the other, the day he died, I would say the same to my son. I'd read through letters my father had written to his mother and discover that he had really wanted to be able to buy me a grand piano. Also among those letters Grandma saved, I'd find one written in an unfamiliar hand, thanking her for the photographs and gifts, for trips to the supermarket, and most of all for letting her see her son, Johnny, over the years, and I'd realize that Grandma knew more about open adoption than she'd let on. At my father's funeral, my grandmother's sister would tell me that we'd get my son back, and she wouldn't explain, but I knew it was connected to the other thing she said, that I am one of the lucky ones in the world because I know what it feels like to be loved. I would commit myself to making sure my son felt the same. Little gifts. Visit more. I wasn't sure. All of those were moments I'd contemplate for a long time after.

But that winter, I was just basking in that moment when Jonathan kept me from freezing to death. We all walked home, and on the way he asked me if I remembered when he was five and he sat in my father's glider but was too afraid to fly. Of course I remembered! I couldn't believe *he* remembered! He said that people perceived him as less brave, or overly cautious, because he was nothing like his brother, but he said he was just strategic about the risks he takes. All of it was amazing, that he could see himself, that he understood something about how others saw him, and that he knew his own perception was an inflection of theirs, not the opposite.

"Do you think you'll be ready to fly someday soon?" I asked him.

"Yes," he said, with certainty. But at that time I only hoped he would get to see my father again before he died.

THIRTY-EIGHT

Y ou slip off the canopy cover and roll the glider out by its wings. Push it out from the hangar, silently, like a horse from its stable. Men sitting under the trees will be talking about the things they wait all week or all month to talk about, standing by patiently for their turn, looking for a reason to get up and help. Some are tow pilots, on call when you have the glider ready. Some of them are kids as young as fourteen, who somehow found this world and got licensed to solo. All of them tuned to the invisible language of the sky, watching the day unfold in wind socks and clouds.

Facilities are nothing fancy here. The runway is a field of grass, bordered on the south by marsh, on the north by Craig's Creek, and on the east and west by the mountains. There are some stables, two small hangars, a few houses, the clubhouse—but no air control tower. Some days the guys sit at the north end of the field under the trees. Some days they sit at the south end, where there's a tiny storage shed with plastic chairs and a radio.

If you don't already know the area, you assess things for miles around beforehand. You look for the flat fields that might make for soft landings, in case you lose altitude too fast and can't get back to the runway.

I remember, as a child, walking across the fields scouting out landing sites as my dad explained that every landing in a sailplane is a kind of crash landing. I guess he meant because you don't have all the controls of a motorized plane. But at the time I understood that they had perfected taking off in gliders, but they hadn't yet figured out how to get back down.

This weekend my son will be flying. He says the only thing he's afraid of is water, and not for the same reasons I am. Of the little bit of online television he's allowed to watch, nature shows are his favorite; what he's afraid of are river monsters and sharks. Flying he can handle.

When we get out onto the airfield, we inspect the plane. My father walks around it weakly, his shoulders shrunken. The wing flaps, the various dashboard indicators, the little hook at the nose of the plane that snatches shut to grasp the towrope and opens wide to let go. I pinched my finger in the little hook once, just as my dad was pulling the trigger to test it, and I was surprised at how strong those tiny jaws turned out to be. We walk the wings, holding their edges to make sure they don't touch the ground as the golf cart pulls the plane into position. I've volunteered to be his passenger for this flight. It will be the first time I've flown in several years. My dad checks my seat belt, which has five straps all radiating to a central buckle. He points to a zippered pouch to my right, where he says, in a whisper, there are barf bags, and I realize he is not kidding. He is speaking as a pilot to his passenger, standard protocol. In the same manner, he explains that he won't be talking much during takeoff because he'll be concentrating, but after that we are free to talk. He has never been so forthright about his silence.

He settles in and begins to murmur to himself. *Altimeter adjusted, dive brakes closed and locked, belts tight, canopy locked, tail dolly off, controls free and clear . . .* The towplane pulls up ahead, dragging the towrope. The glass bubble of the canopy is a tiny, boiling, intimate space: we open the side windows to let in some air. Standing tall above us beside the plane, my brother holds the last five feet of the towrope taut between his hands, like a magician proving it is just a rope, nothing funny about it. He holds it there for my dad's inspection, and this feels more like ceremony than safety check. Through the glass my dad can't possibly detect flaws. He looks at it like a wine label displayed gratuitously and nods his head. I'm surprised this passes for an inspection. The towrope is everything. But then, everything is everything.

Squatting at the nose with his palm in the air, my brother uses his other hand to loop the towrope into the hook of the plane, which my dad holds open. When he makes a fist, my dad closes it. Now my brother is at the wing, swinging his arm to tell the tow pilot there is still slack in the rope. The towplane rolls slowly forward until my brother stops swinging his arm. My dad asks whether I'm ready, and I say yes. What choice do I have? My dad gives the left hand thumbs-up, and my brother starts to swing his arm in a full circle, telling the tow pilot we're ready to go.

What is most amazing about all of it is the degree to which it is not rocket science. You check out every part of the plane because there aren't that many. You trust in the twenty-five pieces that comprise a plane, and beyond that, you trust the same thing the birds are born trusting. And as for me, I'm not trusting a pilot, an anonymous official with a license in magic; I'm trusting my father, who's decided to let the cancer take over.

My brother runs the wing, keeping it from touching the grass as we are towed across the field, but as our speed picks up, he lets go, and we begin to take flight, imperceptibly, even before the towplane has lifted off. For much longer than any commercial plane, we are traveling at the height of what feels no more than your bedroom window. We are still sheltered by the high mountain horizon as we speed forward, our shadow born and racing like a good dog just below us. We ascend so gradually that I have to decide for myself when my fear of heights can relax into disbelief. There is no clear threshold between human heights and heights we can't fathom. Human heights and heavens. Soon we are flying together, towplane and glider, like a big brother pulling his little sister along by the arm, flapping and flying behind.

My dad reads his dials, reads the landscape, looks for other aircraft. Wind is blowing noisily into our little windows so I can't hear him, loud as he tries to whisper. I try to think about anything except the barf bags in the zippered pouch beside me. The towplane ahead of us is sometimes above, sometimes below us, looking like a remote control plane as it bounces in the sky. We rise and fall like a roller coaster, and sometimes I cling helplessly to the sides of the sailplane, searching the sky for signs of an invisible track to tell me where we're going, signs we're moving out of turbulence into smooth sailing. My dad is looking hard for the opposite; turbulence means heat, which is how we get higher. Without telling me, he releases the towrope and the towplane falls away and off to the side, and we speed up over him. My dad gives a wave to thank him for the lift.

And now my dad is doing what he loves most. Now we are a bird. This is what it is all about. All the planning trips up to New Castle, making free weekends, driving here, packing food, the hours preparing the plane, sleeping in the modest quarters of the clubhouse. Flight is a long descent, postponed by invisible lift. We are here to find thermals, and the proof of our detective skills will be our altitude and how long we can float.

Thermals are invisible tornadoes made of upward-moving heat. The world above the ground is like a leaning forest of them, sometimes dense and sometimes loosely scattered. A forest of mobile trees that grow and dissipate as the sun heats the surface of the world unevenly and sends hot air rising in these tunnels. They're invisible except to the birds, so the easiest way to find them is by keeping your eyes out for spread wings. Other evidence is in the subtle circular movements of grass and leaves. You are always descending until you find one and, like an elevator, it reverses the forces of gravity and sends you upward.

Ridge lift is another way to gain elevation, a consequence of the world's wrinkles. Air moves in layers across the surface of the earth, and when it hits a mountain, all the layers bounce; a ghost reverberation of the mountain is made in the sky, two thousand feet above, ready to be climbed. My dad has flown in this valley since 1965, so he knows the precise shape of these echo landscapes. We surf along the ghost–Blue Ridge as though it were a long wave.

My dad enjoys nothing more than taking people up in gliders, but I know that he's in his own world inside the canopy. He is never more present, but he is inaccessible to me. I can see only the back of his head, the canvas bucket hat that every single glider pilot wears to protect his head from the hot sun, and a little of his profile when he turns. My dad facing the universe. The globe of glass containing us giving us a powerful panorama of the valley. I am riding on his back, having the clearest picture I will ever have of what the world looks like to him and what he makes of it.

When I was ten I bought my dad a sweatshirt and I used fabric pens to make a giant heart and across the heart I wrote: *I'm loved*. I guess I was afraid to have it read *I love you*, because that would be too much like just saying it, which I couldn't do. The closest he ever got to acknowledging the sentiment was when he told me a client had popped into his office on a Saturday and caught him wearing it, and he was embarrassed. So I know he must have noticed what it said. Last time I saw it, he'd shrunk from the cancer, and the sweatshirt, which had for twenty years been tight around the ball of his belly, was several sizes too large. During that first bout of cancer, my heart racing as I was rubbing his shoulders, I decided to be an adult and I managed to say the words, in a whisper weaker than his own, and I don't think he heard me.

He sees a bird, the kind whose flying mechanism is the same as a sailplane's, one that soars instead of flaps its wings. One that lazily falls up in the air. He watches closely as the bird shows him the invisible shape of the sky. We follow and pick up altitude.

He dips the wing low and we lean against one side of the plane. I can make out the leaves of the trees on the mountains as we near them. One of the many lies I tell myself: the trees are soft. We are making a sharp turn in the sky, skidding slowly across clouds, with losses of speed and altitude my dad has already accounted for. The runway is not large. I want him to think I am enjoying this as much as he is, but I won't relax until we've landed.

Coming down, the back of my dad's head against a fast-approaching field of green. My heart races. Every landing a crash landing. We float low above the bed of trees and storm in slow motion toward the runway. The wing brakes rise and rip the air, and finally we touch down and roll heavily across the grass, popping up in the air and back down, skipping across the ground until we are riding on the landing gear. Satisfying squeaks of solid mechanics, heavy rubber rolling smoothly. I wish all of flying could be this moment of high-speed travel across a field of grass, bounding without risk, wings and wheels passing off responsibility, freedom in the redundancy, celebrating all the bumps and irregularities of solid ground. We're like a galloping horse.

We extract ourselves as if we're dismounting the saddle, walking funny our first few steps. A golf cart drives up to retrieve the plane, and I walk the wing back to the hangar. We hear that another pilot came down early because of a possible storm. *Dad would never do that*, I think. *He'd fly right into it.* "Perfect landing," I hear someone say. "It's Walter Seek," I hear from another. We guide the glider back into the hangar, where we'll clean the front of the wings with soapy water and stow it away until the next flight. Big Lick, this precious plane is called by the club.

On the way back to the clubhouse, a little bungalow shared by all the glider pilots, its walls covered with photos of men all the way back to the sixties, we might run alongside another glider, steadying the wings like a giant kite. Flying is a kind of team sport. It takes a lot of hands to send a glider into the air, all of them with a silent understanding I never acquired of why it is so important to get up there.

◎ ◎ ◎

My dad had been anticipating this moment for weeks. A tiny window when he could regain some strength, between the end of chemo and the unknown. He rented a house for us and sent long e-mails to Paula and Erik, reminding them of the various offerings of the area. If they didn't like flying, there was a creek; if they didn't like creeks, there were swinging bridges, zip lines, golf carts, hiking trails. He wasn't sure it was enough for them to want to do this thing simply because he wanted so much for them to do it. He sent links to websites that explained flying. None of this: renting a house, cc'ing multiple people on e-mails, finding websites and gathering their links—were things my father knew how to do, until he had this important reason to learn.

Gliders have two sets of controls, front and back, and my dad was always happy to let his passengers take the controls, always with the sneaky hope they'd get hooked. He didn't care whether his passenger was old or young or family or not. He just wanted to pass it on. But at twelve years old, Jonathan was the perfect age to learn to fly—only two years from being able to solo. I'm afraid to know whether it was Jonathan's age, or whether my dad had a special affection for him because he is his first grandson, that made my father so determined to take him flying.

Paula and Erik drove eleven hours from New Haven and we met at the house Dad rented. It's nestled in a valley, with raspberries growing in the back and rainbow trout swimming in a small system of man-made lakes in front. The mountains are beautiful. They're like the Tennessee I remember from my childhood. The Tennessee that makes me roll my eyes when people tell me they've been to Tennessee, and it's beautiful. They don't know how beautiful it is, because it's gone. Now there are Walmarts and Gaps and every store you could ever want to shop at. Dad helped build them; Mom boycotts them. But somehow New Castle still exists. A town of just over a hundred. A place no one has gotten around to destroying yet.

What place will my son remember as home? He won't remember Tennessee. I rode my bike with him in my belly there, swallowing every curve of those hills, hoping he would taste it, too, but that would be as much as he would know of the place I grew up. In the end, our family was just a blip there, emerging and disappearing with me. My son has been all over; he has already moved to North Carolina, to Boston, to New Haven. But his family is from Florida and Indiana. Who will be responsible for all the places we've been? Who will be responsible for the mountains in Tennessee?

I find myself making plans to always love this place of my father's. I have that impulse I had when I fell in love with Ralph Macchio, and I was helpless to do anything about it but suffer, and teach myself karate from library books, and write his name on my high-tops. I decide to admit New Castle onto my list of places to love and, by loving it, to keep it from disappearing. After my father is gone, I will love it for him.

I wonder if my dad will try to crash a plane and die here. I think he would, if it wouldn't mean a lot of inconvenience for the people on the ground.

We claim rooms and settle our suitcases into them. The family room is gigantic, with couches, a fireplace, and a big telescope stationed in the corner, and each of the second-floor bedrooms has windows overlooking it. There are speakers in each room, an intercom system Jonathan, Sarah, and Andrew experiment with excitedly as they run up and down the spiral staircase, slamming doors and yelling at one another across the living room void.

In the morning, we get up early and have breakfast outside on the terrace. My father asks Jonathan if he has any questions in preparation for his flight. I can see how excited my dad is, but the kids are just excited about being in a new place, with a big yard, and trout ponds, and a creek. It is easy to see how much he's suffering just from the exertion of getting up and smiling and speaking.

I should be grateful we are all assembled here, my mother and father, Paula and Erik and the three kids. But little things frustrate me: that my father can't speak loud enough to be heard, that everyone doesn't notice his struggle and so he settles into silence. That Paula and Erik are exhausted from the trip. That my mother is preoccupied with cooking and making sure people are fed instead of sitting down and talking. That my son is too afraid of river monsters to walk the creek the way I used to. That my sister isn't there because of her four kids and that they are always the excuse for everything. That my brother was supposed to be on his way hours ago and probably won't arrive until nightfall. That when he does finally arrive, he regrets not coming sooner, and he says that the bedroom windows overlooking the living room are the perfect launch site for a paper airplane contest, and I'll forever mourn the paper airplane contest we'll never have. That, remembering the astonishing moment I first saw the landscape of the moon through a telescope, I take the telescope outside with my son and find that the moon has already slipped behind the tall mountains that surround us.

As always, I am the only one who knows how precious this moment is. I am scrambling, an invisible facilitator, trying to connect my son directly to my father, erasing the mistake of me, the mistake of giving up my son. I am drawing everyone together to try to make them stick. And I should feel something restored, that my father and mother, though they don't say anything, are demonstrating it isn't over for them any more than it is over for me. Unmitigated disaster, averted. No, the unmitigated disaster is ongoing.

Everyone says that the weekend is turning out to be perfect, and that infuriates me. I am mourning all we've already lost and the inevitable disappearance of everything else. We pile into the cars and drive to the glider field. Big Lick is tangled among the other planes, and it's a geometry exercise my dad didn't anticipate to get it out of the hangar without damaging it. Kids run around, exhausting him, and people aren't listening to him, or can't hear him, as he directs them to lift that wing, or roll that plane back. Paula and my mother chat carelessly in the corner. I worry we won't get to fly. I'm mad that I'm the only one worried. But finally, we get the plane out, and our day of flying begins.

My dad kneels beside the body of the plane, genuflecting to physics, leaning in to speak to my son. I've helped Jonathan strap in, all five belts latched into the circular buckle.

"On takeoff, I won't be talking, I'll be real quiet," he says to Jonathan. "I'm going to be totally focused on flying the plane. After we get up, we can chat a little bit."

Jonathan takes the controls and pushes them left. "That's going to make you turn left," my dad says. "What would you do if you wanted to go straight?" Jonathan slowly releases the stick back to center.

"Yeah. That's it. That's exactly it." He turns to me. "You've got a smart kid here." I think he thinks he may finally have a taker.

"What is all this?" my son asks.

"What is everything, okay. This is the dive brake. Pull that out, that gets you to go down faster. We'll use that during landing. This knob releases us from the towplane. This green knob, you don't need to worry about that, that's—that's called a trim."

My son points to a dial.

"That's a thousand feet. We'll probably go up to almost three."

"Is this the speed?" my son asks.

"That's the speed. Sixty knots, eighty knots. Hundred knots is one hundred fifteen miles an hour. We won't go that fast. Not intentionally, anyway. These two tell you how fast you're going up and down. Like when it says four, means you're going up four hundred feet a minute."

My dad has developed the slow speaking rhythms I remember in my grandmother. The infinite patience and gravity of a storyteller. Every word a stone that sinks deep and certain to the bottom of the riverbed.

Neither one of them talks. The towplane is positioning itself; other pilots are making preparations around them. The other pilots refer to my son as my son and assume Erik is my husband. But then they realize he's Paula's son. They assume Paula is my sister. What is certain is that Jonathan is my father's grandson, because my father has referred to him that way. Probably as much for expedience as anything.

My dad and my son wait. At the end of a period of silence, he asks whether Jonathan has any other questions. It seems he doesn't, except it seems he should.

"Is this—?"

"—That's an air vent . . . That's closed, and that's open."

"Do I want it closed or open?"

"You want it open."

Some things my dad didn't explain because they have certain, stable answers.

Jonathan notices that there are pedals in the front, but not in the back.

"—Oh, I'll work the pedals. What I'll do, I'll use them to try to keep the yaw string straight. You don't need to—you can fly anywhere you want to just with the stick." Some things it seemed my father just couldn't explain.

"What's that?"

"Oh, that's a compass, and I'm not sure what that does; I don't think it's anything important."

My son looks at me, smiling. My dad has so little energy, I'm glad Jonathan can detect levity in him. I'm glad there is still levity left in my father. He's never felt any obligation to admit he was kidding.

And who taught my son what a compass is? When? That he knows it so well he can know it would be a joke not to know what a compass is.

". . . Do I have a parachute?"

"No. No, we don't fly with parachutes."

My son looks at me again, to see if he should smile. That was not entirely a joke, I think, but I'll never know.

"Oh, you'll need to help me look out for aircraft." My dad remembers an important part of copiloting. My son points his arm forward and says, "Twelve o'clock, one o'clock, two o'clock," as he rotates it clockwise. This is how he will indicate the location of the other aircraft. We went over this at breakfast, but my son had already learned it, maybe from Paula's father, who was a commercial pilot.

"Six would be right behind you. Straight back. You won't see anything at six."

My dad taught me to tell time, using a clock by the side of his bed whose entire face glowed pale peach. It seemed to me deeply illogical that for one hand, you take the clock at face value, but for the other hand, just because it's longer, you multiply the values it points to by five. And then you put them together or reverse them in a whole variety of acceptable ways. I remember my father's frustration and my own, and I try to imagine the knowledge of the face of the clock still rather new for my son.

"You'll be able to see from nine o'clock to three o clock," I offer.

My dad cups his head in his hands.

"Dad, you feeling all right?"

"—Oh yeah. I'm just resting."

My knowledge about my dad's condition is like my knowledge of God. I know that my dad is dying, but I don't know what to do about it.

"—What if they're below us, then what do I say?"

My son is not bothered by my dad's weakness. He's always looking for the exception that makes the system fail. The single structural weakness that will make the entire bridge collapse.

A plane comes in for a landing and my dad takes advantage of the interruption to get up and inspect the canopy. The towplanes are always zipping around against the grain, to pick up gliders that are ready to go. I push a hat through Jonathan's little window as my dad lowers himself in and fastens his straps. I ask whether he's had enough to drink. He says he has a drink somewhere. He's not supposed to be drinking Gatorade; too much potassium and too many carcinogenic dyes, but his doctors say he can have whatever he wants now. I hand him the Gatorade that's sitting to the side of the plane. He breathes deliberately, audibly. Like someone who's getting ready to lift a heavy weight.

"All right, Andrew, I won't talk—"

"Jonathan!" I say.

"I won't talk much until after takeoff." My dad is already too focused on flight to correct himself, but I want to make sure he knows who his passenger is.

Soon, I'd be struggling to understand the meaning of my father, the way I've always tried to make sense of my son. I'd be drawn to him like a lover, compelled to press my hand against his heart, feel my own rhythms moved by the power of its beat; it pounded hard, like he was determined to stay. Like I'd so often studied my son, I'd read the slightest shift in his eyebrows, to say he wanted something he didn't have the energy to ask for. I'd massage his neck for hours, a feast of forgetting myself. I'd want to touch the cold stillness creeping up on him, starting at his toes, and I'd pursue togetherness, perpetually receding into the cool, vast mystery of a separate body. We'd sit at his bedside, sending happy things afloat in his imagination; our beloved stories against the groundlessness of night. I would see him sorry to leave, death imparting no special wisdom to make it easier to let go. I'd press my hand to his heart until its last beat, and, still, the weight of his ashes would feel like a lover's touch, resonant with potential. And I'd find my heart doing leaps and bounds as it tried to make sense of an overwhelming new affection for him—butterflies for my dead father.

It shouldn't surprise me that my heart malfunctions in these ways, with everything I've done to test it.

The towplane pulls up. One of the other pilots, Ron, runs to grab the rope. Over the noise of the propeller, I hear my dad saying his prayers: "straps tight, controls free and clear." He has his head in both hands. I walk to the wing and hear Ron say, "Perfect day!" as he approaches the canopy with the towrope. "Good as it gets," my dad says, and smiles up at him. Ron makes a fist to tell my dad he has the towrope in place. "We lucked out," my dad says. "It's not luck," Ron says as he lowers the canopy, and my father sends both red latches forward. My dad and my son, my furthest extents, strapped tightly together in the tiny glass canopy, closed and locked.

My dad has shown me how to run the wing. I've done it many times, since I was little. Sweeping my arm in small arcs till the slack of the towrope is out, and then, when he gives the thumbs-up, in full circles. The towrope pulls taut, and I run alongside the plane, holding the wing level as the rubber wheels squeak and bound across the field. I'm running to keep the wing steady, running to weigh it down. I'm still running as it leaves my hands.

This is a true story, though some names and details have been changed.

ACKNOWLEDGMENTS

I have many people to thank. My sister, for her patient rereadings. Paula Crossfield, for her relentlessness in reminding me to write this story. The many friends who alternately supported me and forgave my absence, most of all Miya, Tatiana, Heather, and David. My editors, Courtney Hodell and Alex Star. My physical therapist, Stephen Rodriguez, for making running and writing almost painless. My son's family, who are always, everywhere, doing immeasurably more than the least they could do. And everyone represented here, for being a part of this story.